Economic Crisis and Mass Protest

'In the global wave of protest against austerity policies during the Great Recession, Iceland played a pivotal role as the early riser. Since the "Pots and Pans Revolution" Iceland's flag became a global symbol of courageous resistance against injustice. Based on in-depth empirical analysis and innovative theoretical thinking, this volume offers a most welcome analysis of the mechanisms through which citizens mobilize under critical circumstances as collective actions create solidarity and feelings of empowerment.'

Donatella della Porta, Scuola Normale Superiore, Italy

Although the triggering effect of economic crises on revolt is a classic sociological topic, crises have until recently mostly triggered large-scale protest in developing countries. The antigovernment protests that occurred in several European countries in the wake of the global financial crisis brought crises to the forefront of protest research in democratic societies, as well as provide important opportunities for studying how crises can trigger large-scale collective action. This volume focuses on Iceland's 'Pots and Pans Revolution', a series of large-scale antigovernment protests that took place in Iceland in autumn 2008 and January 2009.

Iceland was among the first countries to respond to the crisis with large-scale protest. The level of public mobilization was exceptionally high (about 25 percent participation rate) and the protests did not stop until they had brought down the ruling government of Iceland. Using qualitative and quantitative data, this volume situates the Icelandic protests in historical-cultural context and applies social movement theory to explore how the financial crisis triggered them, thus providing a step toward understanding why the global financial crisis has triggered public unrest in other countries.

Jón Gunnar Bernburg is Professor of Sociology at the University of Iceland. He graduated with a Ph.D. in Sociology from the State University of New York at Albany in 2002. His work has cut across several sub-fields of sociology, including stigma and deviance, neighborhood research, social theory, and, in recent years, social movements. In addition to contributing to edited volumes, handbooks, and encyclopedias, he has published articles in leading social science journals, such as *Social Forces*, *Sociology*, *European Sociological Review*, *Criminology*, *Social Science & Medicine*, and *Mobilization*.

The Mobilization Series on Social Movements, Protest, and Culture

Series Editor

Professor Hank Johnston
San Diego State University, USA

Published in conjunction with *Mobilization: An International Quarterly,* the premier research journal in the field, this series disseminates high quality new research and scholarship in the fields of social movements, protest, and contentious politics. The series is interdisciplinary in focus and publishes monographs and collections of essays by new and established scholars.

Other titles in this series

Crisis and Social Mobilization in Contemporary Spain
Benjamín Tejerina Montaña and Ignacia Perugorría

The Brazilian Landless Movement
Critical Dialogues on History, Experiences and Trajectories of a Radical Social Movement
Edited by Alex Flynn and Elena Calvo-González

Austerity and Protest
Popular Contention in Times of Economic Crisis
Edited by Marco Giugni and Maria T. Grasso

Social Movement Dynamics
New Perspectives on Theory and Research from Latin America
Edited by Federico M. Rossi and Marisa von Bülow

Urban Mobilizations and New Media in Contemporary China
Edited by Lisheng Dong, Hanspeter Kriesi, Daniel Kübler

Israeli-Palestinian Activism Shifting Paradigms
Alexander Koensler

From Silence to Protest
International Perspectives on Weakly Resourced Groups
Edited by Didier Chabanet and Frederic Royall

Economic Crisis and Mass Protest

The Pots and Pans Revolution in Iceland

Jón Gunnar Bernburg

Routledge
Taylor & Francis Group
LONDON AND NEW YORK

First published 2016
by Routledge
2 Park Square, Milton Park, Abingdon, Oxon OX14 4RN

and by Routledge
711 Third Avenue, New York, NY 10017

First issued in paperback 2018

Routledge is an imprint of the Taylor & Francis Group, an informa business

British Library Cataloguing in Publication Data
A catalogue record for this book is available from the British Library

Library of Congress Cataloguing in Publication Data
A catalog record for this book has been requested.

ISBN 13: 978-1-138-60012-6 (pbk)
ISBN 13: 978-1-4724-2547-8 (hbk)

Typeset in Times New Roman
by Out of House Publishing

Contents

Figures

Tables

Preface

The winter of 2008 and 2009 was a difficult time in our lives, especially the days and weeks following the October bank collapse. I recall countless moments of disbelief and frustration, and weeks of ongoing anxiety. My home country was being struck by an unprecedented financial, political, and diplomatic crisis. During the first week of the crisis, I remember waking up with an uneasy feeling as I got ready to look at the headlines and turn on the state radio. Every morning the news got worse. First we heard that the country's entire banking system was collapsing and that the stock exchange had been closed. Then we heard that the foreign exchange reserves were drying up, that many of the country's major companies were heading straight for bankruptcy, and that countless businesses and households were about to drown in rising debt. The state too was in big trouble and the outside world was angry with Iceland. The banks had accumulated enormous foreign debt, and to our great surprise powerful entities, including the British and Dutch governments, were holding us accountable for it. Even the countries we had traditionally regarded as well-disposed toward us refused to help unless our authorities accepted legally uncertain claims that were so huge that they threatened to bring down the country's welfare system. Before we knew what had hit us, the British authorities had placed Iceland on their list of terrorist groups. What happened next was no less remarkable, given the context of Iceland's peaceful contemporary history: the crisis spurred a people's revolt. People began protesting in the streets, blaming the authorities for the crisis and demanding the resignation of the government. As participation in the protests grew, protest actions became more radical and threatening, and eventually large-scale mass protests created sufficient pressure to bring the government down.

In the midst of the crisis, I experienced as much anxiety as the next person. But it wasn't mainly my future economic well-being that I worried about (though admittedly I went online a few times to reassure myself of job options in other countries, in case the state actually went bankrupt and I would have no paycheck, and my wife went to the bank to withdraw a substantial sum in case the banks shut their doors). What really shook my nerves was feeling my society tremble, seeing my fellow citizens lose their civility in displays of anger and moral indignation, and witnessing the unleashing of serious public confrontation. It wasn't until things had calmed down a few months later that I started to see what an excellent research project I had on my hands.

The present study was aided by research grants from the Edda Center of Excellence, the Icelandic Centre for Research, and the University of Iceland Research Fund. Moreover, the book is the fruit of collaboration with several individuals. Sigrún Ólafsdóttir and Berglind Hólm Ragnarsdóttir collaborated with me in designing survey measures and obtaining the survey data that I use extensively in this work (the Reykjavík Area Social Survey). Two research assistants, Anna Soffía Víkingsdóttir and Linda Björk Pálmadóttir, conducted many of the qualitative interviews that I rely on, and they obtained the bulk of the textual material that I analyze for substantive content (public meeting speeches, newspaper articles, etc.). In addition, Anna Soffía Víkingsdóttir provided valuable assistance in coding the interview data and obtaining available statistics. I am grateful to Guðni Th. Jóhannesson, Már Wolfgang Mixa, and Sigrún Ólafsdóttir for their invaluable comments on the manuscript and to Jeffrey Cosser for helping me to improve the language of this book. I also benefited from discussing aspects of this work with Giorgio Baruchello, Sara Sigurbjörns-Öldudóttir, Svanur Kristjánsson, Viðar Halldórsson, and Þórólfur Þórlindsson. I thank commentators at the August 2012 "Icelandic Meltdown" workshop at the University of Iowa, especially Dimitra Doukas and Tinna Grétarsdóttir, for encouraging me to expand the empirical focus of this work. I thank the interviewees who gave me and my assistants the time to talk with them about their involvement in the protests. And I thank Gísli Pálsson for suggesting to me that I should write this book, and for mentoring me through the initial steps of the book project. Finally, I thank my former life-partner and dear friend Eydís for her encouragement and support while I was writing this book.

Jón Gunnar Bernburg
Reykjavík, September 7, 2015

1 Introduction

Monday October 6, 2008 is a memorable day for most Icelanders. On that day, in a live broadcast on national television and radio, Iceland's Prime Minister, Geir H. Haarde, delivered a special address to an anxious public. Such addresses are rare in Iceland and due to the enormous traffic on the broadcasting service's website many had to switch on their antenna radios to hear it.[1] Haarde's message was unusually somber: the entire financial system was collapsing.

> Dear Icelanders, I have asked to speak to you now, when the Icelandic nation is facing great difficulties. The whole world is now going through a great financial crisis whose effects can be equated with an economic catastrophe. [...] Some of the largest investment banks have fallen victim to the crisis and liquidity in the markets has in fact dried up. As a result, large international banks have stopped financing other banks and a complete lack of trust has emerged. [...] Due to this situation the position of the Icelandic banks has worsened rapidly in the last few days.[2]

The address came in a context where vague news and rumors had been circulating for a few weeks that the global credit crunch was creating major trouble for Icelandic banks. While the authorities and the bank managers had publicly dismissed these concerns, many Icelanders had sensed that something was wrong. One week earlier, the state had taken over *Glitnir Bank*, one of Iceland's major banks, spurring widespread concern. But even on the night before the address, after a weekend of meetings with the managers of the banks and other leaders in the financial sector, Haarde had announced to the press that there was no need for special action as the banks had agreed to sell assets to reduce foreign debt.[3] But just the next day his message was different; the global bank crisis was also bringing down the other two major Icelandic banks, *Landsbankinn* and *Kaupthing Bank*. This was a scary message. The three banks comprised about 90 percent of the Icelandic banking system, and their overall budget was about eight times larger than the country's annual Gross Domestic Product (GDP), a large part of which was financed with foreign debt (Benediktsdóttir et al. 2011).

The Icelandic banking landscape had changed drastically in the decade leading to this crisis. In the late 1990s the state had owned and operated these exclusively domestic banks. The authorities then began to privatize the banks and in the following years, with easy access to short-term loans on the international market, the banks expanded greatly. By 2007 they had all become large international enterprises. Due to the apparent success of the banks, a discourse emerged in Iceland defining their owners and managers as extremely successful global players, or "business Vikings" (Loftsdóttir 2015). The influx of international capital had raised the standard of living, while in fact the country's economy was accumulating enormous foreign debts.

The global crisis was now blocking the banks' access to credit, making them unable to meet deadlines on their existing short-term loans (Benediktsdóttir et al. 2011). Of course, the global crisis created problems for banks elsewhere, but other states, including the United States and Ireland, hurried to bail their banks out. Runs on the Icelandic banks were imminent but the Icelandic state was too small to rescue them. The lack of a lender of last resort had undermined the trustworthiness of the Icelandic banks, making them vulnerable to the global crisis. Haarde's address went on:

> We should keep in mind [...] that the enormous actions that the United States authorities have decided to implement to rescue their banking system comprise about 5 percent of their GDP. The balance sheet of the Icelandic banks, on the other hand, is many times Iceland's GDP [...] In the threatening situation that now prevails on the world's financial markets a great risk would be involved for the Icelandic nation in any attempt to keep the banks afloat with a lifeline. [...] If the worst came to the worst, there would be a real risk, dear countrymen, that Iceland's economy would be sucked into the turmoil and the result would be a national bankruptcy.

Unable to bail out the banks, the Icelandic authorities hastened to rescue only their domestic operations. On the evening of Haarde's address, his government rushed emergency legislation through parliament, allowing the state to take over (and refinance) the banks' domestic savings and loans, but letting their (much larger) foreign operations become insolvent. The stock exchange had already been closed and on the following day, two of the three banks were insolvent; on the third day, the largest bank collapsed. The banking system of one of the world's most affluent countries had folded in less than a week. One of the largest bank crashes in history had struck one of the world's smallest nations (Jónsson 2009).

Apparently concerned about potential conflict, Haarde emphasized that Iceland had been hit by a global crisis. He concluded the broadcast by asking the nation for support, solidarity, and peace to deal with the volatile situation.

> The government's task in the next few days is clear: to prevent chaos in the event that the Icelandic banks become non-operative to some extent. The authorities have various means to do so and will do so. In the political arena, as elsewhere, it is important to put our differences aside in this situation. It is vital that we remain calm and sober during the hard days ahead, that we do not lose courage and that we support each other in word and deed. Thus, armed with Icelandic optimism, courage and solidarity, we will weather the storm. God bless Iceland!

But Haarde's call for peace and solidarity was not heeded. His framing of the crisis as a global problem, and his intention, and that of the rest of his cabinet, to remain in office, would meet with growing opposition as the crisis unfolded in the following days and weeks. In a remarkable chain of events, especially given a weak tradition of street protest in Iceland's contemporary history, a protest wave emerged – a series of public meetings created a platform for expanding protest, eventually concluding in threatening demonstrations with mass public participation and support, bringing down Haarde's government. This book studies how the financial crisis in Iceland spurred the forces of mass protest.

The first days of the crisis

In the first few days following Haarde's address, the media bombarded the Icelandic public with bad news. The bank collapse instantly wiped out the country's stock exchange, which had multiplied ninefold in value in the years preceding the crisis (Sigurjónsson and Mixa 2011). Widespread capital losses and imminent bankruptcies promised a severe economic recession in the coming months. Moreover, the banking crisis immediately created a fiscal and diplomatic crisis. In the years leading up to the crisis, foreign capital had flowed into the country, enabling banks to offer individuals and businesses easy access to loans. The influx of capital had inflated the value of the króna, raising ordinary people's standard of living and bolstering their economic goals and expectations (Ragnarsdóttir et al. 2013). But in doing this, the banks and the economy as a whole had accumulated enormous foreign debt and now capital wanted out. The global crisis had prompted a constant outflow of foreign currency since early Spring 2008, deflating the exchange rate of the króna. As a result, the country's foreign exchange reserves were drying up. Many worried that the currency shortage could halt imports of basic necessities, such as oil.[4] To stop the outflow of foreign exchange, the authorities imposed capital controls on foreign exchange transactions. Individuals, businesses, and investors who wanted to escape Iceland would find it difficult to take their property and savings with them.[5]

Moreover, a diplomatic crisis emerged as the emergency legislation immediately resulted in liability claims and sudden hostility toward Iceland from abroad. When Landsbankinn fell on October 6 more than 400,000 individuals and businesses in the United Kingdom and the Netherlands lost their savings in the "Icesave" accounts that the bank had operated directly from Iceland (note: the population of Iceland is about 320,000). After compensating their own citizens for these losses, these two nations demanded full compensation from Iceland. The liability claim was colossal relative to Iceland's tiny economy, threatening to plunge the state into unbearable debt. The legitimacy of the claim was uncertain and the authorities reacted to it with ambiguity. On October 8, the British authorities used anti-terrorist legislation to freeze the assets of Icelandic banks in Britain, placing Iceland on their list of terrorist groups.[6] The financial crisis and the authorities' reactions to it were turning friends into foes and creating a risk of state bankruptcy.

In only one week, "the collapse" (*hrunið*) shattered Icelanders' shared reality. After a long period of growing economic prosperity, a severe recession was inevitable, threatening the economic well-being of a population that, like the banks, had accumulated enormous debt in the years leading up to the crisis. But what had seemed like an economic boom had been a bubble that was fated to explode. Iceland, one of the world's most affluent welfare democracies, no longer seemed prosperous and secure. The state was not rich but potentially bankrupt. Major institutions such as banks, which traditionally had been very trustworthy, had lost that trust. The country's image abroad was damaged and financial demands by foreign entities were threatening the foundations of the Icelandic welfare state. The future, which had seemed so bright just a few months earlier, was dark. The Icelandic people were anxious, confused, disappointed, and pessimistic.

The emergence of protest

How the crisis would be defined and explained would clearly have political consequences in this context of a shared sense of disaster, anxiety, and uncertainty. Something had gone terribly wrong, but what? Why did all three banks suddenly collapse? Why did the global credit crunch hurt Iceland so much more than other countries? Why were the private banks able to do so much public harm? Why did the state have to pay for their risky ventures abroad? Why had the public not been aware of danger? Who was responsible for this blunder?

At the moment that the crisis struck Iceland, conflict emerged in public debate about how to answer these questions (Bergmann 2014:6). Haarde's coalition government, which was composed of two parties, the center-right *Independence Party* and the smaller center-left *Social Democratic Alliance*, hastened to neutralize the situation. In addresses, interviews, and press conferences, they referred to the crisis as bad weather; a global storm had struck Iceland – the authorities should not be held accountable for the actions of private banks operating in an international market. Rather, the public should support the authorities in their current "rescue mission"; they were busy rescuing the domestic banking system, and dealing with both a currency crisis and liability claims from abroad.

But criticism emerged in the public discourse. Intellectuals and novelists, journalists and other critics brought up points that would echo in the public discourse in the subsequent weeks and months. Some criticized the authorities for secrecy and white lies; the optimistic Icelandic public had indulged in overspending and extensive borrowing while the system was heading for collapse.[7] Some claimed that the naïve faith of the authorities in free-market principles had made them blind to the danger of their hands-off policy vis-à-vis the financial sector, leading them to allocate insufficient resources into supervising and controlling financial institutions.[8] Others argued that political corruption had resulted in bad decisions in the past, including the sale of the state banks to "men with party connections but no experience of directing banks" in the early 2000s.[9]

Moreover, while it is common for conflict to arise in Iceland's political debate, what was novel was that protesters began to challenge the authorities in the street. The collective challenge started in the midst of the bank collapse. Two days after Haarde's somber address, a well-known musician, Bubbi Morthens, held a "protest concert" in downtown Reykjavík. About a thousand people attended it, some carrying anti-government slogans. Later in the week, two public protest meetings were held in downtown Reykjavík. While only about a hundred individuals showed up for each of these meetings, they brought a message of challenge: they carried anti-government slogans, and speeches were held with allegations of corruption and flawed democracy, demanding the resignation of the government and certain government officials.[10]

These early protests received considerable attention and, despite very limited public participation, were mentioned by the foreign press covering the banking crisis in Iceland.[11] In a context of emotionally charged, national, focus, the crisis was being framed as a crisis of democracy and government. The seeds of collective challenge were being sown.

The unfolding crisis and the evolution of the protest

Over the following weeks, the anxious Icelandic public witnessed the crisis unfold through constant media coverage. All the news was bad. First of all, a severe economic recession seemed inevitable; the media carried reports of a wave of bankruptcies and lay-offs anticipated in the near future, along with dropping real-estate values, ongoing depreciation of the króna, and inevitable inflation.[12] The depreciation of the króna and high inflation meant not only a reduced standard of living for most individuals but severe financial trouble for many in-debt households (prior to the crisis it had been easy to obtain loans from the banks to buy a larger house, to renovate one's kitchen, buy a new car, and so on). Since all loans were index-linked, reflecting changes in the cost of living ("price-ensured loans") or the exchange rate of certain foreign currencies ("currency loans"), the outstanding balance of many of them rose by as much as 100 percent, while real-estate values dropped. The monthly payments faced by in-debt households were on the increase as they headed into deep crisis.[13]

The fiscal and diplomatic crisis became more serious as the days went by. Between the cost of re-financing the entire domestic banking system and taking measures to meet the enormous foreign debt that appeared to be falling on the state, there was no light at the end of the tunnel. Iceland desperately needed foreign currency, and on October 24 the authorities applied to the International Monetary Fund (IMF) for assistance. But the IMF was apparently unwilling to provide Iceland with a currency loan unless the Icelandic authorities agreed to compensate the United Kingdom and the Netherlands for the Icesave accounts (Jóhannesson 2009:249); both these countries had representatives on the IMF board. Even the other Nordic countries, which are frequently assumed in Iceland to be sympathetic toward the country, refused to provide Iceland with currency loans unless it first agreed to meet the British and Dutch demands in connection with the Icesave claim. Despite legal uncertainty regarding the claim, the Icelandic authorities soon agreed to enter into a negotiation process concerning reimbursing the United Kingdom and the Netherlands for compensation paid to Icesave account holders. Humiliated and coerced, Iceland then became the first Western nation in 30 years to enter an IMF program on November 19, 2008 (Matthíasson 2008).

During this time the media bombarded the public with news about scandalous practices and alleged criminal behavior in the financial sphere. Through intricate patterns of cross-ownership, the banks had seemingly invested in themselves to conceal their problems and maintain high stock values. Major shareholders in the banks had apparently borrowed enormous amounts from their own banks. News came out about high-up bank employees being granted relief on huge loans that they had been encouraged to take to buy bank shares during the good times. The emerging image was that of a thoroughly corrupt financial system.

As the crisis unfolded, public protest meetings became regular in downtown Reykjavík, attracting a growing number of individuals. The meetings became a platform for challenging the way in which the authorities framed the crisis as a global, as opposed to a local, problem. In the course of a few weeks, thousands of individuals began to attend the meetings, including nationally known intellectuals, critics, and activists, who argued that Iceland's political leadership had led the nation into crisis due to corruption and blind faith in market forces. Collective demands emerged: the ruling government was called on to resign, along with the Chairman of the Board of Governors of the Central Bank, and the Director of the Financial Supervisory Authority. One protest event, a large public meeting on November 24, was broadcast live on national television. The Prime Minister and most of the cabinet attended it as members of a panel to answer questions from the public. That night the public witnessed angry citizens scolding the political leaders and booing at their replies.[14] Collective challenge had become a real feature of the unfolding crisis.

As the weeks went by and government leaders showed no intention of stepping down, protest actions became more threatening to public order. Activists began resorting to disruptive tactics to force the government to step down, spicing up the public meetings with an anticipation of public disorder and organizing contentious performances outside of the platform of the meetings. Eventually, on January 20, 2009, threatening mass protest broke out. Thousands of demonstrators gathered on Austurvöllur square in downtown Reykjavík, facing the parliament building and, imitating South American *cacerolazo* demonstrations, banged on pots and pans, shouting slogans, chanting, and singing. Most were committed to peaceful action, but some frontline protesters engaged in vandalism and confrontation with riot police who lined up with shields to protect the parliament building. The protests went on for three successive days and created an atmosphere of civil unrest and disorder throughout the downtown area, and the noise could be heard kilometers away. In the evenings, bonfires were lit, and the demonstrations turned into riots; police used gas and batons to disperse the crowd. Referring to their use of kitchen utensils, the protesters claimed that a "pots and pans revolution" (*búsáhaldabylting*) was in process.[15]

The pots and pans protests attracted widespread participation and support among the public, and involved a serious threat to public order, creating strong pressure on government leaders to step down. Eventually, on January 26, Prime Minister Haarde announced that his government was stepping down. The protests had broken the partnership of the Independence Party and the Social Democratic Alliance.[16] A temporary, minority left-wing coalition government was formed in the next few days, and general elections were promised in the spring.[17] After the government resigned, activists continued protesting for a time, but public participation waned rapidly and institutionalized politics prevailed again in Iceland. The financial crisis had spurred a protest wave which, in the end, had brought down Haarde's coalition government, sixteen weeks after his memorable, somber address to the nation.

The significance of the Icelandic case: Iceland in global context

We now know, several years later, that Iceland was not the only country to experience popular protest in the wake of the global financial crisis. After striking Iceland in early October 2008 the financial crisis spread and triggered popular protests in many other European countries.[18] In January 2009, three months after the Icelandic protests started, mass protests broke out in Lithuania (Woolfson 2010). Like Iceland, the Baltic countries had gone through a period of enormous economic growth fueled by foreign credit, followed by sharp economic contraction, growing unemployment, falling property prices, and reduced income and consumption. As in Iceland, in the context of an unfolding crisis, protesters directed their anger against their national authorities. In the following months and years, anti-government protests broke out in other Eastern European countries, such as Slovenia (Razsa and Kurnik 2012), the Czech Republic (Navrátil and Císař 2013), and Romania (Burean and Badescu 2014). Moreover, between 2010 and 2012 the implementation of austerity measures led to large-scale popular protests in Southern Europe, including Portugal (Accornero and Pinto 2014), Spain (Calvo 2013), and Greece (Johnston and Seferiades 2012; Rudic and Karyotis 2013a).

This international wave of popular protest associated with the global financial crisis has naturally evoked the interest of social movement scholars. Research is still in its early stages, but important observations have been made. One emerging view has been to define the protests in Europe as a part of a global protest wave that includes the Arab Spring uprisings in 2011, the Occupy Wall Street movement, also in 2011, and even the protests in Turkey and Brazil in 2013 (della Porta and Mattoni 2013; Tejarina et al. 2013). Thus, della Porta and Mattoni (2013:2) have emphasized that all of these different national protests should be seen:

> not as isolated instances of protest that happened to have a few characteristics in common but rather as linked to one another as part of the wave of protest that began to develop in 2008 with the revolts in Iceland and continued with the protests in Turkey and Brazil.

By identifying the different national protests as parts of a global protest wave, della Porta and Mattoni (2013) emphasize that they were not isolated national reactions to a spreading global crisis, but affected one another through transnational diffusion of protest repertoires, that is, ideas (e.g. ideas of participatory democracy) and methods (e.g. formation of protest camps, or occupation of public spaces). As social movement research indicates (Andrews and Biggs 2006; Myers 2010), protests in one place may inspire protest in other places through diffusion of ideologies, frames, identities, protest methods and innovations, and by giving examples of successful action. In this vein, della Porta and Mattoni (2013) define the different national protests as the "movements of the crisis"; they are driven in part by transnational diffusion of frames and methods across countries hit by the crisis, and eventually also to countries hit less severely by the crisis (such as Brazil).

The Icelandic financial crisis protests hold a special place in this global protest wave. Iceland was one of the first hard-hit victims of the global credit crisis, and thus was the first country to react to it with popular protests, starting shortly after the bank collapse in October 2008. Notwithstanding the importance of other early protests (Sakellaropoulos 2012; Woolfson 2010), this "early start" enhances the significance of the Icelandic case. It enables us to isolate the national-local conditions created by the financial crisis from the subsequent spreading of protest frames and methods (e.g. Kousis 2013; Roos and Oikonomakis 2013). In other words, the Icelandic case allows us to study how the local conditions created by the financial crisis are conducive to protest, without the "contamination" of crisis protest repertoires spreading from other countries. But, this is not to say that global protest repertoires played no role in the Icelandic protests. As it turns out, they certainly did.

The global financial crisis did not evoke mass protest in all countries struck by it, nor did international currents of protest repertoires gain momentum everywhere. If the Icelandic protests represent the beginning of the global protest wave, they provide a microcosm, a particular national context, for studying how the financial crisis triggered the forces of protest. Importantly, della Porta (2013) has argued that despite the global nature of the financial crisis, and despite the fact that the spreading protest repertoires were rooted in the late 1990s global movement against corporate globalization, the recent crisis protests have all been focused on national, as opposed to global, issues. The recent crisis protests have involved citizens protesting against their own national governments, and the protest discourses have focused on political corruption, lack of representation, and weakening of national sovereignty vis-à-vis global capitalist forces and interests (della Porta 2012b; della Porta and Mattoni 2013; Fominaya and Cox 2013). Although research is still very limited, scholars have suggested that the crisis may have had a particularly strong impact on popular protest in countries where popular discontent with national democracy already existed prior to the crisis (Pappas and O'Malley 2014). Indeed, a major theme to be treated in this book is that the financial crisis spurred the forces of protest by amplifying pre-existing discontent with the state of democracy.

Another important feature of the recent crisis protests, which also distinguishes them from the earlier "global justice" protests, is that many of them have involved a high level of participation by the general public. Social surveys indicate that in recent years public participation in protest has increased drastically in countries such as Portugal and Spain (Accornero and Pinto 2014). In some countries, public participation has been enormous. For example, survey work has indicated that about one third of the population of Greece participated in anti-austerity demonstrations in 2011 (Rudig and Karyotis 2013a). As can be expected given such enormous participation, protesters are not merely the "usual suspects," that is, young grassroots activists and radical leftists, but "ordinary" people of various backgrounds, many of whom have never protested before (Rudig and Karyotis 2013b).

Thus, the financial crisis has in many places made the general public highly receptive to protest mobilization and the protests have often created a substantial threat to public order and spurred political instability. This fact makes the global protest wave particularly interesting from the point of view of social movement research and the Icelandic setting provides a case in point. As I show later in this book, about one quarter of adult Icelanders participated in the financial crisis protests, and a substantial majority supported them. This enormous protest mobilization created enough pressure to bring down the government and force the authorities to hold new elections. In affluent democratic societies, street protests rarely attract enough participation and support to bring down the government.

Moreover, this high level of protest mobilization is even more remarkable given that Iceland has almost no tradition of street demonstrations threatening public order. While social movement organizations, such as movements for gay rights, women's liberation, or workers' solidarity, regularly plan peaceful marches and demonstrations in Iceland, recent Icelandic history contains no instances of threat to public order mass protests of the type that emerged after the bank collapse.[19] In fact, we need to go back as far back as 1949, when Iceland joined NATO, to find an instance of protest confrontation with the police (Jóhannesson 2006:49–137). This absence of any tradition of mass protests makes it even more interesting to study how the crisis spurred the forces of mass protest in Iceland.

Finally, the global protest wave has compelled researchers to address new ways in which "human agency" (goal-driven behavior of individuals) plays a role in protest mobilization. Many of the crisis protests have been characterized by an absence of formal organization, established political actors and central organizational planning, and often they have had no clear leadership (della Porta and Mattoni 2013:8). New actors unaffiliated with formal movements have played major roles in the protests, in conjunction with the "usual" grassroots activists and radical leftists. A major reason for this development may be that social media networking sites have become major arenas of protest mobilization, enabling individual actors and small groups to perform mobilization work and innovate effectively (Postill 2014). Another reason may be that in many places the financial crisis had a life-shattering effect on many individuals, potentially making many of them receptive to protest mobilization. The current work on the Icelandic case will confirm the pivotal role of independent actors in the development of the protests. By illustrating the "spontaneous" nature of mobilization in the crisis protests, we can also come to understand why the "movements of the crisis" have rarely lasted beyond the shared momentum of the financial crisis.

Aims of the book

This book examines how the financial crisis spurred a protest wave in Iceland in the fall of 2008 and January 2009. The broad objective is to identify the major forces underlying the evolution of the protests, thus contributing to social movement theory as well as to the emerging research on the global crisis protest wave. The study is case-centered (George and Bennet 2005), and thus uses multiple methods – qualitative and quantitative – that cut across levels of analysis and address several major issues in social movement research.

Specifically, the study addresses three major research topics. First, I examine how the historical-political context of the financial crisis was conducive to the emergence of protests in Iceland. Ever since Marx (1967 [1887]) placed economic crisis at the heart of his theory of rebellion, the role of crises in spurring revolt has been an important, albeit understudied, issue in social movement theory. While crises have only recently become the focus of attention in research on protests in affluent democratic societies (della Porta and Mattoni 2013; Pappas and O'Malley 2014; Woolfson 2010), the triggering effect of crises has been a major topic in work on historic revolts (Davies 1962) and on revolts and protests in Third World countries (e.g. Walton and Ragin 1990). Taken together, the work implies that crises spur revolts and major protests not merely by creating widespread economic strain (Davies 1962; Gurr 1970), but by changing the political context (Almeida 2003, 2010; Auyero 2001; Auvinen 1996; Gemici 2013; Ortiz and Béjar 2013; Skocpol 1979; Walton and Ragin 1990) and perhaps by disrupting established lives and the shared world-views of many people at the same time (Borland and Sutton 2007; Snow et al. 1998).

If research on the link between crisis and protests has been limited, especially in the context of affluent democratic societies, the recent global protest wave spurred by the financial crisis has brought the issue to the forefront of social movement research. The Icelandic case provides an important opportunity to illustrate the intermediate processes translating the financial crisis into mass protests. This book studies not merely the economic effects of the crisis, but how it changed the historical, political, and social context in Iceland.

The second major topic of the book is to study the role of "human agency" in translating crisis into mass protests. Contemporary social movement theory emphasizes that the actions of goal-driven individuals – human agents – are pivotal in linking broad social change and protest mobilization. No matter how conducive a given change in the social or political context (crisis, war, etc.) may be for collective action, it does not "automatically" lead to such action, but can do so only through the interpretations and deliberate actions of goal-driven actors (Jasper 2012; McAdam et al. 1996). Such key actors need to interpret a given change as opportunity for mobilizing others, and they need to act on this perception by engaging in protest planning, protest actions and innovations, and meaning-making (Benford and Snow 2000; Oberschall 1996; Snow and Benford 1988; Snow et al. 1986; Swidler 1986, 2003; see Johnston 2009).

Moreover, goal-driven actors play a key role in driving the dynamics of expanding protest (della Porta 2012a). Ongoing protests may create opportunities for more protests (Koopmans 2004), by attracting new protest actors and strengthening activist networks; they may create a shared sense of collective efficacy and solidarity and may facilitate the emergence and diffusion of shared frames that call for more protests. The present study explores the developing interpretations, innovations, and framing work of major actors in the Icelandic protest wave. The major actors include not only protest organizers and activists staging contention at protest events, but also prominent public intellectuals and social critics who assumed an active role in framing the crisis in the public debate.

The third major aim of the book is to study the individual-level processes underlying protest participation by individual citizens. The Icelandic setting provides an opportunity to examine and juxtapose the processes underlying protest behavior in a time of crisis. Early "breakdown" theories argued that crises were conducive to mass protests because when they end prosperity, many individuals perceive their losses as unjust and frustrating, thus motivating them to participate in protests (Davies 1962; Gurr 1970). This theory has rarely been applied in the "appropriate" historical setting of a sudden crisis (for an exception, see Rudig and Karyotis 2013a, 2013b), but Iceland provides a case in point, as in fact does the recent global wave of protest. As in many other countries, the Icelandic crisis ended a long period of growing prosperity, creating widespread perception of economic loss (Ragnarsdóttir et al. 2013).

But, as we will see, the crisis created not only economic strain, but also evoked political and cultural processes that probably motivated many individuals to protest on the basis of "frame alignment" (Snow et al. 1986), that is, on the grounds of their political attitudes, beliefs, and allegiances. As cultural theorist Swidler (1986; 2003) argues, ideology influences behavior in "unsettled" times; when people need to choose a side in emerging conflict, they rely on their existing frames and ideologies. I use mixed methods to address these and other processes influencing protest behavior, including social (McCarthy and Paulsen 1993) and situational-emotional incentives (Jasper 1998), and biographical availability characteristics (McAdam 1986).

Methods

The case study relies on mixed methods. In addition to using available statistics from police and public agencies, I obtained original data by using qualitative interviews, discourse analysis, and social surveys. Iceland is a convenient place for conducting a case study focused on a particular national context. The country is small. It has only about 320,000 inhabitants and it has only one metropolitan area, the Reykjavík area. Most of the protest action took place in downtown Reykjavík, making it manageable to study most of the main protest events that took place in the fall of 2008 and January 2009 and also to contact and interview the key actors who instigated and planned protest events and to study the bulk of the signifying performances from the period. It also made it easier to survey the general public.

I used three methods of data collection: semi-structured interviews, a discourse analysis, and social survey work. I conducted semi-structured interviews with thirty individuals. First, I interviewed leading protest organizers, that is, individuals who directed the scheduled public meetings and large protest events. Second, I interviewed both "active" and "passive" protest participants. Thus, I interviewed participants who assumed an active role in staging acts of contention at the protest meetings as well as outside of them (I frequently refer to such actors as "ground-level activists" in this work) and individuals who joined the protests, for example, by shouting slogans and beating pots and pans, but did not lead or take part in planning any protest performances. Third, I interviewed individuals (intellectuals, social critics) who were prominent in framing the crisis in the public debate, that is, in the news and social media. Finally, I interviewed police officers who managed police operations at the protests. Appendix A details the methodology of the interview work. I draw on the interviews in all chapters of this book. Aside from a few well-known individuals (that is, well known in Iceland) who agreed to be named in this work, I assign pseudonyms to my interviewees. Table 1A in Appendix A presents a list of the interviewees showing their characteristics and main roles in the protests.

I performed a discourse analysis of "framing work," including speeches, articles, interviews, press conferences, blogs, and other texts from the post-collapse period between October 2008 and late January 2009. The discourse analysis is presented in Chapter 4, which focuses on the substantive content of the protest discourse. In this part of the analysis I use the term "signifying agent" to refer to the actors who played prominent roles in framing work after the collapse. These include protest organizers and ground-level activists as well as intellectuals and critics who spoke at public meetings and appeared in the news and social media to frame the crisis. This analysis also studies the framing performed by government leaders. Appendix A details the methodology of the discourse analysis.

Finally, I use two population-representative surveys that measure participation in, and support for, the protests. First, the Reykjavík Area Social Survey measures participation in, and support for, the January 2009 pots and pans demonstrations. Second, the National Voting Study measures participation in, and support for, the financial crisis protests more generally. Appendix B presents the methodology of the two surveys, and reports descriptive results produced by all survey instruments that are used in the book. Appendix C reports the full regression models for the analysis of the statistical predictors of protest participation and protest support. I present the results of this analysis in a simplified manner in Chapter 5.

Book outline

The chapters move across the historical context of the crisis, through the role of agency, to the level of individual mobilization. Chapter 2 (Context of Crisis) studies the historical-political context of the crisis, and aims to explain how it was conducive to the development of popular protests. The chapter identifies the historical convergence of two major factors. First, using the terms of Snow et al. (1998), the crisis disrupted the Icelanders' "quotidian"; it produced a perceived threat to people's way of life and taken-for-granted social reality. In a shared moment of confusion and anxiety, many individuals needed to make sense of the crisis and restore moral order. Second, the crisis harmed the credibility of the authorities, undermining the ability of government leaders to avert blame for the situation. Not only did the outspoken commitment of the authorities to neo-liberal reforms in the decades leading up to the collapse appear naïve and misguided in the midst of the crisis, but having to negotiate with foreign entities made them vulnerable to criticism for serving foreign capitalist interests. Furthermore, since Iceland was the only country suffering the collapse of its entire banking system at the time, it was difficult to blame only global forces for the crisis.

In the language of political process/opportunity theory (Tarrow 2011), the crisis created an opportunity for mobilizing a challenge against the authorities. This brings us to the second major topic, which is a study of the role of individual actors, or human agents, in using the crisis to mobilize others in protest. Chapters 3 and 4 do this by studying interpretations, actions, and framing by protest organizers, activists, and signifying agents.

Chapter 3 (Evolution of Protest) uses qualitative interviews, police data, and survey work to study the development of the protests. I discuss how, during the initial unfolding of the crisis, inspired by a perception of opportunity, and motivated by their political goals, a handful of individuals initiated a novel platform for contention in Iceland, namely, public meetings. As the crisis evolved in the next few weeks, public participation grew and the meetings became an epicenter of protest innovation and framing. Participation then waned for a while during the holiday month of December 2008, but ongoing activism kept the protests alive. After the holidays, in January 2009, growing participation and activism concluded in "pots and pans protests" involving enormous public participation and support. In the final protest phase, after the unifying demand for government resignation had been met, protest no longer attracted public participation and faded out after a few weeks.

Chapter 4 (Evolution of Discourse) examines the substantive content of the protest discourse that emerged in Iceland after the bank collapse. Relying on a discourse analysis of texts and performances, I discuss how various types of signifying agents – protest organizers, activists, social critics, intellectuals, and journalists – framed the financial crisis, at public meetings and elsewhere, not merely as an economic crisis but as a political and moral crisis calling for democratic reform. The historical-political context of the crisis enabled the signifying agents to amplify pre-existing discourses about political corruption and unbridled neo-liberal reforms. Interestingly, however, the most unifying element of the emerging collective action frame, namely, the demand for government resignation (a claim strategically extracted by the key players at the public meetings), pre-determined the end of the protest wave, leaving many activists dissatisfied with the success of the campaign.

Chapter 5 (Individual Mobilization) addresses the individual-level processes underlying the behavior of protest participants. Using both semi-structured interviews with protesters and survey work with samples representative of the population of the Reykjavík area, I explore the frames and experiences of protesters "on the ground" and test the predictors of protest participation and protest support. This work reveals that several types of incentives combined to mobilize individual citizens to participate in and support the ongoing protests. Thus, "frame alignment" (Snow et al. 1986) created strong political incentives for many individuals to protest. But, social and emotional incentives also played a role. Interpersonal ties entailed incentives to protest, and for many the protest site was an exciting location to meet with people and enjoy "magical" moments of affective solidarity. Economic loss played a role in protest behavior, but its effects were limited to individuals who thought that the crisis was harming them more than others. Furthermore, the work reveals the role of disincentives and costs. Some individuals struggled with identity issues when they thought that others went too far and when they themselves crossed the boundaries to become protesters. Finally, I find that greater age, having children, and living far from the protest site significantly reduced a person's probability of participating in the protests. Still, participation was prevalent in most social groups: protesters came from many different backgrounds.

Chapter 6 (Conclusion) summarizes the findings and discusses how the application of social movement theory helps to explain the evolution of the Icelandic financial crisis protests, thus addressing the "usefulness" of the theories. In particular, I discuss how the study contributes to research about 1) the link between crises and popular protests, 2) the role of human agency in translating "opportunity" into protest mobilization, and 3) the incentives (and disincentives) underlying the protest behavior of individual citizens. I also address the implications of the work for current research on the global protest wave.

Notes

1 Jóhannesson (2009) has written about many of the historical details discussed in this chapter.

2 Haarde, Geir H. "Prime Minister's Address Due to Special Circumstances in the Financial Market." Special broadcast on Iceland's National Radio and Television. Reykjavík, October 6, 2008. Like most of the other quotes in this book, this text was originally in Icelandic and appear here in the author's translation.

3 "Ekki þörf á aðgerðapakka" (No need for an operation packet) (article). (2008, October), *Mbl.is*. Available online at www.mbl.is/frettir/innlent/2008/10/05/ekki_thorf_a_adgerdapakka/

4 "Hætta á að landið verði olíulaust" (A risk that the country may become without oil) (article). (2008, October), *Viðskiptablaðið*. Available online at www.vb.is/frettir/12986/?q=and

5 "Lög um gjaldeyrismál samþykkt" (Legislation on currency issues passed) (article). (2008, November), *Mbl.is*. Available online at www.mbl.is/frettir/innlent/2008/11/28/log_um_gjaldeyrismal_samthykkt/

6 "Hryðjuverkalögum beitt gegn landsbanka" (Terrorist act enforced against Landsbankinn) (article). (2008, October), *Mbl.is*. Available online at www.mbl.is/vidskipti/frettir/2008/10/08/hrydjuverkalog_gegn_landsbanka/

7 Björg Eva Erlendsdóttir. (2008, October). "Þögn er gull en kjaftæðið króna" (Silence is gold but nonsense is króna) (article). *Mbl.is*. Available online at www.mbl.is/greinasafn/grein/1247798/; Jón Trausti Reynisson. (2008, October). "Við brugðumst ykkur" (We failed you) (article). *DV.is*. Available online at www.dv.is/leidari/2008/10/10/vid-brugdumst-ykkur/

8 Þorvaldur Gylfason. (2008, October). "Saklausir vegfarendur" (Innocent bystanders) (article). *Visir.is*. Available online at www.visir.is/saklausir-vegfarendur/article/2008350689856; Einar Már Guðmundsson. (2008, October). "Herhvöt úr norðri" (Call for arms from the north) (article). *Mbl.is*. Available online at www.mbl.is/greinasafn/grein/1250149/

9 Þorvaldur Gylfason, speech at a public meeting in Háskólabíó, Reykjavík, November 24, 2008.

10 "Mótmæla Davíð Oddsssyni" (Protest against Davíð Oddsson) (article). (2008, October), *Visir.is*. Available online at www.visir.is/motmaela-david-oddsssyni/article/2008944858393

11 "Mótmæli á Arnarhóli vekja athygli" (Protest at Arnarhóll receives attention) (article). (2008, October), *Mbl.is*. Available online at www.mbl.is/frettir/innlent/2008/10/10/motmaeli_a_arnarholi_vekja_athygli/

12 "Hundrað manna hópuppsagnir um mánaðamótin" (Hundreds laid off by the end of the month) (article). (2008, October), *Visir.is*. Available online at www.visir.is/hundrad-manna-hopuppsagnir-um-manadamotin/article/2008873968238; "Verðbólgan mælist 18,1%" (Inflation is 18.1%) (article). (2008, December), *Mbl.is*. Available online at www.mbl.is/vidskipti/frettir/2008/12/22/verdbolgan_maelist_18_1_prosent/

13 "Íbúðalánasjóður gæti hrunið" (The Homeloan Fund might collapse) (article). (2008, December), *Dv.is*. Available online at www.dv.is/neytendur/2008/12/9/ibudalanasjodur-gaeti-hrunid/

14 Lára Hanna Einarsdóttir. (2008, November). "Magnaður borgarafundur" (An amazing citizen meeting) (blog post). *Lára Hanna*. Available online at http://blog.pressan.is/larahanna/2008/11/25/magnadur-borgarafundur/

15 "Kröftug mótmæli við Alþingishúsið" (A strong protest by the Parliament building) (article). (2009, January), *Visir.is*. Available online at www.visir.is/kroftug-motmaeli-vid-althingishusid/article/2009271666814; "Piparúða beitt á mótmælendur – tíu í handjárnum" (Pepper spray used on protesters – ten in handcuffs) (article). (2009, January), *Visir.is*. Available online at www.visir.is/piparuda-beitt-a-motmaelendur–tiu-i-handjarnum/article/200952240833; "Táragasi beitt á Austurvelli" (Teargas used at Austurvöllur) (article). (2009, January), *Mbl.is*. Available online at www.mbl.is/frettir/innlent/2009/01/22/taragasi_beitt_a_austurvelli/

16 Gunnarsson, Valur and Mark Tran. (2009, January). "Icelandic PM becomes world's first leader to step down over banking system crisis" (article). *The Guardian*. Available online at www.theguardian.com/world/2009/jan/27/iceland-prime-minister-resignation

17 "Jóhanna þakkaði traustið" (Jóhanna said thanks for the trust) (article). (2009, February), *Mbl.is*. Available online at www.mbl.is/frettir/innlent/2009/02/01/skjaldborg_slegid_um_heimilin/

18 For brief overviews of recent European protests, see: http://councilforeuropeanstudies.org/critcom/enough-dispatches-from-researchers-studying-europes-exploding-social-movements-3/

19 I should note that earlier in the year 2008, in March and April, truck drivers protested increasing oil prices by blocking traffic on main roads, on several occasions. One of these protests escalated into physical conflict with police, attracting a group of youths who took part in the drivers' conflict with the police. See: Evening news, Icelandic National Radio and Television, April 23, 2008.

2 Context of crisis

> I have this photo from one of the demonstrations on the wall of my office. It shows a boy holding up a sign reading "HELVÍTIS FOKKING FOKK!" I think that this sign captures what was going on inside the heads of many of us. Everything was collapsing and people had a hard time grasping what was going on and why.[1]

Icelandic authors and popular commentators have often used the "HELVÍTIS FOKKING FOKK!" sign to capture the collective mood in Iceland during the days and weeks following the October 2008 bank collapse. As these words of 44-year-old protester Kári bear witness to, the bank collapse disrupted Icelanders' shared reality, creating anxiety, frustration, and confusion. Furthermore, as the unfolding fiscal and diplomatic crisis rapidly undermined the credibility of the country's authorities, many individuals felt left without a perspective on these disorienting events. This convergence of social disruption and a political credibility crisis would provide a fertile ground for the growth of popular protest in the coming weeks.

This chapter examines the historical and political context of the Icelandic crisis, identifying how it was conducive to popular protest. It addresses a classic, but understudied, topic in social movement theory, namely, the question of why crises sometimes spur mass protests and uprisings. Social theorists have long noticed that economic crises often precede revolts and mass protests. Karl Marx (1967[1887]) famously placed economic crisis at the heart of his theory of revolt, arguing that crises intensify and unleash pre-existing conflict and thus increase the probability of uprisings.[2] Moreover, early social movement theory on revolts and uprisings was preoccupied with the impact of sudden changes and disruptions on uprisings and mass protest (Davies 1962; Gurr 1970). Rooted in classical social theory (Durkheim 1951 [1897], 1984 [1893]), the early scholarship assumed that sudden changes and disruptions were conducive to rebellions because they caused a breakdown in mechanisms of social control; they undermined social cohesion and created widespread individual strain (Buechler 2004; Goldstone 1980; Snow et al. 1998; Useem 1998).

In the past few decades, however, social movement research has not focused much on the role of crises or other types of social disruptions in uprisings and protests, with the exception of research on protests in Third World countries (Ortiz and Béjar 2013; Walton and Ragin 1990). In fact, contemporary social movement research has largely abandoned the breakdown approach (Buechler 2004; Snow et al. 1998), emphasizing instead the political and cultural processes underlying revolts and mass protests. The prevailing assumption in current scholarship has been that collective action is to be explained in terms of the historical and political context (Aya 1979; Foran 1993); analysis should be concerned with how particular political, cultural, and social dynamics lead to collective action.

Empirical research on the processes that sometimes translate crises into major uprisings and mass protests has been limited. But if the global wave of the "movements of the crisis" has brought the issue to the forefront of protest research in affluent countries (della Porta and Mattoni 2013), then the Icelandic case provides an excellent opportunity to address the issue empirically. This chapter uses both breakdown and political process/opportunity theories to identify how the context of the Icelandic financial crisis was conducive to protest.[3]

Breakdown theories: disruption of personal and social realities

Two variants of the breakdown tradition are particularly relevant to the present study. These are theories of 1) relative deprivation, and 2) quotidian disruption. Relative deprivation theory implies that crises and other types of disruptive changes create fertile ground for revolt because they create widespread individual experience of frustration of expectations and goals. Such perceived deprivation presumably results in frustration and perception of injustice, motivating individuals to take part in rebellious action (Davies 1962; Gurr 1970). Thus, Davies (1962) described several historical revolts that all occurred after a prolonged period of growing prosperity ended in a sudden reversal. Davies proposed that frustration was a major intermediate process linking crisis and revolt in such historical contexts. Since prosperity increases expectations and goals of the population – during periods of growth people learn to anticipate increased prosperity in the future – a sudden reversal can create "a mental state of anxiety and frustration when manifest reality breaks away from anticipated reality" (p. 6). A crisis thus creates a mismatch between expectations and goals, on the one hand, and the objective reality of reduced opportunity, on the other hand, creating feelings of unjust deprivation and frustration, resulting in "a revolutionary state of mind" (p. 8).

Thus, relative deprivation theory focuses on the role of individual strain in translating pressures experienced during crises into protest behavior. It proposes that in a crisis, experiencing or anticipating economic loss motivates many individuals to participate in protest. I use survey data to test this process later in this book (in Chapter 5), when I examine at the individual level the processes underlying the protest behavior of ordinary protesters.

Another, more recent, variant of breakdown theory emphasizes that abrupt events such as accidents and disasters can undermine taken-for-granted assumptions and expectations and threaten an established way of life. Snow and his colleagues (1998) have argued that an important consequence of accidents, disasters, and other disruptive events is that they disrupt "the quotidian", that is, the routine life of individuals and their taken-for-granted ideas and expectations. Events that disrupt, or threaten to disrupt, routine life undermine "the taken-for-granted substrate of everyday life" (Snow et al. 1998:4): they create doubt, uncertainty, and confusion about practices and taken-for-granted understandings. Borrowing from Mead's (1938) notion of the "specious present", Snow et al. (1998:5) argue:

> In the specious present doubts, uncertainties, and inhibitions are not at the forefront of consciousness, and action is largely habituated and routinized [...] in the problematic present action is inhibited, routine is stymied, and uncertainties emerge. The problematic present thus arises when the specious present, or the quotidian, is disrupted.

According to Snow et al., events that threaten to disrupt an established way of life, including threats to taken-for-granted subsistence routines, are particularly conducive to the emergence of social movements. Not only do such disruptions cast doubt on taken-for-granted assumptions, but they make individuals more risk-seeking than usual because they are faced with actual or anticipated loss of what they have, making them "powerfully motivated to engage in collective action to reconstitute the quotidian and recoup what they have lost" (p. 17). Thus, in a time of collectively experienced quotidian disruption, individuals are impelled to participate in action to repair the social fabric.

Very few studies have applied this theory directly. One exception is Borland and Sutton's (2007) study of the experiences of women in the Argentinian crisis in the early 2000s. Illustrating the usefulness of this theory for studying activism in times of crisis, Borland and Sutton found that disruption of subsistence routines and threats to ways of life made women open to adopting new (activist) frames and identities. For many women, activism became the new quotidian as it provided them with purpose, solidarity, and identity. Moreover, quotidian disruption led many to question established social practices, including gender inequality, so illustrating the role of quotidian disruption in unveiling the socially constructed character of inequalities previously perceived as natural.

In short, like relative deprivation theory, the theory of quotidian disruption implies that a crisis may motivate individuals to participate in rebellious action due to the experience of actual or anticipated loss. But the theory has macro-social implications as well, emphasizing cultural breakdown; it implies that the disruption of routine existence in a crisis may render taken-for-granted assumptions and shared meanings open for reinterpretation and thus create a shared need for restoring or repairing taken-for-granted reality. Such a situation may provide an opening for the emergence of radical frames and identities.

Implications for the current study

Breakdown theories provide only a partial explanation of how and why crises may spur rebellious action. As scholars have long emphasized, even widespread discontent does not necessarily give rise to the political, cultural, and social forces and dynamics that social movement theorists today consider fundamental in protests and revolts. Zagorin (1973:44) summarized this point nicely years ago:

> [*A*] very long distance separates discontent from revolution. In order for one to lead to the other, many factors must intervene, such as developments in the social and economic structure, conflicts and changes in the political system, the emergence of ideologies, and the like. Such factors are crucial to the dynamic causal process of revolution. Furthermore, they are not attributes of states of mind, but properties of political and social situations or systems.

The failure to study collective intermediate processes and dynamics, and particularly the lack of attention to political context (Aya 1979), has in fact been a major reason for the tendency to ignore breakdown theory in contemporary social movement studies (Buechler 2004). Still, breakdown theories seem useful for studying a case such as the Icelandic one. After all, crises often result in widespread experience and anticipation of economic loss and a threat to people's way of life, and so did the Icelandic crisis (Ragnarsdóttir et al. 2013). But, as the theory's critics have emphasized, disruptive effects of change need to be situated in a historical-political context and subsequent intermediate processes need to be studied.

The current work uses breakdown theory to identify how the disruptive features of the Icelandic crisis contributed to the emergence of protests. Later in this book (in Chapter 5) I study the effects of personal disruption on protest behavior. Specifically, I test whether and how personal economic loss motivated individuals to participate in the protests. In the current chapter, however, I focus on the group-level implications; discussing how the crisis disrupted the shared reality of the Icelandic public, undermining taken-for-granted assumptions and expectations, and creating a shared need for restoring taken-for-granted reality.

Political process/opportunity: change in the political context

Crises may do more than cause economic harm: they may also change the political context. Scholars have pointed out that crises may spur revolts and uprisings by weakening state power and undermining the legitimacy of the authorities. Such effects have been found in pre-modern times. For example, a fiscal crisis undermined state power prior to the French Revolution (Skocpol 1979). Moreover, research on protest in the Third World has found that fiscal crises are conducive to political protest, especially if they entail intervention by international agencies into domestic political-economic policy (usually as austerity measures). Walton and Ragin (1990) compared political protests across Third World debtor countries in the late 1970s and 1980s, and found that countries experiencing austerity pressure from the IMF experienced more political protest than other countries. Though they were unable to observe intermediate processes, these authors suggested that debt-induced austerity created specific targets of protest (namely, international actors such as the IMF, and domestic political actors collaborating with them) while also having far-reaching effects throughout society, providing a broad basis for widespread mobilization.

Likewise, Ortiz and Béjar (2013) examined instances of contentious collective action (demonstrations, strikes, and politically motivated riots) in Latin American countries in the period from 1980 through 2007. Statistical analysis found, after controlling for economic, political, and social-compositional factors, as well as prior protests, that participation by a country in an IMF program greatly increased the likelihood of contentious collective action. Based on these findings, the authors argued that participation in IMF programs render the authorities vulnerable to criticism for giving up sovereignty in the service of foreign capitalist interests.

> This, in turn, decreases the government's legitimacy and makes them more likely to be perceived as caving to the pressures of international agents [...;] people thus lose their belief in the notion that the existing political institutions represent the interests of the society and engagement in contentious action increases as a measure to demand accountability.
>
> (Ortiz and Béjar 2013:508)

Like Walton and Ragin's work, however, this study did not study the intermediate processes.

The political context of democratic Iceland is different from the authoritarian state context of many of the Third World countries studied in previous research. But the general lesson derived from extant work is that crises may change the political context in ways that make collective action more feasible than otherwise (Almeida 2003, 2010; Auyero 2001; Auvinen 1996). How this may occur depends on the historical-political context. Negotiating with foreign entities in times of crisis may damage government legitimacy (Ortiz and

Béjar 2013) and provide specific targets for protest (Walton and Ragin 1990); in other cases the authorities may respond to crisis with neo-liberalist reforms that enrage groups who feel deprived of their entitlements (Gemici 2013). Attention to historical specificity is a key to analyzing changes in political context and their consequences for collective challenge.

Political and discursive opportunities

Focusing on how crisis changes the political context, sometimes by undermining government legitimacy, inevitably brings us to the widely used, but debated (Jasper 2012), notion of political opportunity. Prominent social movement scholars have emphasized that political opportunity often plays a key role in igniting protest waves or cycles, and revolutions (Goldstone and Tilly 2001; McAdam et al. 1996; Tarrow 2011). Goldstone and Tilly (2001, cited in Tarrow 2011:160) define political opportunity as "the perceived probability that social protest actions will lead to success in achieving a desired outcome." For these authors, various changes and developments in the political system or outside it may lead to the emergence of opportunity. Opportunities may arise due to:

> changes that shift the balance of political and economic resources between a state and challengers, that weaken a state's ability to reward its followers or opponents or to pursue a coherent policy, or that shift domestic or outside support away from the regime.
>
> (Goldstone and Tilly 2001, cited in Tarrow 2011:160)

For example, studying the revolutions in Eastern Europe in 1989, Oberschall (1996) argued that the historical convergence of weak legitimacy of the communist regime and the withdrawal of potential military support from the Soviet Union jointly presented an important political opportunity for challenge in that context.

Thus, political opportunity can unleash underlying conflict, enabling dissidents to mobilize others in a challenge against the authorities. Since underlying conflict is embedded in the historically specific context (the distribution of power, elite relations, class relations, political alignments and parties, ideologies and beliefs, ethnicity and nationality, etc.), an insight into the relevant features of the historical context is vital for understanding the meaning of conflict and the motives of those engaged in it. I adopt this approach in the current work.

Social movement scholars have argued that focusing on political opportunity risks ignoring other types of opportunity, including discursive opportunity (della Porta and Diani 2006:219; Koopmans and Olzak 2004). While political opportunity refers to a shift in institutionalized politics which renders the ruling authorities vulnerable to challenge, discursive opportunity refers to the capacity of movement actors to use available ideas, beliefs, and values to transform or create new frames to mobilize others in collective action. Later in this work (in Chapter 4), we will see how efforts to frame the Icelandic crisis as a democratic crisis proved successful because they resonated with the available discourses in society.

Before the collapse: the historical context of the Icelandic financial crisis

The perceptions and conflicts that arose in Iceland after the financial collapse can be understood only if they are situated in the context of the historical, political, cultural, and economic developments that took place before it. The country's political leadership had not only played a leading role in liberating capital from state constraints during the past decade, but had endorsed the subsequent financial expansion, celebrated myths about the superiority of Icelandic bankers and businessmen, and dismissed warning signs that began flashing at least two years in advance. After the bank collapse, in the midst of the shared disruption created by the unfolding financial, economic, fiscal, and diplomatic crisis, these actions and inactions would create a huge credibility deficit for the Icelandic authorities.

State protectionism and constraints: Iceland through the 1980s

A latecomer to the community of Western industrialized societies, Iceland modernized rapidly in the post-World War II period. Still a poor, traditional agricultural society and a Danish dependency at the beginning of the twentieth century, Iceland gained full independence in 1944, and by 1980 had developed into an industrialized, highly affluent welfare democracy (Grímsson and Broddason 1977; Ólafsson 1993). But even as late as the early 1980s, tiny Iceland was homogeneous both culturally and economically; it was a society of dense social relations, acquaintances, high social and institutional trust, and strongly unifying values and norms emphasizing egalitarianism (Bernburg and Ólafsdóttir 2012; Tomason 1980), nationalism (Hálfdanarson 2001), hard work (Ólafsson 1996), and sobriety (Gunnlaugsson and Galliher 1986). Icelanders thought of themselves as having an unusually high degree of social equality (see Broddason and Webb 1975; Grímsson and Broddason 1977; Tomason 1980), and many experienced upward intergenerational social mobility due to the expansion of the middle class in the modernizing economy (Ólafsson 1982; Thorlindsson 1988).

In the early 1980s the state still played a fundamental role in the central planning of major spheres of the economy, culture, and morality. The state had a legal monopoly on radio and television broadcasting (Broddason 2005); political parties controlled the major newspapers (Kristjánsson 1993); extensive state control ranged from price and currency controls to restrictions on opening hours of stores to a ban on the sale of beer (Gunnlaugsson and Galliher 1986). While secular in outlook, more than 90 percent of the population belonged to the Lutheran state church. The state owned and directly operated the major banks and credit was rationed (Ólafsson 2011).

In this context of cultural homogeneity and minimal ethnic diversity, the protectionist role of the state was rarely challenged. Importantly, however, the Icelandic state bureaucracy had always been weak and vulnerable to political manipulation (Kristinsson 1993) and in the 1980s, despite an increasingly complex economy, clientelism and nepotism were die-hard features of Icelandic politics and public administration (Kristjánsson 1993). Positions in state administration and state organizations were often handed out on the basis of political connections and political criteria (Kristinsson 2006; Kristjánsson 2012), and financing of major projects often came through political channels – in a state-run financial system (Kristjánsson 1993).

In this era, labor-capital struggles and polarized ideological conflict about the Cold War still shaped the politics. Four major parties represented the political camps in the Icelandic parliament. In contrast to the neighboring Nordic countries, political power was tilted to the right of the political spectrum (Ólafsson 2011). Thus, the largest political party was the urban-based, center-right Independence Party, which was backed by business and controlled the largest newspaper in Iceland. Supported by about 40 percent of voters, this party usually controlled the executive branch of government in coalition with a minority party. The second largest party was the Progressive Party, a center-pragmatist party also backed by business as well as the rural economy. Last, the political left comprised two small parties: the center-left Social Democratic Party, and the Socialist Party.

Globalization and invasion of free market logic: the 1990s

The 1980s witnessed a shift away from state welfare politics to neo-liberalist economic reforms and reduction in the welfare state in the United States (led by President Reagan) and United Kingdom (led by Prime Minister Thatcher); this shift began to shape Icelandic politics and society in the late 1980s. Furthermore, in the 1990s and 2000s, the global tide of free-market logic changed Icelandic politics, economy, and culture in fundamental ways, rendering the economy, particularly the financial sphere, increasingly "disembedded" (Polanyi 1957) from other social institutions and ultimately leading to unrestrained accumulation of systemic risk for Iceland.

The Independence Party led these developments in the political sphere. In the late 1980s and early 1990s, younger party members began to replace the party's traditional pragmatic conservatism with an outspoken neo-liberal agenda of cuts in welfare spending and business freedom (see Bergmann 2014:41). According to this agenda, state central planning and market and capital restraints were outdated means of running an economy; they needed to be replaced by entrepreneur initiative driven by unrestrained free-market competition. Releasing the forces of private enterprise would benefit society by fueling economic growth. As elsewhere, the end of the Cold War fueled the rise of the free-market ideology in Iceland and, with the most powerful political party adopting it, it ushered in changes in welfare policies, regulation of business and finance, taxation, and state ownership in the following years.

In 1991 the Independence Party formed a coalition government, and the party's new Chairman, Davíð Oddsson, became Prime Minister. In the years to come, under the leadership of Oddsson and his successive cabinets, major moves toward financial liberalization and decreased income redistribution through taxation and welfare benefits occurred (Ólafsson 2008). The Iceland Stock Exchange was established at the beginning of the decade. In 1991 the state made permanent the adoption of a transferable quota system in Icelandic fisheries; permission to catch fish became the private property of individuals who could sell it or rent it out (Árnason 2008). The fishing quotas became a major source of rent-seeking and soon became concentrated in the hands of large companies. This became a topic of fierce political debate in Iceland, especially when quota selling began to leave fishing communities around the country without any catch permits (Einarsson 2015). In 1994 Iceland became a member of the European Economic Area (EEA) Agreement (a type of half-way membership of the EU). Becoming an EEA member was an important change in that it entailed freedom of trade and movement of capital and labor among the member countries. Subsequently, restrictions on capital flow across countries were abolished. In 1997 the authorities decided to spur investment by taxing individuals' capital gains by only 10 percent.[4] Welfare benefits began to lag behind real income (Ólafsson 2011), and flatter income tax rates (with a low tax on capital gains) led to increased inequality in real income (Kristjánsson and Ólafsson 2009). But economic growth was substantial, as it had been in the previous decades. The Icelandic public continued to experience absolute increases in the standard of living, but the rich were becoming richer than the rest of the population.

Capital liberation, "the Outvasion" (Útrásin), and debt accumulation: the 2000s

At the turn of the twenty-first century, the Icelandic authorities put in motion major privatization projects. Between 1998 and 2003 the government, led by Independence Party leader Oddsson, sold several state organizations, including large production and construction companies, the National Telecom of Iceland (one of Iceland's largest organizations), and all of the major financial organizations in Iceland including the three major banks (Sigurjónsson 2010; Icelandic National Audit Office 2003).

This large-scale privatization, and especially the sale of the state banks, created expanding opportunities for business entrepreneurs in Iceland. Domestic and foreign capital became available, leading to multiplied investment capability within the economy. Icelandic investors now operated in a global financial market. The newly privatized banks grew enormously when they began to invest in companies abroad. Released from state restraints, they became international enterprises. By the end of 2003 the total assets of the banks amounted to 174 percent of Iceland's GDP; by the end of 2005 they amounted to 376 percent of GDP (Benediktsdóttir et al. 2011). The market value of companies listed on the Iceland Stock Exchange grew twenty-five-fold between 1996 and 2006, and many companies became investment companies, even hedge funds, without even changing their names (Jónsson 2015:29). Figure 2.1 shows the growth of the Icelandic stock market in the 2000s. A much-used term, "the outvasion" (Icelandic: *útrásin*, implying a dynamic event, the opposite of an invasion), was adopted in media discourse to refer to these developments as a whole (Bergmann 2014:25). With access to the international, short-term financial market, Icelandic entrepreneurs were conquering the outside world.

A new social class of the financial elite emerged and the Icelandic media and yellow press frequently displayed its success and conspicuous consumption. The leaders of the outvasion, that is, the managers and major shareholders in the banks, were extremely well rewarded. One of the Icelandic financial moguls (and main shareholder of Landsbankinn) became the first Icelander to appear on Forbes Magazine's list of the world's wealthiest people (Jóhannesson 2015:17). Even artists became dependent on the generosity of

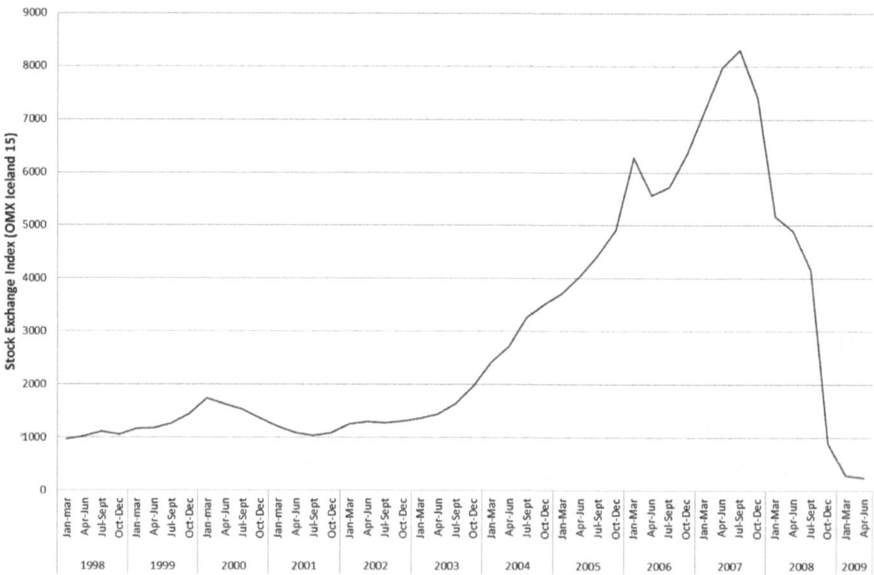

Figure 2.1 The Iceland Stock Exchange main index (OMX Iceland 15), 1998–2009
Source: www.nasdaqomxnordic.com

the financial moguls (Grétarsdóttir et al. 2015). Iceland finally had its own subculture of the super-rich, who

> utilized the newly privatized banks to embark on one the greatest shopping sprees in world history, buying up businesses and investing their borrowed cash around the world. The simultaneous leveraged *outvasion* of Icelandic companies was also caused by fierce internal competition between the groups of Viking Capitalists.
>
> (Bergmann 2014:82)

Moreover, "they indulged in conspicuous consumption on an unprecedented scale, buying an English football club, a Formula One racing team, a yacht formerly owned by Armani, and England's most prestigious bank, Singer & Friedlander" (Jónsson 2015:30).

As ordinary Icelanders felt their standard of living rising every year, their expectations and goals rose as well (Ragnarsdóttir et al. 2013). Iceland's GDP increased 10 percent annually in the mid-2000s (Benediktsdóttir et al. 2011), and the buying power of disposable income rose annually by 4 to 8 percent (Ólafsson 2011:239). An influx of capital into the Icelandic economy strengthened the exchange rate of the króna, lowering the cost of imported products and bolstering the public's buying power both domestically and abroad. With access to loans on the international banking market, the banks offered individuals and businesses in Iceland easy access to loans. Prices of real-estate took off, as did the construction industry. All parts of the economy were running briskly, and companies and owners of capital were tempted to use their position to access credit and invest. The optimistic public did the same; individuals and households accumulated debt to keep up with the Joneses, buying larger homes, new and expensive cars, and so on. In the years leading to the 2008 collapse, total Icelandic household debt more or less doubled (Ólafsson 2011:244).

> Illustrative of the excess is that in 2007 more luxury Range Rovers were sold in Iceland than in Denmark and Sweden combined. The money supply increased [*by up to a half each year and house prices*...] doubled in only a few years, while the rise in real wages lagged behind. Iceland was clearly living well beyond its means. [... *Capital*] inflow was driving the whole economy with both asset prices and the currency rising way beyond their underlying values.
>
> (Bergmann 2014:81)

There was a downside to this of which the public was unaware. Domestic and foreign investment and increased buying power among the public were driven by an accumulation of national debt. When the banks and other investment companies began to invest internationally, they began to accumulate foreign debt, and as investments expanded, national debt became enormous relative to the tiny Icelandic economy. The rising prosperity was an "illusion" (Johnsen 2014:1–11).

Figure 2.2 shows the amount of credit granted to the private sector (by deposit money banks or other credit institutions) as a share of Iceland's GDP. The credit ratio rose by more than 100 percent between 1995 and 2002, but after the privatization of the banks was completed in 2003, accumulation of credit rose exponentially; by 2005 it had grown by more than 300 percent since 1995, and the following year it had grown by 500 percent. By 2005 Iceland was one of the most heavily in-debt economies in the world (Ólafsson 2008:243). But, although the financial expansion was unsustainable, the people leading it had no incentive to slow it down. On the contrary, they had strong incentives to continue on this course. In the words of Ólafsson (2011:27), "external debt escalated and excessive risk behavior became predominant in the Icelandic financial and business environment, driven by the quest for accumulation of assets, profits and bonuses."

The accumulation of national debt did not stop managers and owners of the banks from continuing their aggressive investment strategy, nor did the Icelandic authorities restrain the banks in any significant way. The banks kept growing and in August 2008 their total assets amounted to 865 percent of Iceland's GDP (Benediktsdóttir et al. 2011). In actual size the banks had grown ninefold in only five years. A major share of the total lending by the banks was to their largest owners and related parties (Mixa 2015), a trend that became more pronounced in the final years and months leading up to the bank collapse (Benediktsdóttir et al. 2011:195).

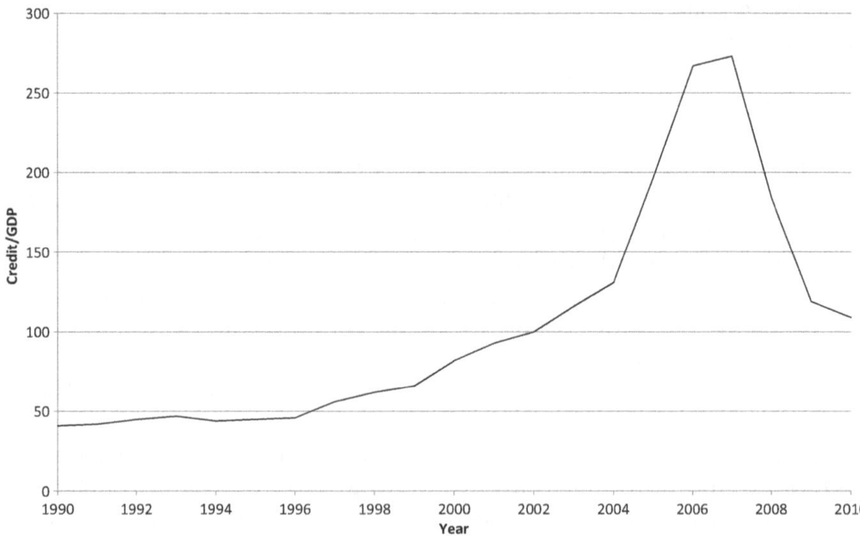

Figure 2.2 Credit to the private sector as a proportion of Iceland's GDP, 1990–2010
Source: Johnsen (2014:7)

Success myths

In the years leading up to the bank crisis, the media in Iceland did little to raise concerns about the growing national debt, but instead delivered celebratory news about Icelandic banks and holding companies buying up companies and banks overseas (Árnason 2015).[5] The National Broadcasting Service concluded its evening news by reporting the values of the Dow Jones and other major stock indexes. With rare exceptions (e.g. Önundarson 2005), Icelandic intellectuals and political commentators expressed little concern about the way things were going.

A "Viking" metaphor appeared in the Icelandic media discourse that combined a reference to the alleged unique qualities of Icelanders with the national roots of Icelandic business entrepreneurs (Bergmann 2014; Jóhannesson 2015; Loftsdóttir 2015). An invented term, "outvasion Viking" (*útrásarvíkingur*) or "business Viking" appeared, referring to the bold invasion of Icelandic entrepreneurs into other countries. As Bergmann (2014:25) points out, in Iceland "the Viking image symbolizes Iceland's Golden Age ... a time of political autonomy and cultural greatness." The implication of the Viking metaphor was that Iceland's cultural heritage and national origins explained how the aggressive and innovative business strategies of the Icelandic entrepreneurs gave them what seemed to be a superior advantage on the international financial market.

The authorities were eager to associate themselves with the economic miracle and the outvasion (Jóhannesson 2015; Loftsdóttir 2015), and despite the exponential accumulation of national debt that was taking place in the mid-2000s, they outspokenly encouraged and apparently supported the ongoing expansion of the financial sector. In 2005, Prime Minister Halldór Ásgrímsson expressed his "dream" of Iceland becoming an "international financial center" (Jóhannesson 2009:97), and the following year a government-appointed committee, led by a top manager of one of the Icelandic banks, concluded that Iceland could become such a center if the authorities created a fruitful environment for financial business (Prime Minister's Office 2006). Iceland's president, Ólafur Ragnar Grímsson, also celebrated the brilliance of the outvasion Vikings, relating it to the country's settlement heritage (Bergmann 2014:84–86). In 2007 a new government comprising the Independence Party and the Social Democratic Alliance listed the expansion of the financial sphere as one of its major goals (Jóhannesson 2009:98).

The uncritical acceptance of the celebratory discourse used by the media and the authorities when referring to the outvasion left the public in no position to suspect that it actually entailed accumulation of systemic risk for Iceland. In this sense, the public was living in an illusion.

Undercurrent of discontent

An undercurrent of left-wing discontent about this political, social, and cultural development emerged in the late 1990s and early 2000s. Left-wing politicians, social critics, and intellectuals criticized how neo-liberal policies (such as the special 10 percent capital gains tax) led to more social inequality and a weakened welfare state. The perception that Iceland was a country of great social equality was vanishing as top earners were leaving the general public behind.[6] The critical voices were often directed at the political leadership of the Independence Party and its strongman leader (and later Chairman of the Board of Governors of the Central Bank), Davíð Oddsson.

Moreover, along with such traditionally leftist criticisms, "new-left" currents reached Iceland, changing the political debate. Socialists, environmentalists, and feminists formed an alliance and founded a new political party, the Left-Green Movement, in 1999, replacing the traditional Socialist Party. Supported by about 10 percent of Icelandic voters, this party represented the alliance of new-left discontent in the parliament during the 2000s.[7] Also, inspired by the global justice movement, activist groups emerged and organized occasional environmental and human rights protests. In particular, a small activist group, "Saving Iceland", organized several protests to direct attention to environmental damage caused by government-led construction of hydro-electric plants and aluminum smelters in Iceland. However, although Icelandic activists were acquiring protest experience and establishing international connections, these protests attracted very limited public participation.

Importantly, another oppositional discourse emerging in the 2000s was that of political corruption and power consolidation that was allegedly associated with the ruling parties. The Independence Party and the Progressive Party formed successive governments from 1995 to 2007, and despite their emphasis on free-market capitalism, many claimed that old-boy nepotism influenced their politics (Kristjánsson 2012). Specifically, in the 2000s several corruption cases surfaced, spurring waves of criticism. First, when the banks were privatized, accusations were made that the leaders of the two ruling parties had intervened in the privatization of two of them, Landsbankinn and Búnaðarbankinn (later Kaupthing). Critics argued that political favoritism had influenced the choice of prospective buyers of the banks. In a rare gesture of protest, the Chairman of the Privatization Committee resigned from his post during the process (Bergmann 2014:68).

Also, cases of political hiring were given great prominence in the media in the mid-2000s (Kristjánsson 2012). District Court and Supreme Court judges were hired seemingly due to their political affiliations with the Independence Party, and on two occasions it was claimed that kinship connections with the party's leader, Davíð Oddsson, influenced the hiring process. Oddsson was appointed as Chairman of the Board of Governors of the Central Bank in 2005 after stepping down as Prime Minister in 2004, spurring widespread criticism of unprofessionalism in the Icelandic government.

As I argue in Chapter 4, the discourse of discontent became a vital resource ("discursive opportunity") in the collective action framing which took place after the bank collapse. But in the pre-crisis period of growth and optimism it did not move the public to act in protest. The majority of Icelandic voters supported the government while their living standards kept rising in a booming economy. It hardly occurred to anyone that it was possible to mobilize the public in a large-scale protest against the authorities.

Warnings dismissed

Although the chain of events leading to the collapse of all three major Icelandic banks in October 2008 surprised almost everyone, warning signs began flashing two years earlier about the non-sustainability of the credit-based investment strategies of the banks and their owners, and about the accumulation of systemic risk for the Icelandic economy. But all warning signs were openly dismissed both by the banks and the Icelandic authorities.

Early in 2006, the Icelandic banks encountered serious difficulty in raising funds on the short-term financial market, resulting in a temporary setback in their asset building (Johnsen 2014:76–79; Figure 2.1 shows how stock market values decreased in early 2006). However, this setback did not halt the financial expansion and the accumulation of debt continued. Rather than soft-pedaling their financial expansion and debt accumulation, the banks found novel ways to raise more funds by initiating high-interest depositing schemes in other countries (Bergmann 2014:88–109). In particular, Landsbankinn opened branches in the United Kingdom and in the Netherlands and launched a savings scheme under the name "Icesave." Making use of European single-market passport regulations, the bank operated like a domestic bank in these countries and collected deposits via high-interest internet-based savings accounts. By the time of the bank collapse in October 2008, the Icesave scheme had collected a sum roughly amounting to the equivalent of Iceland's GDP (Bergmann 2014:110–132). As I discuss below, the Icesave accounts would create a major crisis for the state after the collapse, as the United Kingdom and the Netherlands would claim that the bank's "home country", that is, the Icelandic state, was directly responsible for all the deposits.

While few Icelandic analysts raised any concern about these developments (Sigurjónsson et al. 2011),[8] in early 2006 international credit-rating firms such as Moody's and Standard & Poor's expressed concern about the overheating of the Icelandic economy, the accumulation of national debt, and the fact that the financial system was becoming overly large relative to Iceland's GDP (Bergmann 2014:89–92; Jóhannesson 2009:93). Analysts at international banks, such as the Royal Bank of Scotland and Danske Bank (2006), expressed similar concern. But the Icelandic authorities reacted to the warnings by dismissing them, implying that they were based on faulty information and incompetence, and even that they were motivated by envy and that those who voiced them were acting from malicious motives. Even in the months leading up to the crash, when the credit default swap (CDS) spread applying to the banks had increased substantially (an indicator of the risk that a bank may default), government leaders insisted that warnings were unwarranted.

Thus, one cabinet minister dismissed the Danske Bank (2006) critic by stating that he was in need of "rehabilitation" (Jóhannesson 2009:91).

The authorities were committed to protecting the trustworthiness of the banks right up until the collapse in October 2008. From a speech by Prime Minister Haarde to the Iceland Chamber of Commerce on February 13, 2008:

> In the past few weeks, the CDS spread on the Icelandic banks has increased considerably, probably in part because international investors lack information on the actual position of the banks. […] this spread is in itself a serious issue because it prevents the banks from raising credit in the normal way on the markets, which are already difficult due to the credit shortage. [… *Despite these positive reports and statements*] from the Financial Supervisory Authority, Moody's, Credit Sights and others, we still see negative coverage by *individual* analysts and media. There we *typically see* [… *plain misrepresentations of the facts*] and *the descriptions of the Icelandic economic system are grossly exaggerated.* It is a matter of concern that these parties do not pay attention to the detailed information which is available to everyone and shows the strong position of the banks and the Treasury. *There seem to be forces at work here other than a search for the truth* [italics added by the author].[9]

Such statements were reinforced by state supervisory agencies. On August 15, less than two months before the crash, the Director of the Financial Supervisory Authority issued a press release saying that according to stress tests the Icelandic banks could withstand even a serious market crisis.[10] The night before Prime Minister Haarde delivered his somber address to the Icelandic nation, his message was that the authorities did not need to act on the situation, expressing his satisfaction that the banks now intended to downsize by selling foreign assets. It would become difficult for him and his cabinet to maintain credibility when the banks came down over the next few days.

After the collapse: convergence of quotidian disruption and credibility crisis

If prospects for mobilizing the public in protest were slim in Iceland during the boom years, the crisis changed this context. First, it disrupted the quotidian, creating a shared, emotional focus on defining the crisis. Second, it harmed the credibility of the authorities, making it difficult for them to avert blame for the crisis.[11] The convergence of quotidian disruption and a credibility crisis created a rare opportunity for dissidents at variance with the political leadership to mobilize other Icelanders in protest against it.

Disruption of the quotidian and the shared problematic present

The financial crisis created a breakdown in social order by disrupting the "quotidian" of ordinary people in Iceland. The financial crisis disrupted the taken-for-granted realities of many individuals, creating not only widespread anxiety and relative deprivation due to perceived personal loss, but also undermining shared taken-for-granted assumptions. Using the terms from the breakdown theory of Snow et al. (1998), the crisis disrupted the "specious present" and gave rise to a "problematic present"; it disrupted habit and produced confusion and doubt, hence creating a shared emotional focus on defining the crisis.

The crisis shattered the positive economic expectations of the majority of people. After experiencing a long period of growing prosperity, Icelanders had become used to economic security; most of them were accustomed to anticipating a bright economic future. But the bank collapse changed this perceived reality in a matter of days, creating widespread anticipation of bankruptcies and lay-offs in the following weeks and months, along with falling real-estate values, ongoing depreciation of the króna, and high inflation.[12] Figure 2.3 presents findings of quarterly opinion polls on expectations regarding the economy in Iceland in the near future in the period 2002–2009. Prior to the crisis, the majority were optimistic about the economic future. This optimism peaked in 2007. By the end of 2008 the great majority had become very pessimistic; a major change had taken place in people's perception of their economic future.

The situation created widespread anticipation of personal difficulties and economic loss. Aside from worrying about job losses and reduced buying power in the weeks and months to come, many households had accumulated debt prior to the crisis, when it had been easy to obtain loans from the banks

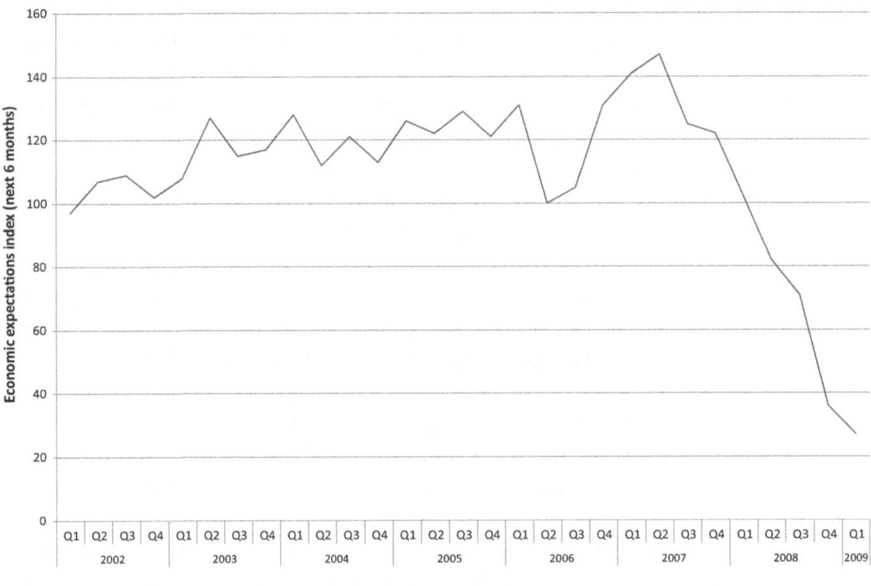

Figure 2.3 Economic expectations of the Icelandic public, 2001–2009
Source: Capacent Gallup. URL: http://data.is/1sV3CyJ

to buy larger houses and new cars. Since loans had been indexed in terms of the consumer price index or linked to specific foreign currencies ("currency loans"), the outstanding balance of these loans increased substantially, even by as much as 100 percent, while real-estate values were dropping. The monthly payments of in-debt households were constantly increasing.[13] Some individuals would lose their jobs in the coming weeks and months: the unemployment rate would go from 1 to 8 percent. Moreover, the majority of people would experience some reduction in their standard of living.[14]

But the crisis did more than create widespread anticipation of personal economic loss. It produced a collectively experienced disruption in taken-for-granted reality; it disrupted taken-for-granted assumptions and ideas about Icelandic society, thus resulting in a shared experience of a problematic present. Icelanders were used to the idea of living in one of the most affluent and secure societies in the world, but Haarde's address on October 6, 2008 threw them into a state of shared uncertainty about their current and future way of life.[15] At that moment Iceland was no longer prosperous and secure. What had felt like economic prosperity was an illusion.

Moreover, the crisis undermined the trustworthiness of major institutions, particularly banks. Banks, which traditionally had been highly trustworthy in Iceland, suddenly could not be trusted. After the bank crash the media bombarded the public with reports of alleged scandalous practices, even criminal behavior, by top managers of the banks and their owners, who apparently had been running wild in a non-regulated zone. The reports implied that in the final months leading to the crash the banks had deliberately concealed their true position; they had kept their stock values high by means of schemes of cross-ownership and bond-buying, while at the same time the owners of the banks had borrowed enormous sums from them, especially in the final years leading up to the collapse (Mixa 2015). High-up bank employees had been granted relief on huge loans that they had been encouraged to take to buy bank shares during the good times. The crisis created a new image; that of a thoroughly corrupt financial sphere. According to opinion polls, in 2008 the public's trust in banks fell by 36 percentage points (Bjarnason 2014).

Also, the crisis threatened Icelanders's shared national identity. Loftsdóttir (2012) has pointed out that while the media had described Icelanders as world players during the boom years, often celebrating the "presumed surprise and admiration of other nations in regard to the Icelandic business venture" (p. 606), in the wake of the collapse many worried that Iceland might fall into the category of a Third World country (see also, Loftsdóttir 2014).

The breakdown theory of Snow et al. (1998) implies that shared quotidian disruption impels individuals to participate in collective action to "reconstitute the quotidian and recoup what they have lost" (p. 17). My interviews with protest participants illustrate how the problematic present created a need for a shared definition of the situation, encouraging many individuals to attend public meetings. Interviewees experienced the crisis as a "shock," "a surreal situation," and "total chaos," and they felt an urge to "understand what was going on" by "discussing it with others." In the words of 29-year-old protester Sigurður, "the crisis was a moral collapse. [...] Icelanders had projected the image that we had conquered the world and we were outvasion Vikings – and then this all collapsed."[16] Saga, a 22-year-old protester, described in an interview how her anxiety during the crisis made her go to the public meetings for a shared perspective:

> the confusion, it was just such a shock [...] we did not know anything, everyone was just clueless with their lives on the line. [...] I went to get information, you know, just to meet other people and talk together, to find out what was going on.[17]

From credibility crunch to foreign threat to legitimacy crisis

The crisis created shared doubt as well as a need to restore moral order and collectively define the situation; it also changed the political context by undermining the credibility and legitimacy of the authorities. While endorsing the financial expansion had been a bullet-proof political strategy in the years leading up to the crisis, it created a credibility crunch for the authorities after the collapse. First of all, the collapse of the banks contradicted the way in which the government and its supervisory institutions (the Central Bank and the Financial Supervisory Authority) had spoken about the banks in the years and months preceding the crash; they had dismissed warnings about the banks' unsustainability, insisting that they were trustworthy. It was as if the authorities had been conducting a public relations campaign on behalf of the failing banks. Moreover, the real and anticipated effects of the bank collapse on the state harmed the legitimacy of the authorities. The same political leadership that had liberated capital from state restraints in the name of free-market efficiency had lost face due to a painful realization: liberation of capital does not indemnify the state and the public against harm if private capital goes wrong.

In the immediate aftermath of the collapse it was widely anticipated that the Icelandic state would take a devastating blow due to the crisis. In the months leading up to the crash it had become clear to international bankers that the total size of the Icelandic banks meant that the tiny Icelandic state would be unable to play a role as a lender of last resort; this undermined the banks' trustworthiness on the international market and ultimately made them vulnerable to runs (Benediktsdóttir et al. 2011).

As a result, the Icelandic state now faced serious fiscal threats. Two major problems surfaced. First, a currency crisis emerged. In the years prior to the crisis, an influx of foreign capital into Iceland had inflated the value of the króna and raised the standard of living, but the country's foreign currency reserves were now drying up due to a capital flight. It came to light that in the weeks before the crisis, repeated attempts by the Central Bank to secure agreements about borrowing foreign currencies from other countries had all failed.

Other countries had been unwilling to help Iceland on its course of unsustainable financial expansion (Jóhannesson 2009:30–61). The Icelandic authorities initially responded to the currency crisis by placing capital controls on foreign exchange transactions. But Iceland desperately needed foreign currency. On October 24, after a failed attempt to borrow currency directly from Russia, the Icelandic authorities applied to the IMF for assistance, as well as asking the other Nordic countries for help.

But the second major problem made much-needed currency loans from the IMF and neighboring countries possible only at a high price for the authorities. As discussed in Chapter 1, when the banks fell, the authorities passed emergency legislation allowing the state to take over and re-finance the domestic operations of the banks, letting the international part of the banks become insolvent. The state hurried to guarantee all domestic savings accounts to assure Icelandic citizens that their savings were secure (so avoiding a run on the new domestic banks). But this huge act of nationalization resulted in enormous liability claims and outright hostility toward Iceland from abroad. The Icesave accounts created the most serious and immediate political problem. When Landsbankinn crashed, more than 400,000 individuals and businesses in the United Kingdom and the Netherlands lost their savings in these accounts. The governments of the two countries had to compensate their citizens, but since the Icesave scheme was run via a branch of Landsbankinn, both governments demanded full compensation from Iceland, arguing that the Icesave accounts were like any other savings accounts in Iceland, and therefore that the Icelandic state was directly responsible for them.[18] The liability claims were immense relative to Iceland's tiny economy (again, roughly amounting to the equivalent of its GDP), and thus threatened to plunge the state into unbearable debt.

From the moment of the bank crash, the media began to focus exclusively on the Icesave affair, causing widespread anxiety and disbelief among the public. Since the legal issues were uncertain, the Icelandic authorities reacted to the Icesave claims with ambiguity, implying that they should be resolved in court. Adding to the intensity of the situation, and the public's worries, the British authorities used anti-terrorist laws to instantly freeze all assets of Icelandic banks in Britain, officially categorizing Iceland as a terrorist group. Icesave thus posed a threat to the country's economy and to the state's financial situation, creating widespread anxiety among the public; it seemed as if the authorities had allowed the banks to take enormous risks at the expense of the Icelandic public.

Despite the legal uncertainty of the Icesave claims, it soon came to light that a currency loan from the IMF would not be granted unless the Icelandic authorities agreed to accept responsibility for Icesave (both the United Kingdom and the Netherlands had representatives on the IMF board; Jóhannesson 2009:249). Even the other Nordic countries (with the exception of the Faroe Islands and Norway) refused to provide Iceland with a currency loan unless it agreed to compensate the United Kingdom and the Netherlands for Icesave. The Icelandic authorities finally agreed to enter into a negotiation process about reimbursing the compensation paid to the holders of Icesave accounts. On November 19, Iceland became the first Western nation to enter an IMF program in 30 years. Foreign entities were thus forcing vulnerable Iceland to take on a part of the banks' enormous liabilities, and the Icelandic authorities complied.

Thus, the unfolding crisis undermined the legitimacy of the authorities, especially in the period from early October through November, 2008. After liberating capital from state restraints and privatizing the banks, neither the present nor the previous government, nor the supervisory agencies (the Central Bank and the Financial Supervisory Authority) had sufficiently restrained the financial sector from outgrowing the Icelandic economy (Johnsen 2014), threatening state insolvency and jeopardizing the country's welfare system. Ambitiously unleashing market forces, the authorities had seemingly done nothing to prevent the public from potential harm; they had stood by watching the banks accumulate risk at the expense of the public. After the crash, critics could frame them as ideologically naïve and incompetent (see Chapter 4). In this historical context, the Icesave affair in particular created the perception that Icelandic government leaders had failed to protect ordinary people's interests, due to their neo-liberal agenda, or incompetence, or both, apparently allowing irresponsible expansion without considering the possible implications for ordinary people and the nation as a whole if something went wrong.[19]

The international dimension played an important role in the emerging legitimacy crisis. First, it shaped how the public initially perceived the bank crash and its causes. Iceland was the first major victim of the global credit crunch, and the only country to lose its entire banking system in the crisis. Governments in other countries, such as Ireland, hurried to bail out their major banks, but the Icelandic state could not do so due to its smallness. The crisis thus had not created a comparable financial system breakdown elsewhere. As a result, the collapse of the Icelandic banks, and the Icesave crisis in particular, became a center of attention in the international press, where it was implied that the Icelandic authorities were incompetent, having failed to restrain the banks despite the warning signs. Between this discourse and being placed on Britain's list of terrorist states, the Icelandic authorities faced a credibility crunch on the international level as well as domestically. The unique situation of Iceland in the global crisis made it difficult for the authorities to blame it on global forces.

Second, the financial crisis made the authorities vulnerable to criticism about giving up sovereignty to foreign capitalist pressure. Entering into an IMF program meant that foreign agents would be in charge of implementing austerity measures in Iceland. Again, austerity measures demanded by foreign agents such as the IMF have been known to undermine government legitimacy and trigger protest in Third World countries (Ortiz and Béjar 2014; Walton and Ragin 1990). Moreover, agreeing to accept the Icesave bill for diplomatic-political reasons, without testing the legal issues in a court of law, spurred criticism of the authorities (Bergmann 2014:8). To many it was unfair to make the Icelandic public liable for the profit schemes of private banks in other countries. Moreover, many Icelanders felt that the crisis thus posed a threat to the country's sovereignty (Loftsdóttir 2014). The issue of Icelandic sovereignty would become a major theme in the framing of the crisis at public meetings and elsewhere in the following weeks (see Chapter 4).

Conclusion

The aim of this chapter has been to explain how the Icelandic financial collapse created fertile ground for the development of mass protest. After reviewing major features of political history, and of the financial expansion and subsequent collapse, I argue that the historical convergence of two major factors was pivotal in creating a context conducive to protest: 1) the disruption of shared social reality, and 2) a credibility crisis for the authorities.

The financial collapse disrupted the quotidian of ordinary people in Iceland. First, it posed a threat to the established lifestyles of many individuals, who were suddenly plunged into uncertainty about fundamental aspects of their current and future way of life. We will see in Chapter 5 how such experiences motivated some individuals to participate in and support the protests. Moreover, the crisis disrupted people's shared taken-for-granted social reality: it disrupted shared, optimistic ideas about prosperity and security, it shattered the trustworthiness of major social institutions, and it threatened Icelanders' national identity. Using the terms of Snow et al. (1998), the crisis created a shared experience of a "problematic present" which, as my interviews with protesters reveal, in turn produced a widespread need to define the situation in some collective manner.

The bank collapse and the fiscal (and diplomatic) crisis changed the political context in Iceland, undermining the credibility of the authorities. Inspired by the global tide of free-market ideology, the authorities, led by the Independence Party, had in the 1990s and early 2000s freed capital from state constraints and privatized the country's state banks. Then they had endorsed the expansion of the newly privatized banks, celebrating myths about their successes and dismissing all warnings about the unsustainability of their growth, both for the banks and for the Icelandic economy. After the collapse, these actions (and lack of action) created a credibility crunch for government leaders and their delegates. In the context of the crisis, their outspoken faith in free-market forces appeared naïve and ill-guided, and the enormous cost of the collapse for the state made them vulnerable to criticism for having allowed reckless gambling in which only the public stood to lose if the game went sour. As the Icesave affair illustrated, the banks had been able to take enormous risks at the expense of the Icelandic public, while the authorities stood by. Entering into an IMF program and agreeing to pay the Icesave compensation claims made the authorities vulnerable to criticism about giving up the country's sovereignty to serve foreign capitalist interests. That no other country had suffered a comparable system collapse due to the global crisis made it even more difficult for them to blame the crisis on global forces.

Notes

1 Interview #10. The slogan, an original formulation in a slangy register, translates as "DAMN FUCKING FUCK!"

2 Karl Marx (1967[1887]) did not develop a theory about processes, but generally argued that crises intensify and unleash existing structural conflict, increasing the odds of revolt. Marx's concern with the possibility of workers' revolt against capitalist modernization led him to argue that economic crisis was a crucial trigger for revolt. As Boswell and Dixon (1993:684) explain, for Marx, crises trigger revolts by intensifying class conflict and capitalist exploitation – "over the need for increased work effort with fewer workers in production, and over wage or job losses in the labor market." Moreover, by halting and even reversing growth, crises reduce the perceived cost of revolt. In short, crises intensify and expose class conflict and reduce the perceived cost of revolt, raising the likelihood of rebellion. Boswell and Dixon (1993) compared violent uprisings among 61 countries and found that "market crises are most likely to precipitate rebellion if exploitation is high" (p. 691).

3 Buechler (2004) has discussed how these two theories are not contradictory but are in fact complementary. He argues that they partially overlap as they use different language to describe the same processes. Thus, from the point of view of those who want to protect the status quo, political opportunity represents breakdown, whereas from the challengers' point of view, breakdown represents opportunity.

4 Website of Iceland's Director of Internal Revenue. Available online at www.rsk.is/einstaklingar/skattar-og-gjold/fjarmagnstekjuskattur/

5 The business Vikings in fact owned one of the major Icelandic newspapers, the free morning paper *Fréttablaðið*, and another major newspaper, *Morgunblaðið*, was by tradition associated with the Independence Party (on this point, see Árnason 2015).

6 Kristjánsson and Ólafsson (2009) have found that between 1993 and 2007 the ratio of average income of the richest 1 percent to median household income increased by about 500 percent (from 4.6 to 28.7 percent). Inequality in disposable income (that is, after taxes) also grew (again, the main source of income at the top of the income scale, that is, capital gains, was taxed at only 10 percent). Thus, households in the top 10 percent received about 19 percent of the total disposable income in 1993, but in 2007 their share was 40 percent. The share of the top 1 percent of households increased even more dramatically, from 3 to 21 percent (thus, by 600 percent).

7 At the same time, the Social Democratic Alliance was founded to unite the center-left. This party looked favorably upon privatization and liberation of capital, but it aimed to protect the welfare system.

8 Sigurjónsson et al. (2011) have examined the social causes of this collective silence.

9 Haarde, Geir H. "Prime Minister's Address at the Annual General Meeting of the Iceland Chamber of Commerce." Speech, Reykjavík, February 13, 2008. Reykjavík: Prime Minister's Office.

10 "Bankar undir álagi" (Banks under pressure) (article). (2008, August 15), *Viðskiptablaðið*. Available online at www.vb.is/skodun/bankar-undir-alagi/14699/

11 My study does not analyze the complex causes of the bank collapse and its effects on the Icelandic state and economy. Rather, my aim is to explain how the crisis appeared to ordinary people in its immediate aftermath. Scholars who have tried

to explain the causes of the Icelandic crisis include Benediktsdóttir et al. 2011 and Johnsen 2014.

12 "Hundrað manna hópuppsagnir um mánaðamótin" (Hundreds laid off by the end of the month) (article). (2008, October), *Visir.is*. Available online at www.visir.is/hundrad-manna-hopuppsagnir-um-manadamotin/article/2008873968238; "Verðbólgan mælist 18,1%" (Inflation is 18.1%) (article). (2008, December), *Mbl.is*. Available online at www.mbl.is/vidskipti/frettir/2008/12/22/ verdbolgan_maelist_18_1_prosent

13 "Íbúðalánasjóður gæti hrunið" (The Homeloan Fund might collapse) (article). (2008, December), *Dv.is*. Available online at www.dv.is/ neytendur/2008/12/9/ibudalanasjodur-gaeti-hrunid/

14 The effects of the crisis on the lives of individuals would turn out to be less severe than most people feared at the beginning. As my survey work indicates (Appendix B, Table 2B), only about one fifth of the population had experienced a substantial reduction in their standard of living about a year after the collapse.

15 I myself recall the unforgettable moment of shared anxiety when I heard Haarde's address with a group of co-workers. Unable to access the televised broadcast on my computer (the link was down due to the overload), I went to my department's office where about ten people had gathered around a small radio to hear the address. As I stood listening to the broadcast with the others, I could see my own growing anxiety reflected in their faces. No one said much afterwards, but just left for home wondering what had just happened and what it all meant. I recall going to sleep that night unsure of whether I would be able to access my bank savings in the morning; and I wondered whether I would be able to perform any money transactions with no banks operating.

16 Interview #6.

17 Interview #4.

18 The two states argued that the Icelandic state was responsible for funding the Icelandic Depositors' and Investors' Guarantee Fund, which in turn was responsible for providing a minimum guarantee for all savings accounts in the country. Being administered by a branch of Landsbankinn, the Icesave accounts should be viewed like any other savings accounts in Icelandic banks. Moreover, the Icelandic authorities could not guarantee all Icelandic savings accounts without the same applying to the Icesave accounts. For reviews of the Icesave affair, see Benediktsdóttir et al. 2011, Bergmann 2014, Jóhannesson 2009, and Hallgrímsdóttir and Brunet-Jailly 2015.

19 Years later, several court rulings validated the legitimacy of the emergency legislation, thus freeing the state of many of the liability claims that looked so extremely serious in fall 2008 (including Icesave).

3 Evolution of protest

> Prior to the collapse people lived on some cloud [...] if you tried to talk to them about the structure of society they had no interest, but rather asked "Where did you buy this sweater?" or "Did you get a new car?" They talked in money and about having things.
>
> I decided to call a meeting [...] to gather intellectuals and artists who had knowledge of and insights into the issue, to give speeches and try to explain it to us.[1]

These words are taken from my interview with Hörður Torfason, the leading organizer of the outdoor public meetings that were held every Saturday in midtown Reykjavík from when the banks collapsed in October 2008 until the pots and pans protests broke out in January 2009. As we will see, the "Saturday meetings" became the epicenter of a developing protest wave, and Torfason's words illustrate a point that is fundamental to contemporary social movement scholarship: that the interpretations and actions of goal-driven actors (human agents) are pivotal in translating an emerging mobilization opportunity into mass mobilization. In the words of prominent social movement theorists McAdam et al. (1996:8):

> Most political movements and revolutions are set in motion by social changes that render the established political order [...] vulnerable or receptive to challenge [... *But*] such changes only become an 'opportunity' when defined as such by a group of actors sufficiently well organized to act on this shared definition of the situation.

According to this, social change spurs collective action only if individual actors who are both able and motivated to engage in protest define the changing context as an opportunity for collective challenge and, furthermore, engage in deliberate efforts to mobilize others in challenge. Such actors organize protest events, initiate and perform acts of contention, usually by employing well-known protest methods but often in novel ways and at important moments, as well as building social networks to expand the protest. Moreover, since shared meanings shape how people react to their situations, such actors also perform framing work to mobilize others in contention (Snow et al. 1986; Snow and Benford 1988). Hörður Torfason's decision to call a meeting in the midst of the crisis illustrates how timely actions of individuals who perceive an opportunity for mobilizing others in protest may ignite protest. He perceived a widespread need among the public to define the crisis as a mobilization opportunity and started to organize public meetings. Although, as we will see, participation in the first meetings was limited, Torfason planned a new meeting every Saturday over the ensuing weeks and this effort became pivotal in creating a platform for other actors to counter the authorities' "global problem" framing of the crisis and plan and perform acts of contention.

This chapter and the next study how individuals used the opportunity provided by the crisis to mobilize the Icelandic public in protest. This chapter studies the dynamic progression of perceived opportunity, innovative employment of protest methods, and public participation in the evolving protests. In addition to police data, survey work, and historical accounts, I use interviews with individuals who played prominent roles in organizing protests and innovating at protest events. Specifically, I interviewed leading protest organizers, ground-level activists, that is, individuals who played an active role in planning and performing acts of contention at large protest events and elsewhere, and public intellectuals and social critics who were prominent in blaming the authorities for the crisis. The next chapter (Chapter 4) examines the evolving protest discourse; it studies how these actors framed the crisis at public meetings and in the media in the wake of the bank collapse.

Studying the Icelandic financial crisis protests

Social movement scholars use different concepts to describe periods when conflict and contention increase and become diffused throughout society. Whether these are referred to as *cycles of contention* (Tarrow 2011:199) or *protest waves* (Koopmans 2004), the broad point is that such periods do not comprise merely a series of isolated protest events, but developing, interconnected protests that comprise different (and sometimes repeated) phases of waxing and waning participation, activism, and innovation (Jung 2010; Koopmans 1993).

Protest waves are thus driven not only by changes or disruptive events (for example, crises), but by internal protest dynamics. Protest waves are often ignited due to the initiatives of "early risers," that is, individuals who perceive a change in the social or political context as a mobilization opportunity (Tarrow 2011:201). Such actors are crucial for the development of protest. As Koopmans (2004:24–26) argues, at such moments novel forms of contention may start the wheel of collective action, as they disrupt established arrangements. The emergence of new protest actors and novel protest methods, and of new demands and frames, and so on, may create expanding opportunities for other actors (della Porta 2012a). Successful protest actions and increasing participation increase the sense of efficacy among protest actors, encouraging them to innovate and expand the protest.

The period following the financial collapse in Iceland had many characteristics of a protest wave. The collapse of the banks in early October 2008 marked the beginning of it. Prior to the crisis, prospects for mobilizing the Icelandic public in protest were slim. As in many other countries, the late 1990s and early 2000s witnessed the emergence of grassroots activism in Iceland, inspired by Global Justice Movement repertoires (Beyeler and Kriesi 2005; della Porta 2012b, 2013). Activist organizations such as the *Coalition for Military Base Opposition* (originally founded to protest the NATO military base in Iceland) organized occasional protests focused on global human rights (e.g. the war in Iraq), and environmental activists formed a small organization, *Saving Iceland*, and protested government-led construction of huge hydro-electric plants and aluminum smelters in Iceland's uninhabited and largely unspoiled countryside.[2] But the general public did not participate in protest action; such protests rarely attracted more than a few dozen participants. Although support for the substantive issues was often widespread,[3] the public was not receptive to protest.[4]

The 2008 financial crisis changed this situation; the aftermath of the bank collapse witnessed a period of heightened collective contention. But the crisis did not instantly spur mass protest. The wheels of protest were put in motion by innovations by a handful of actors, followed by phases of waxing and waning public participation and ongoing changes in protest tactics that, many weeks later, concluded with threatening mass protest.

Counting protesters and police: a methodological note

In addition to historical accounts and survey work, this chapter uses police data to examine participation in the protest. Figure 3.1 shows police estimates of the number of individuals attending protest events and the number of officers assigned to each event in Reykjavík, from October 8, 2008 through February 11, 2009. The period is restricted to these dates since police data do not exist on the number of protesters after February 11. The figure shows how the number of protesters (and police) grew in the latter part of October and through November. December participation waned although there were many events that attracted a substantial police presence. Then in January participation increased again and reached a peak in the pots and pans protests on January 20–22.

It is important to note that while data on the number of police officers assigned to an event are reliable, estimates of the number of protesters are not reliable for all dates. For certain days the figures probably underestimate the actual number of protesters. Police used camera images of the protest site to estimate the density of people located at the site at one point in time. While roughly estimating the correct number of protesters at one moment in time, this method does not account for individuals who come and go during events

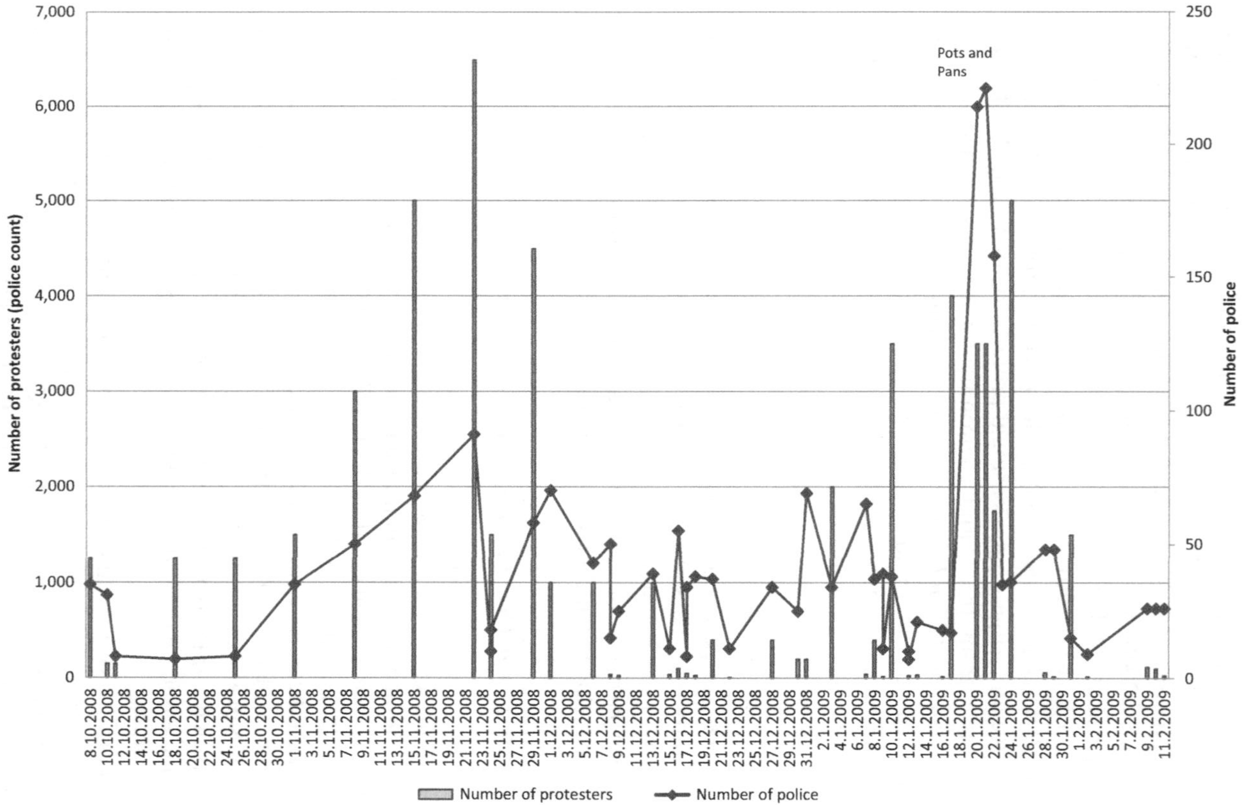

Figure 3.1 Number of police and the estimated number of protesters at protest events in midtown Reykjavík, October 8, 2008 to February 11, 2009

Source: Capital Area Police Authority (unpublished data)

that last many hours. This problem applies, in particular, to the explosive pots and pans protests on January 20–22; the estimated number of protesters was much higher than reported in Figure 3.1 (I address this limitation with survey data below).[5] But, in combination with historical accounts, we can use police data to estimate the number of protesters at most other events precisely enough to study the broad pattern of the protests.[6]

The emergence and expansion of protest, October and November 2008

My interviews illustrate how protest organizers and activists, as well as public intellectuals and social critics, came to define the crisis not merely as a reason and opportunity to express their long-standing discontent with the country's political leadership, but as an opportunity to mobilize others in challenge. But this shared sense of opportunity did not emerge overnight; it evolved in a dynamic of innovation and growing participation during the unfolding of the financial crisis in October and November 2008.

In the midst of the bank crash, individuals who had engaged in social and political criticism prior to the crisis sensed a sudden change in the reactions of others to their messages. For example, in the months leading to the October 2008 bank crash, an Icelandic novelist and left-wing critic, Einar Már Guðmundsson, had appeared on talk shows and written columns in newspapers criticizing the societal and economic developments that had been taking place. To him, neo-liberalism had been leading Iceland on a path of excessive materialism, power consolidation, and political corruption. Guðmundsson's input had hardly been noticeable in public debate prior to the crisis, but the bank crisis changed the situation. In the days following the crash, he sensed a change in the reactions of others. Many people were suddenly moved by his message. In his own words:

> All of a sudden what I had been saying fitted in [...] It is like with poems and songs or literature that become popular, years later, because they suddenly touch something that is going on [...] My columns right after the crash [,...] I've never experienced such enormous instantaneous reaction to anything I've written.[7]

To some social critics, having revealed the failures of neo-liberalism, the crisis presented an opening for ideological debate. One critic recalls the aftermath of the crisis in this way:

> [*I sensed the situation*] as an opportunity for all to bring up their opinions [...] a dominating ideological system had fallen and everyone was open to something new to commit to. [...] I felt very strongly that society could change.[8]

During the initial confusion of the bank crash, in the second week of October 2008, a few individuals began to create a novel platform for collective challenge; specifically, they organized outdoor meetings in downtown Reykjavík. Perceiving a widespread need among the public to define the confusing situation, such actors saw public meetings as a means to join with others to define the crisis in a venue outside of institutionalized politics. While public "town meetings" are well known globally as a method of contention, they were a novelty in Iceland. The handful of individuals organizing the first meetings had no formal organizational basis; they acted on their sense of injustice, and on their own initiative. As leading protest organizer Hörður Torfason put it: "I stepped out in my role as an artist [...] to unite people because they were frightened."[9]

The first protest event took place on October 8, on the same day that the last bank became insolvent (and two days after Prime Minister Haarde's address to the Icelandic nation, see Chapter 1). Popular musician Bubbi Morthens gave a "protest concert" in downtown Reykjavík. About 1,000 people attended this free concert, at which Bubbi criticized the hostility of the British authorities over the Icesave issue. A few individuals carried protest signs.[10] Two days later a small crowd gathered at Arnarhóll, a grassy hill next to the Central Bank in midtown Reykjavík. Speakers at this meeting focused their attention on Davíð Oddsson, Chairman of the Board of Governors of the Central Bank, and former Prime Minister and strongman leader of the Independence Party, and demanded his resignation.[11] Well-known gay rights activist and artist Hörður Torfason attended the meeting. Though he was inspired by the attempt to create collective action, he was disappointed by the absence of strategic action:

> I went to this protest, on that first Friday [*after the bank crash*]. I had seen it on Facebook. It was a typical Icelandic protest. People were just staring at each other, and a man was singing [*a protest song*...] I found the organizer, a young man, a known activist and protester. [...] I asked him where he was going with this. He was just kind of scared, had not expected so many, he said he just wanted to talk to the press. He had no plan for what to do next. I asked him: "Do you mind if I say something?" [...] I got the loudspeaker and announced that I would be having a meeting at noon the following day.[12]

Torfason's decision to take charge and call for another meeting led him to organize a public meeting every Saturday for the next 15 weeks. He strategically located the first meeting on Austurvöllur, the square facing the national parliament building in midtown Reykjavík.[13] With its central statue of the nineteenth-century independence leader Jón Sigurðsson, the square is traditionally used for celebrations of the national day. Like the day before, only a small crowd attended the protest meeting; but the message of challenge was clear. People carried signs with anti-government slogans (e.g. "CORRUPT

GOVERNMENT"), and the two meeting speakers, one of whom was Torfason himself, described the bank crash as the manifestation of political corruption. Torfason asked those present whether they agreed with him in demanding the resignation of the government and concluded the event by announcing another meeting for the following Saturday.[14]

Despite the limited public participation during the first week of protest, Torfason organized a second Saturday meeting on Austurvöllur on October 18. By this time, the bank crisis was changing into a fiscal and "foreign threat" crisis (see Chapter 2). The second meeting had a more definite structure than the first, and a lot more participants. Police estimates in Figure 3.1 indicate that about 1,250 people participated in the meeting. Torfason had placed a stage with a powerful sound system at one end of the square, and invited a few nationally known individuals to deliver short speeches.[15] "I told people not to be consumed by anger, but to turn to the next person and [...] form a connection and talk together about our system."[16] Torfason concluded the meeting by asking whether those present wanted to meet again in one week. "Saturday meetings" were held for the subsequent 14 weeks.

For experienced performer Torfason, creating a platform for protest involved strategic planning, persistence, and hard work:

> [*In my prior work as a social activist,*] I had come to understand the power of repetition [...] I started calling around to see who was available and wanted to come [*and speak at the meetings...*] I knew as a director that the meetings had to be short because long meetings are tiring, and it is all about the psychological effect. [...] I was working 18 hours a day, talking to people, and my phones did not stop ringing.[17]

Torfason used the days between the meetings to find intellectuals, artists, and social critics to give short speeches. His conditions were that the speakers could not be formal members of political parties. He relied on informal ties and volunteers, and used social media to deliver announcements. But he had to fight to maintain control of the first few meetings:

> [*At the first meetings*] I had to fight off people who did not respect rules. [*I had rented the stage and the sound system and got permission from the city to organize the meeting, but*] they tried to take over the stage, shouting and screaming about burning down the parliament. I told them I wanted them out of there. [...] I made a deal with two strong guys, they were my bodyguards. [...] It took three weekends [*until I felt I had gained full control of the meetings*].[18]

Torfason minimized conflict and unsophisticated speech and shouting from the stage by creating a list of speakers a few days in advance. In his view, he was creating "a platform to inform people."[19]

In the following weeks the novel outdoor meetings created a public platform for other actors to challenge the authorities and their framing of the crisis, and for making collective demands. The message of the meetings, which reached the news and spread via social media, was that Iceland's long-standing political leadership had led the nation into crisis (I examine the content of this discourse in more detail in Chapter 4). Torfason concluded each meeting by asking participants to indicate support for three specific demands, namely, that the government and its two delegates, the Chairman of the Board of Governors of the Central Bank and the Director of the Financial Supervisory Authority, accept responsibility for the crisis and step down. Novelist Einar Már Guðmundsson delivered a speech at an early Saturday meeting. He experienced the meetings as a platform for individuals to engage in a shared definition of the evolving situation:

> There we were in October 2008 and *it just became so clear how absurd it all had been*, like the insider trading and how the banks had been run and how the neo-liberal religion had become widespread in the society [...] and then [... *the collapse*] just happens and people start giving speeches, and there are people everywhere talking about these things and meeting; *there emerges this longing among people to meet and to express themselves and listen to others and to mirror oneself in the experiences of others.* [*The protests were not just about conflict, particularly the public meetings at Austurvöllur*,] [...] only like 20 percent engaged in conflict but the other 80 percent were just people down there discussing the issues, with each other, even with the police [italics added by the author].[20]

The unfolding crisis and emerging collective action inspired other actors to expand the platform for contention. A relatively unknown person, theatrical director Gunnar Sigurðsson, began to organize "citizens' meetings", that is, indoor public meetings where invited speakers talked about specific topics (e.g. the media, politics, etc.), and cabinet ministers were asked to come and answer questions from the floor.[21] Sigurðsson recalled feeling a strong urge to bring citizens and politicians together in a forum to define the crisis:

> I just sat at home trying to get to the bottom of what was going on. The banks had gone to hell. [...]. The news was saying nothing, just some shouting. And protests were starting, so I just decided, yeah, on the spur of the moment. I just thought that we needed some answers straight from the politicians and decided to organize a citizens' meeting. [...] I called my daughters and asked them to help. [...] It was a kind of a coincidence really.[22]

The citizens' meetings focused on defining the financial crisis, especially its historical and political causes. The largest citizens' meeting was broadcast live on national television on November 24. Prime Minister Haarde and the majority of his cabinet agreed to be lined up in a panel to answer questions from people attending the meeting. About 1,500 citizens attended the meeting, asking critical questions and booing at the ministers' replies.[23] Icelanders watched this humiliation of the country's political leadership on their television screens.

In November, foreign entities pressured the Icelandic authorities to agree to demands for compensation to the British and Dutch authorities in connection with the Icesave accounts (see Chapter 2). Participation in public meetings grew every week and similar meetings began to be held in larger towns outside of the Reykjavík area as well.[24] As shown in Figure 3.1, from November 1 to November 22, the number of participants in public meetings in Reykjavík rose from about 1,500 to 6,500 (the latter figure amounting to about 7 percent of Reykjavík's adult population). The largest meeting (on November 22) was held three days after the authorities indicated that they would pay compensation for the Icesave accounts and subsequently enter into an IMF program (Jóhannesson 2009:260–261). At the meeting, protesters covered the front door of the parliament building with a poster made to look like an official stamp reading "Sold. IMF." The message was that foreign capitalist entities had bought the Icelandic state (through the IMF).

Perceived efficacy and activist innovation

As participation in the public meetings grew, activists attending them began to experience growing protest efficacy. They noticed that participation was spreading beyond the "usual suspects", to the general public; middle-aged and older people, and people from all sorts of backgrounds were turning up to the meetings (survey data presented in Chapter 5 confirms that protesters came from very dissimilar backgrounds), bolstering the growing sense of efficacy – creating the perception that the protests might lead to social change. Sigurður, a 29-year-old writer recalled that:

> There was a definite moment I think around mid-November [...] when I saw that [*thousands*] were showing up [...] I remember thinking "YES!"[25]

And Baldur, a 30-year-old journalist noted that:

> I've been going to protests since I was a kid and a teenager and often there is this feeling that you are always seeing the same faces, but that was not the case in this protest. There were new faces and new people.[26]

The perception that participation was not only increasing but spreading beyond the group of "usual suspects" encouraged activists to step up and invent ways to make the protests effective. The experience of Stefanía, a 32-year-old college student, was typical:

> What was so beautiful was the enormous number of older people, you know, people who were perhaps 55 plus, who were there dead-serious, both at the protests and at the citizens' meetings, listening and talking calmly. [...] Then you realize "OK" that's the way it is, it's not just us, the usual suspects, talking back in our wool sweaters. It is a cross-section of the nation demanding that something change and this is incredibly liberating also, because then you just *know* that it will happen.[27]

Stefanía sensed a "movement of energy" and no longer "felt completely powerless": "You are no longer just some fucking barcode who has no say." Feeling a strong duty "to find a way to do something," Stefanía assumed an active role in planning acts of contention at the meetings and elsewhere, and asking others via Facebook to participate in the protests. While performing her duty as an activist, she experienced joy and excitement, especially when stretching the boundaries of the protest. Later Stefanía spoke at a Saturday meeting.

Meanwhile, government leaders refused to step down, outspokenly dismissing the concerns and demands of protesters. On November 10, while acknowledging that "people have a right to protest," Prime Minister Haarde referred to intensifying acts of contention (discussed below) as "acts of a mob,"[28] and at the aforementioned November 24 citizens' meeting, which was broadcast on national television, Minister of Foreign Affairs Ingibjörg Gísladóttir responded to the audience by implying that those present at the meeting "may not necessarily represent the opinions of the entire nation" (Sveinsson 2013:89). Protesters interpreted such statements as representing an arrogant stance on the part of the authorities.

In November, speeches at the meetings became more action-oriented and activists used the meetings to perform contention and disrupt public order. Providing examples for others to do the same, activism created anticipation of public disorder. The following passage describes one innovative protest act. At a large Saturday meeting held on November 8:

> [*After meeting organizer Hörður Torfason had just asked people at the meeting to remain calm and peaceful*], to everyone's surprise a man appears on top of the parliament building. He pulls up the flag of the Bónus food chain stores in a symbolic gesture that is supposed to show who really controls the country. The man is a young college student [...] who is known for his participation in [... *environmental*] protests.
>
> (Sveinsson 2013:47)

Such acts were not planned in cooperation with organizers of the meetings, but were unexpected and sometimes grew out of the situational dynamics and shared emotions evolving at the protest site. In the words of 59-year-old truck driver Daði, "you just had to find something to do inside all this action. I never saw any overall organization."[29] The activism at the meetings creates, one the one hand, a sense of intensifying protest, solidarity, identity, excitement, and purpose among many protesters. Activist Sigurður noted that:

> I felt this increase very strongly, you know, when the anarchists started to realize [*that this was an opportunity for them*], when they started showing up they dragged all kinds of people along with them [...] they were doing all kinds of little things that had very good effects on the group. [...] One moment, you know, when one of them climbed up onto the parliament building and put up the Bónus flag, that made the crowd go wild. [...] These moments really weld the group together.[30]

Such performances encouraged others to engage in and even plan their own acts of contention. In the words of 29-year-old college student Ingimar:

> It was a mixture of the mass of people that Hörður Torfason summoned and the bravery of the anarchists to always go further, and then the others saw that "we can do this too!" And that's how things happened, you see, then the avalanche started.[31]

On the other hand, disruptive acts such as throwing paint at the parliament building, wearing black masks at the protest meetings, or throwing things at the police created discontent among many protesters who did not want to be associated with unlawful behavior or acts of aggression (see Chapter 5). Acts of aggression worried protest organizers who wanted to attract the public by means of peaceful protest. At times they sent out people to calm down the aggressive individuals in the crowd.

By late November, public meetings were characterized by anticipation of public disorder. In the words of Police Chief Eiríksson, "In November the rhythm of the protest changed and became harder and harder."[32] During the meetings, which were still organized for speech-making and stage performance, paint, eggs, and other things were thrown at the parliament building. The boundaries of protest were expanded, and a larger part of those attending the meetings participated in provocation, for example, throwing eggs at the parliament building.[33] The explosive mixture of public participation and activism peaked at a large Saturday meeting on November 22. After the large and highly emotional meeting ended, about 500 people marched from Austurvöllur square to the Reykjavík police station to demand the release of a known activist who had been arrested on the previous day. The crowd attempted to burst into the police station.[34] The police used pepper spray to disperse the crowd, but then released the young man on bail and the crowd cheered as he walked out of the police station.[35] Remarkably, no arrests were made. The incident received attention in the media; to the general public it signified an intensification of the protests and an increased threat to public order. That no one was arrested for the attack on the police station is understandable only in the light of the predicament of the Icelandic police authorities. Due to their small size, they had to avoid an escalation of direct conflict with protesters (see discussion below).

Waning participation, ongoing radicalization: December 2008

The second phase of the protest, in December 2008, was characterized, on the one hand, by increasingly radical actions by small groups of activists and, on the other, by waning public participation in the protests. December is a month in which all normal routine is interrupted by preparations for traditional celebrations in the Christmas and New Year period. The data in Figure 3.1 show how waning participation of the public in protest went in hand with the holiday season. Participation in public meetings reached a low point around the Christmas holidays. Still, protest organizers and activists kept contention alive during the holidays.

As participation began to drop off after almost two months of public meetings, at the beginning of December activists began to push for stronger protest actions. Capturing the change in the mood of activists was an anonymous flyer distributed at the Saturday meeting on December 6. It read:

> Time for action! It is important to come together, listen to speeches and discuss our struggle. This is kind of a "first stage" in our struggle for change. But now there has been enough of that. Almost everything that needs to be said has been said. We all know how much injustice there has been and how much injustice will be imposed upon us in the future if the authorities and our political leaders are not stopped. [...] Join the action against the authority, join the revolution!
>
> (Þórisson 2014:58)

On December 7, waning participation prompted Torfason to announce that peaceful "quick actions" were to be expected, and would be "announced to the media at one hour's notice."[36]

Protest organizer Torfason persisted in engaging in strategic behavior to keep the protest alive during the holidays. On December 27, expecting very limited participation, he tactically planned a "silent" Saturday meeting; only about 500 individuals gathered on Austurvöllur in a moment of silence that day. As Torfason commented:

> We sent out announcements saying we respected the Christmas tradition and we encouraged people to celebrate it with loved ones [...] and take a good rest [... *while we*] would stand there both Saturdays as their representatives until they were ready to come back right after Christmas.[37]

In December, small groups of activists planned many protest events outside of the platform of the public meetings. Such events usually attracted small crowds of activists and captured the ongoing attention of the

Icelandic news media. Despite waning public participation, anticipation of contention and threat to public order was kept alive in the public mind during the December holidays. The data in Figure 3.1 show a substantial and ongoing police presence at many smaller events during the month of December. There were seven protest events in November and sixteen events in December, most of them involving a small number of protesters but a substantial police presence.

I will describe three separate events to illustrate the disruptive nature of the December demonstrations and the spontaneous group dynamics that they entailed.[38] The first of these events took place on December 1, a national holiday celebrating Iceland's acquisition of sovereignty. Via social media, separate groups jointly announced that a "national assembly" would be held on Arnarhóll. Only about 1,000 people attended the meeting, but after it a smaller group of about 100 headed to the Central Bank to demand the resignation of Davíð Oddsson, the Chairman of its Board of Governors. Protesters performed a symbolic gesture, throwing an effigy of Oddsson out of the door of the bank. Shouting "Davíð burt!" ("Davíð out!"), the group pushed through the front door and into the bank's lobby and occupied it for several hours. Police described the situation as "sensitive" and "explosive" (Þórisson 2014:51–57). The police threatened to use gas on the protesters, but nothing came of this threat after the protesters sat down and refused to move. After prolonged negotiations with the police, the protesters left the lobby, but only after the police agreed to leave first. The event was reported by the news media and received national as well as international attention.[39]

The second event happened one week later, on Monday December 8. After a citizens' meeting, about thirty people walked to the parliament building, and some of them managed to enter it; a few of them were wearing black masks to hide their faces. The situation degenerated into a tussle when guards tried to eject the protesters, causing a major disruption and fear to others inside the building. The event was unexpected and therefore the police did not arrive right away. Sveinsson (2013:96) has described this event as follows:

> Four men ring the doorbell of the parliament building. Guard María [...] opens the door. [...] One of the men holds the door open while the other three walk in. When María tries to close the door one of them [... *grabs her and holds her*]. The majority of the group had been hiding in the Alþingi garden and now run in with masks covering their faces and run up a narrow staircase. Two stories above is the public gallery. Meanwhile two other guards react to the situation and try to prevent the group from barging in. A fight develops and the guard, María, falls backwards [... *and suffers various injuries...*]. Three guards against 30 demonstrators are overwhelmed. [... *One man manages to run past the guards and enter the public gallery*]. The man shouts "OUT! GET OUT! THIS HOUSE NO LONGER SERVES ITS PURPOSE!"

Some members of the group were arrested, and later nine were charged with an offense. Some parliamentary members described feeling fearful during the incident.[40]

The third event was one of the most memorable of the entire protest period. A group of activists disrupted and effectively ended the live broadcast of an annual last-day-of-the-year program. The show, "Kryddsíld," invites the chairmen of the Icelandic political parties to Hótel Borg, located on Austurvöllur square, to discuss the past year in a live broadcast on December 31 each year. The following story appeared in one of the major online news media websites in Iceland, on December 31, 2008:

> The show *Kryddsíld* suddenly ended earlier than scheduled. The broadcast first switched to a commercial break but then there appeared a screen message saying that *Kryddsíld* was over due to intentional damage to broadcasting equipment.
>
> The police used pepper spray to get protesters out of the lobby of Hótel Borg. They were angry and prevented Prime Minister Geir H. Haarde from entering. He arrived later than the other participants because he had been recording his annual New Year address.
>
> Protesters burned the broadcasting cables and damaged the property of Hótel Borg. Ingibjörg Sólrún Gísladóttir, Chairman of the Social Democratic Alliance and Foreign Minister, said she doubted that those protesting outside Hótel Borg represented the Icelandic people. She said she drew a clear distinction between these protests and the peaceful protest meetings on Austurvöllur over the past weeks.
>
> Ambulances have arrived at Austurvöllur so that those who got pepper spray in their eyes can be taken care of. About ten people need care now.[41]

Threatening mass protest, January 2009

At the beginning of 2009 the public was pessimistic (see Figure 2.3 in Chapter 2). No light had appeared at the end of the tunnel as far as the crisis was concerned. The beginning of January witnessed increased participation in public meetings. About 2,000 individuals attended the first Saturday meeting of the year, and two weeks later, on Saturday January 17, 4,000 individuals attended the meeting. Participation was approaching the mid-November level and small groups of militant activists continued to stage acts of civil disobedience in between meetings; as in December such events involved small groups engaging in disruptive actions that attracted substantial police and media attention.[42]

The protest had reached a new phase. A developed activism in combination with growing public participation created widespread anticipation of threatening, even violent, mass protest. Police Chief Eiríksson recalled the anticipation: "At the beginning of January we had a strong feeling that the second half was about to begin."[43] Organizer Torfason deliberately bolstered anticipation with public announcements. For example, on January 11 Torfason announced to the press that the protest was "just beginning," it would now "start for real," and up until now "protesters had just been practicing."[44] In his own words, his tactic was to "imply things vaguely to create tension and anticipation."[45] A plan was already in the making. Several days earlier, Torfason had mounted a small protest event by the parliament building. The reactions of the police had given him an idea:

> [*A police officer*] came to me and asked me to move away from the building to the other side of the street. I asked him why? He told me my speech had disturbed parliament members who were having a meeting inside the house. I was very surprised [...,] the house was so badly sound-insulated! [...] I thanked him for giving me a very [*good idea*]. The idea was to ask people to meet up in front of the parliament building on January 20 when the parliament members returned from their holidays and bring their pots and pans so the parliament members would hear us clearly. Now was the time to make ourselves as visible as possible to them; for too many months and weeks we had simply been ignored.[46]

While the idea of using South American-style *cacerolazo* protests, that is, the banging of pots and pans, had been around since the very first meetings in October, organizers now saw it as a timely tactic. They called on the public via social and news media (and from the Austurvöllur meeting platform) to "polish their pots and pans" and show up to protest by the parliament building on Tuesday January 20 when the parliament started back after the Christmas vacation.[47] The first issue on the parliament's agenda that day, a proposition about a change in the alcohol legislation, seemed almost painfully trivial under the circumstances.

"The Pots and Pans Revolution"

On Tuesday January 20, protesters began to gather on Austurvöllur square. As the protest took place on a weekday, the members of the parliament (including part of the cabinet) were now working inside the building. In this new context, the mood of the protest changed; it became much more aggressive than the public meetings had been. "Yeah, people had been encouraged to show up with pots and pans," protester Guðmann recalled, "but when we saw the mass of people that was there, you realized that something new was happening."[48]

The national media reported live from the protest site from the beginning, spreading the information about the mass turnout. Protesters now faced the parliament building, banging pots and pans with spoons, shouting slogans, chanting, singing, and throwing eggs and paint, and even stones and dirt, at the parliament building. Most protesters were committed to peaceful action, but frontline protesters provoked police officers by pushing and kicking their shields.[49] The police dressed in riot gear, with helmets and plastic shields, and formed a cordon in front of the parliament building. As before, their orders were to allow the protest, and make no arrests unless there was direct physical violence (Gíslason 2014). This "soft" approach resulted in only twenty-one arrests that day, and, remarkably, no more arrests were made in the subsequent days.[50] Despite the intensifying unrest, the police avoided escalation of conflict. Later in the night, a riot-like situation developed on Austurvöllur, and the police resorted to forceful methods to deal with aggressive protesters. The protest was not confined to midtown Reykjavík, as "solidarity protests" broke out in smaller towns around the country; these were smaller and less threatening.[51]

On the following day, January 21, the aggressive protest intensified and created even more public disorder and a greater threat of violence. At times, protesters moved between government buildings, creating an atmosphere of disorder throughout the midtown area. Loud noise from strident wind instruments used by some protesters could be heard kilometers away. The protest lasted into the evening when bonfires were lit. In the recollection of protester Sigurður:

> [*That night*...] midtown Reykjavík was just ruled by chaos, when people were burning benches and tearing down the Oslo Christmas tree, and there was just total confusion and the police had lost control [...,] they used pepper spray very often but only used tear gas once, I think.[52]

As on the previous night, a riot broke out on Austurvöllur later on. The police used tear gas and batons to deal with protesters. A few police officers were injured when they were hit by stones thrown by protesters; very few of the protesters were injured.

As in the preceding weeks, the small groups of activists assumed an important role at the site of the pots and pans protests. In addition to the ongoing provocations, including lighting bonfires and assuming the role of frontline aggressors, they provided examples and encouragement to provoke the police, sometimes by giving out tactical advice and by "activating those who were passive" (e.g. saying "you need to be in their faces to provoke them"). They also provided first aid to the victims of pepper spray. As 19-year-old activist Guðmann recalled:

> [...] we knew that the police would use teargas or pepper spray [...] so we who had been in at the core of these small protests here and there. [...] we read about how to react [...,] we got some milk to help people who got it in their eyes.[53]

Protest threat and government breakup

On the evening of the second day of the protest, it was announced that the Social Democratic Alliance Association of Reykjavík was meeting in the National Theater Cellar in midtown Reykjavík to deliberate on how to react to the political situation (that is, whether to suggest to the national party that it should withdraw from the coalition government with the Independence Party). As the news spread about the location of the meeting, thousands of protesters marched from Austurvöllur to gather outside the meeting building. A large bonfire was lit outside the building and a "carnival" atmosphere emerged as protesters banged their pots and pans, chanting and singing.[54] The presence of the huge crowd and the awareness of a potentially explosive situation created fear among the group of politicians who were meeting inside the building (some of them were members of parliament). They feared that protesters might come barging in through the front door (Árnason 2014). The meeting concluded by proposing that the Social Democratic Alliance should discontinue its partnership with the Independence Party, thus dissolving the coalition government.[55] The protests were beginning to break up the partnership of the Independence Party and the Social Democratic Alliance.

Later in the night, a dangerous situation arose (Gíslason 2014). A group of aggressive (and probably drunk) people were about to throw stones at an isolated group of about five police officers, when other protesters decided to form a defensive line to protect the officers. The incident received considerable attention from the media. The following morning, on the third day of the pots and pans protest, Torfason asked protesters to wear orange ribbons to signify their commitment to peaceful protest. The protests quietened down and many protesters wore orange ribbons that day. The threat of violence was reduced and protesters were peaceful in their actions.[56] From the perspective of the police, the moment of danger had passed.[57]

But although the threat to public order had diminished, the momentum of mass public participation had not been lost. The following day's Saturday meeting attracted about 5,000 people and speakers there used the expression "pots and pans revolution" (*búsáhaldabylting*) and emphasized that the protests would not stop until their demands had been met. On that day the Minister of Commerce announced his resignation from office, and the following Monday, January 26, Prime Minister Haarde announced that the coalition government was stepping down. Within days, a new, minority left-wing coalition government was formed and promised new elections in the spring.

Protest participation and support among the general public: survey findings

Once again, police estimates of the number of protesters participating in the pots and pans protests on January 20–22 are not valid, because of the long duration of the events. To my knowledge, no representative survey data exists on protest participation in the earlier phases of the protest (October through December 2008). However, such data exists on participation in the January

Table 3.1 Public participation in the January 2009 pots and pans protests

	(%)
Never	74
Once	10
Two or three times	10
Four times or more	6

Data: Reykjavík Area Social Survey (sample size = 609)

pots and pans protests. These data reveal a high level of protest participation and support among the general public. The findings in Table 3.1 show that 26 percent of a representative sample of 609 survey respondents from the Reykjavík area participated in these protests in some capacity (see Table B1, Appendix B). Given a 95 percent confidence level (26 +/- 3.5 percent), and given that the adult population of the Reykjavík area was about 151,000 in 2009 (www.statice.is/), I estimate that between 34,000 and 44,500 people attended the pots and pans protests in midtown Reykjavík in January 2009 (note: as shown in Table B3, Appendix B, this result is confirmed by another survey, showing a 25 percent participation rate among the Reykjavík area population in the post-crash protests).

Since the survey simply asked respondents how many times (if ever) they had gone to the protest site "to participate in a protest," this large estimate includes all of those who attended the protests, irrespective of their protest role and intention. The pots and pans protests went on continuously for three successive days, January 20–22, so a better idea of the number of individuals assuming an active protest role can be obtained by examining repeat participation. About 16 percent of the survey respondents indicated having gone more than once to protest, of which 6 percent indicated going four times or more often. Thus, using the 95 percent confidence level, I estimate that between 11,500 and 18,500 people went repeatedly to Austurvöllur to participate in the pots and pans protests, of which about 6,200 to 12,000 highly determined individuals went at least four times. Clearly, active protest participation involved many people apart from the "usual suspects" of grassroots activists. It is indicative of the level of the threat to public order that the police authorities were able to assign only slightly more than 200 police officers to the protest site at the peak of the protests on January 20–21 (once again, see Figure 3.1).

I can also use the survey data to estimate the level of public support for the protests. The findings indicate widespread support: a majority supported the protests. The findings in Table 3.2 show that 56 percent of survey respondents from the Reykjavík area were in favor of the actions of the participants in the pots and pans protests, while a little under a quarter were opposed to them.

Even more pronounced protest support appeared when respondents were asked whether they generally supported the post-collapse protests. The estimates in the second row of Table 3.2 come from another survey of a sample representing the adult population of Iceland. These data show 70 percent support for the post-crash protests, with only 17 percent opposed to them. Participation in protests was less pronounced in towns and rural areas outside the Reykjavík area, while the level of public support for the protests outside Reyikjavík was similar to that for protests in the city.

Despite the widespread support for the protests, a large part of the public felt that protesters had gone too far in their actions in the pots and pans protests. As is shown in Table 3.3, 57 percent of survey respondents from the Reykjavík area expressed the view that the protesters had "gone too far," while only 9 percent felt that they "should have gone further." This finding illustrates a theme that emerges in the protesters' narratives explored in Chapter 5, namely, that many of them felt that activists and others at times went too far with disruptive action and acts of aggression, both at public meetings and at the pots and pans protests. In their view, such acts "spoiled the protests." Of course, the fact that many protesters and the majority of the public were committed to peaceful protest does not override the fact that disruptive actions were probably important in creating anticipation of public disorder and a threat of violence, putting pressure on the Icelandic political leadership.

Table 3.2 Public support for the post-collapse protests

	Opposed (%)	*Neutral (%)*	*In favor (%)*
Were you in favor or opposed to the actions of protesters in the pots and pans protests?[a]	23	21	56
Did you support or oppose the post-collapse protests?[b]	17	13	70

[a] Data: Reykjavík Area Social Survey (sample size = 609)
[b] Data: Icelandic National Voting Study (sample size = 1,295)

Table 3.3 Public attitudes to the protesters' actions in the January 2009 pots and pans protests

	%
Protest actions went too far	57
Protest actions were just about right	34
Protest actions should have gone further	9

Data: Reykjavík Area Social Survey (sample size = 609)

Fading protest mobilization, February and March 2009

Once the government had resigned and new elections had been promised in the spring, protest participation waned rapidly. The last Saturday meeting, on January 31, attracted 1,500 people, and was a peaceful gathering at which participants listened to a soft music performance. No further Saturday meetings were held. Still, in the subsequent weeks small activist groups continued to stage protests, but participants rarely exceeded 100 people.[58] Accounts of protest from this period are scarce. I have found police records of several protest events in February and March, but they did not receive much attention from the media. Both the public and the media had lost interest in protests, at least for the time being.

Summary: four phases of protest

I have described the evolution of the financial crisis protests by dividing them up into four phases. Table 3.4 provides an overview of this discussion. In the first phase, during the unfolding of the crisis in October and November 2008, a handful of actors perceived the crisis as a mobilization opportunity and organized public meetings. Meeting participation was limited at the beginning, but organizers persisted and participation grew as the crisis unfolded. The meetings offered a novel platform for individual actors to voice criticism, counter the government's framing of the crisis and make shared demands (I discuss this discourse in the following chapter). In the second phase, during the holiday month of December, participation waned, though small activist groups continued to stretch the boundaries of contention, capturing media attention and creating anticipation of trouble. In the third phase, in January 2009, participation in public meetings increased again, but now in conjunction with developed activism. This phase concluded with a threatening pots and pans protest that lasted for three days and involved enormous public

Table 3.4 Four phases of the Icelandic financial crisis protest wave, 2008–2009

Phase 1 *October–November 2008*	*Phase 2* *December 2008*	*Phase 3* *January 2009*	*Phase 4* *February–March 2009*
Perception of opportunity prompts actors to plan public meetings, creating a platform for framing, demand-making, and activist innovation; public participation grows, creating a shared sense of collective efficacy	Waning public participation during the holidays; protest organizers and activists keep contention alive, protest acts become more radical (threatening, disruptive)	Growing public participation in conjunction with radical activism, anticipation; threatening mass protest leads to the resignation of the government and promise of a new general election	Demands made at the protests have been met, participation wanes, activism fades out in a few weeks

participation and support. The protests brought down the coalition government. In the final phase, in February and March 2009, the key stated goal of the protests had been achieved and public participation waned. Small activist groups protested for a time but the momentum of mass mobilization vanished and protest faded out.

Protest policing

Data on the police presence at protest events, shown in Figure 3.1, illustrates that police presence at public meetings increased constantly in October and November, reflecting not merely the growing numbers of participants, but also the growing threat to public order. But the police authorities realized at the very beginning of the protests that Iceland's tiny police force would have a huge problem containing the escalating mass protest.[59] Therefore, as we have seen above, they adopted a "soft" approach. Thus, borrowing the terminology of della Porta and Diani (2006:198), the Icelandic police adopted a "negotiated" opposed to an "escalated-force" model to deal with the protests. Thus, instead of trying to prevent the protest, the police tolerated it, allowing protesters to engage in disruptive forms of protest, such as burning benches and throwing eggs and paint at the parliament building and police officers. Police usually tried to negotiate with protesters, avoiding using any coercive methods that might provoke them. Their aim was to prevent the escalation of physical conflict. As the protests grew in size police officers on the site were ordered not to arrest anyone unless there was physical violence (Gíslason 2014; Þórisson 2014). In the words of a sergeant overseeing police operations on site:

> At the protest meetings we had two old guys walking around, we weren't provoking people by putting out a bunch of officers, but we kept the others ready behind the building. Even though things were being thrown at the parliament building and other things were going on, [*we did not react with arrests or other harsh methods*]. We are such a small police force [...] which is really the reason why we took a soft approach. If we start something, we have to be able to finish it and not do things worse.[60]

The "soft" approach by the police arguably played a role in the evolving pattern of the protests. Icelandic sociologist Gíslason (2014) has interviewed police officers who were at the protest site. His work illustrates how the Icelandic police refrained from using physical force, most of the time, and thus avoided escalation of conflict in highly sensitive situations where protesters vastly outnumbered the police. Thus, despite enormous strain on police officers, due to the clarity of their orders, their training and their tradition of non-violence, and their sympathy with the protesters, police actions were usually remarkably restrained, resulting in very few injuries (almost all of those suffering injuries were police officers hit by stones thrown by protesters). As

I discuss in Chapter 5, the soft approach by the police made the protest site relatively "risk free," reducing the perceived cost of protesting for individuals. It also made the protests more "harmonious" in the eyes of protesters.

Conclusion

Studying the evolution of the protests, we have seen how the shared problematic present arising in the crisis inspired actors to organize public meetings that became the epicenter for the dynamics of protest action and participation. Neither formal organizations nor established political actors planned the protests, nor did protesters rely on pre-existing formal organization.[61] The main instigators were independent actors who relied on informal networks and social media to mobilize others in challenge against the authorities. No single mind or organization planned the myriad of protest actions; sometimes protest organizers and ground-level activists cooperated, but usually they did not. A few key actors initiated and planned public meetings, prompting others to plan and perform acts of contention. While the unfolding crisis provided the conditions for mass mobilization, the development of the protest was contingent on the initiatives of individual actors, their timely employment of tactics, and specific chains of events. At times, conflict and disagreement emerged among organizers and activists. Actors employed global tactics of contention, including "town meetings" and South American-style *cacerolazo* (pots and pans) protests. But the methods were novel in Iceland, and their timely deployment played a crucial role in sparking protest dynamics.

The financial crisis did not automatically spur mass protest, nor did it do so immediately. Icelanders are not used to heading to the streets; threatening mass protest emerged after many weeks of ongoing meetings and small, but disruptive, protest events. The initial actions of a few goal-driven individuals perceiving the crisis as a mobilization opportunity set the wheels of collective action in motion. At the height of the bank crash, these "early risers" began to organize a platform for collective contention. Perceiving the shared problematic present and emotional need among the public to define the crisis (see Chapter 2), and motivated by their ideologies and ideas of justice, they planned public meetings focused on defining the crisis and making shared demands. Although public participation was limited at first, the actors persisted in organizing more meetings, making them regular occurrences in midtown Reykjavík.

As protest scholars have pointed out (della Porta 2012a; Koopmans 2004), protest events may expand opportunity for subsequent protests; such events may produce new or transformed frames and create and reinforce social networks, collective efficacy, and solidarity among protesters. We have seen how such dynamics influenced the evolution of the protests. As the fiscal and diplomatic crisis unfolded in the latter part of October and November, participation in public meetings grew, and by mid-November the meetings attracted thousands of people. The expanding platform for contention not only enabled actors to perform collective action framing (see Chapter 4), but encouraged activists to innovate and organize themselves in staging acts of contention, first at the meetings and then elsewhere. Such acts created solidarity on the protest ground (see Chapter 5) and received substantial media attention, leading to an anticipation that the protests might develop into a major threat to public order.

In December, opportunity for large-scale protest mobilization was reduced, because Icelanders are by tradition busy with holiday preparation and family time. In this period, protest organizers responded to the waning participation by keeping the protest alive through the holidays, and small activist groups stretched the boundaries of the protest by staging disruptive events outside the public meetings. Protest thus received ongoing media attention while participation waned. When participation increased again in January 2009, it did so in conjunction with an anticipation of protest entailing threat to public order. January concluded with threatening protests entailing enormous public participation and support, creating enough pressure to bring down the government 16 weeks after the bank collapse.

Notes

1 Interview #24, with Hörður Torfason.

2 "Mótmæli erlendra gegn Kárahnjúkavirkjun" (Protest of foreigners against the Kárahnjúkar Power Plant) (article). *Fréttablaðið*, February 24, 2003.

3 For example, opposition to the decision by the Icelandic authorities to support the invasion of Iraq in 2003 was overwhelming among the Icelandic public, yet protest mobilization was very limited. See: "Þorri landsmanna vill af Íraks-listanum" (The majority of people wants off the Iraq-list) (article). (2005, January: page 6), *Fréttablaðið*. Available online at www.visir.is/ExternalData/pdf/fbl/050106.pdf; "Efasemdir um Kárahnjúkavirkjun" (Reservations about the Kárahnjúkar Power Plant) (article). (2005, April), *Visir.is*. Available online at www.visir.is/efasemdir-um-karahnjukavirkjun/article/2005504070413

4 Beyeler and Kriesi (2005) similarly found in their work on the Seattle protests in 1999 that although there was widespread support among the public for the issues motivating protesters, public support for the protest actions was quite low.

5 I asked the police sergeant overseeing the police operations to re-examine pictures and camera work from public meetings where, based on media reports, the number of demonstrators seemed to have been miscounted (interview #29 with Hávarður, Reykjavik). In a few cases the count was revised but in most cases the counts are reasonable (except that participation in the pots and pans protest of January 20–22 is likely underestimated by a huge margin).

6 Most indoor meetings and a few small peaceful protest events are missing from this data. With the exception of one large indoor meeting shown live on national television on November 24, indoor "citizen's meetings" are not defined as protest events in the police data. Figure 3.1 covers a total of 51 protest events in midtown Reykjavík in the period. I have obtained a list of all reports of protest events in major news media in Iceland in the period from October 8, 2008 to February 11, 2009. This list shows that the actual number of protest events was somewhat higher, over 60 events.

7 Interview #23, with Einar Már Guðmundsson.

8 Interview #15.

9 Interview #24, with Hörður Torfason.
10 "Ládeyða á Austurvelli" (Little action at Austurvöllur) (article). (2008, October), *Mbl.is*. Available online at www.mbl.is/greinasafn/grein/1248750/
11 "Kröfðust afsagnar bankastjórnar Seðlabanka" (Demanded the resignation of the Central Bank's governor board) (article). (2008, October), *Mbl.is*. Available online at www.mbl.is/ greinasafn/grein/1249373/
12 Interview #24, with Hörður Torfason.
13 Interview #24 with Hörður Torfason.
14 "Ástandi efnahagsmála mótmælt" (The economic situation protested) (article). (2008, October), *Mbl.is*. Available online at www.mbl.is/greinasafn/ grein/1249585/
15 "Krefjast þess að Davíð víki" (Demand Davíð's resignation) (article). (2008, October: page 2), *Fréttablaðið*. Available online at www.visir.is/ExternalData/pdf/fbl/081019.pdf
16 Interview #24, with Hörður Torfason.
17 Interview #24, with Hörður Torfason.
18 Interview #24, with Hörður Torfason.
19 I do not intend to exaggerate Torfason's role in the protests. As I illustrate in this chapter, many actors that are not named in this work also played crucial roles in the protests, by performing their own acts of contention at protest events, by planning protest events outside of the meetings, and by performing framing in the media and at public meetings (see Chapter 4). I focus on Torfason here because he played a leading role in igniting the protests; he planned and directed the Saturday meetings that became an epicenter of the evolution of the protests.
20 Interview #23, with Einar Már Guðmundsson.
21 For example, Steinþór Guðbjartsson. (2008, November). "Ráðamenn tali við fólk en ekki til þess" (The authorities talk with people but not about them) (article). *Mbl.is*. Available online at www.mbl.is/greinasafn/grein/1251814/
22 Interview #30, with Gunnar Sigurðsson.
23 For example, Lára Hanna Einarsdóttir. (2008, November). "Magnaður borgarafundur" (An amazing citizen meeting) (blog post). *Lára Hanna*. Available online at http://blog.pressan.is/larahanna/2008/11/25/magnadur-borgarafundur/
24 For example, Rakel Sigurgeirsdóttir. (2008, December). "Við sem mótmælum okkur miðar áfram" (We who protest are making progress) (blog post). *Rakel Sigurgeirsdóttir*. Available online at http://raksig.blog.is/blog/raksig/entry/743711/
25 Interview #6.
26 Interview #21.
27 Interview #26.
28 Helgi Bjarnason. (2008, November). "Munur á mótmælum og skrílslátum" (Difference between a protest and a mob) (article). *Mbl.is*. Available online at www.mbl.is/greinasafn/grein/1254283/
29 Interview #13.
30 Interview #6.
31 Interview #18.
32 Interview #25, with Reykjavík Police Chief Stefán Eríksson.
33 For example, "Á fjórða þúsund mótmælti" (About four thousand protested) (article). (2008, November: page 4), *Fréttablaðið*. Available online at www.visir.is/externaldata/pdf/fbl/081109.pdf
34 "Fanganum sleppt" (The prisoner released) (article). (2008, November), *Mbl.*is. Available online at www.mbl.is/frettir/innlent/2008/11/22/fanganum_sleppt/
35 Interview #28 with Reykjavík Assistant Police Chief Hörður Jóhannesson.
36 "Boða skyndiaðgerðir" (Announce sudden actions) (article). (2008, December), *Fréttablaðið*. Available online at http://timarit.is/view_page_init.jsp?pageId=4013366
37 Hörður Torfason, unpublished speech entitled "When I becomes we" (sent to the author by Torfason via e-mail on March 12, 2014).

38 Detailed descriptions of protest events can be found in the journalistic work of Sveinsson (2013), and in Þórisson's (2014) police report of the protest period.
39 Anna Sigríður Einarsdóttir (2008, December), "Hrópuðu "Davíð burt" (Shouted "Davíð out") (article), *Mbl.is*. Available online at www.mbl.is/greinasafn/grein/1258202/; "Áhlaup á Seðlabankann – varnaúða hótað" (Attack on the Central Bank – defense-spray threatened) (article). (2008, December), *Visir.is*. Available online at www.visir.is/ahlaup-a-sedlabankann–varnaruda-hotad/article/2008104292779
40 "Sjö handteknir – átökum lokið" (Seven arrested – fight over) (article). (2008, December), *Visir.is*. Available online at www.visir.is/sjo-handteknir–atokum-lokid/article/2008171271402
41 "Kryddsíld lokið vegna skemmdarverka" (Kryddsíld over due to vandalism) (article). (2008, December), *Mbl.is*. Available online at www.mbl.is/ frettir/innlent/2008/12/31/kryddsild_lokid_vegna_skemmdarverka/
42 "Óviðunandi ógn við ráðherra" (Unacceptable threat to minister) (article). (2009, January), *Visir.is*. Available online at www.visir.is/ovidunandi-ogn-vid-radherra/article/2009138876888
43 Interview #25, with Reykjavík Police Chief Stefán Eiríksson.
44 "Mótmælin rétt að byrja" (The protests are just beginning) (article). *Morgunblaðið*, January 11, 2009.
45 Interview #24, with Hörður Torfason.
46 Hörður Torfason, unpublished speech entitled "When I Becomes We" (sent to the author by Torfason via e-mail on March 12, 2014).
47 "Mótmælastaða við Alþingishúsið þriðjudaginn 20. Janúar" (A protest stand by the Parliament on Tuesday January 20) (article). (2009, January), *Raddir Fólksins*. Available online at http://raddirfolksins.info/?p=370
48 Interview #7.
49 For example, "Fjölmenni á Austurvelli" (Many people at Austurvöllur) (article). (2009, January), *Mbl.is*. Available online at www.mbl.is/frettir/ innlent/2009/01/20/fjolmenni_a_austurvelli/; "Allt á suðupunkti við Alþingi" (Things at a boiling point by the Parliament) (article). (2009, January), *Mbl.is*. Available online at www.mbl.is/frettir/innlent/2009/01/20/allt_a_sudupunkti_vid_althingi/
50 Data on arrests was provided to the author by the Capital Area Police in November 2014.
51 For example, "Mótmæli á Ráðhústorgi" (Protest at a town-hall square) (article). (2009, January), *Mbl.is*. Available online at www.mbl.is/frettir/ innlent/2009/01/21/motmaeli_a_radhustorgi/
52 Interview #6. Note that the Oslo Christmas tree is an annual gift from Oslo, Norway to the people of Iceland. By tradition, the tree had been placed in front of the parliament building at Austurvöllur square.
53 Interview #7.
54 "Mótmæli við fundarstað" (Protest by a meeting place) (article). (2009, January), *Mbl.is*. Available online at www.mbl.is/frettir/innlent/2009/ 01/21/motmaeli_vid_fundarstad/
55 "Samþykktu ályktun um stjórnarslit" (Resolution about a government breakup) (article). (2009, January), *Mbl.is*. Available online at www.mbl.is/frettir/ innlent/2009/01/21/samthykktu_alyktun_um_stjornarslit/
56 "Appelsínugul mótmæli" (An orange protest) (article). (2009, January), *Mbl.is*. Available online at www.mbl.is/frettir/innlent/ 2009/01/22/appelsinugul_motmaeli/
57 Interview #25.
58 Data provided to the author by Capital Area Police Authority, November 2014.
59 Interview #25, with Reykjavík Police Chief Stefán Eiríksson.
60 Interview #29.

61 After the protests a debate emerged in Iceland about the alleged role of the Left-Green party in playing a central role in planning the protests and mobilizing the public in it (see Sveinsson 2013). Although many members of this party, including some of its representatives in the parliament, publicly supported the protests, and even took part in them, my data do not support claims about the role of this party in the planning of protest events.

4 Evolution of discourse

> The current economic and political bankruptcy is neither a natural catastrophe nor an accident. [*It is*] the consequence of a man-made global financial system that Icelandic politicians [... *allowed to take control of*] Iceland's economy. There were men who made those decisions, in the name of an ideology created by men. It is that ideology, and those men, who are responsible for our current situation.[1]
>
> As long as no one has resigned, we are all guilty.[2]
>
> The authorities say that they are on a rescue mission and that we must not spoil this work or interrupt it with The Democracy. [...] But we, the people of this country, must get rid of the fear, rely on ourselves and make the necessary changes.[3]

These passages are taken from speeches given at public meetings in midtown Reykjavík in the wake of the October 2008 bank collapse. Typical of the speeches at these events, they bear witness to efforts to define the financial crisis in a way that would inspire listeners to participate in, or to support, ongoing protests. Thus they identify the target of the protests by blaming the authorities' failures for the crisis (as opposed to emphasizing the role of global forces or blaming the banks themselves); they evoke motivational emotions among listeners by appealing to democratic ideals and moral duty; and they propose a specific remedy: the government must step down. In the language of framing theory (Benford and Snow 2000), these speeches exemplify *collective action framing*, that is, they convey meanings and symbols that rationalize protest and provide motivations for individuals to participate in protest.

In the spirit of the theoretical tradition of symbolic interactionism (Mead 1938), framing theory emphasizes that people react to their problems on the basis of how they define them, and since objective reality is subject to different interpretations, efforts to define problems and their remedies constitute an important part of what mobilization actors do. Therefore, studying framing processes, especially the framing efforts of actors aiming to mobilize others in challenge, may help to explain how a given historical context results (or fails to result) in mass action (McAdam et al. 1996). This chapter focuses on this issue. After briefly introducing a few theoretical concepts, I examine the debate that emerged in Iceland about how to frame the crisis. After addressing how government leaders framed the crisis, I study the protest discourse that evolved at the public meetings and in the media in the wake of the bank collapse. We will see how various signifying agents – protest organizers, speakers at public meetings, ground-level activists, and intellectuals and social critics appearing in the media – framed the financial crisis as a moral-political crisis calling for protest and democratic reform.

Framing as bounded (and strategic) innovation

Framing theory implies that objective problems cannot trigger mass protest unless many individuals define them through a shared *collective action frame* (Benford and Snow 2000; Snow and Benford 1988). Such a frame comprises three elements. First, "diagnostic definitions" identify the target problem and attribute causality and blame, pointing out the target of contention. Frames promoting protest against the authorities often define the authorities as responsible for illegitimate (undemocratic) practices or injustices that victimize people (Gamson et al. 1982). Second, "prognostic definitions" specify what collective action is needed to remedy the identified problem. Prognostic definitions specify tactics and targets, for example, they call for mass protest against a government diagnosed as corrupt, or promote suicide bombings of targets that are highly valued by those who have been defined as adversaries (Snow and Byrd 2007). Finally, "motivational definitions" provide motives, often emotional reasons, for individuals to participate in contention. As Benford (1993) has found, such definitions often emphasize the severity and urgency of the problem as well as the efficacy of collective action. Moreover, such definitions may define participation in collective action as honorable or as a moral duty (Benford 1993; Snow and Benford 1988). Such definitions can be powerful as they can motivate individuals to engage in dangerous actions, even suicide (Einwhoner 2003; Snow and Byrd 2007).

Framing theory assumes that collective action frames emerge, in part, due to the efforts of goal-driven actors aiming to mobilize others by creating and recreating frames. As Snow and Benford (1988) argue, social movement agents tend to have an explicit interest in attracting and mobilizing new participants, and they do so not only by transmitting existing ideologies, but by strategically producing, reproducing, and invigorating meanings and ideas. Thus, they "frame, or assign meaning to, and interpret, relevant events and conditions in ways that are intended to mobilize potential adherents and constituents, to garner bystander support, and to demobilize antagonists" (Snow and Byrd 2007:198).

But, the social-cultural context always places constraints on potentially successful efforts to construct mobilizing frames. According to framing theory, collective action framing has mobilizing potential insofar as it "resonates" in a given social context. Specifically, the mobilizing potential of a collective action frame depends on two factors: 1) *credibility* and 2) *relative salience* (Benford and Snow 2000). First, frames have more appeal if they are credible, that is, if they "ring true" in a given cultural-historical context. Claims that can cite ongoing events or an apparent state of affairs for support are more likely to ring true than other claims. But, a frame's credibility is not simply a direct function of whether claims are factual or valid, but rather whether they are "culturally believable" (Benford and Snow, 2000:620). Widespread perceptions of the "real world" may be valid, but they may also be shaped by myths. Furthermore, claims are more likely to ring true if they are made by actors perceived as credible by others.

Second, frames have more mobilizing potential if they raise issues that matter to people. Effective framing appeals to values, beliefs, or ideas that are deeply held by many individuals, and it tackles issues that are relevant to people's everyday experiences. Frames that focus on issues far removed from the everyday lives of individuals have weaker mobilizing potential. Finally, frames that resonate with cultural narratives – myths, stories, folk tales – are more likely to raise issues that people care about (or focus on the issues in a way that makes people care about them).

Framing thus is a bounded activity that involves "the connection and alignment of events, experience, and strands of moral codes so that they hang together in moral directives or callings that are assembled, collated and packaged" (Snow and Byrd 2007:130). Swidler's (1986) well-known discussion of the cultural "tool kit" encapsulates a related notion. For Swidler, culture comprises a "tool kit" of meanings and symbols that actors can build on and use to construct meanings and strategies of action, often in strategic or opportunistic ways. Strategic framing involves craftsmanship on the part of the signifying agent who acts as a "cultural handyman" who uses the tools – ideas, symbols, beliefs, sentiments, narratives – available at the moment (Johnston 2009:22). Studying how such agents use culture to frame a situation thus reveals the strategic nature of framing. It also reveals how existing conflict is often reproduced and amplified in dynamic situations (Swidler, 2003).

Studying framing in the Icelandic setting

As discussed in Chapter 2, the financial crisis threatened the way of life of many individuals as well as their shared, taken-for-granted social reality, resulting in national media and widespread public focus on defining it. In a sense, framing the crisis was "in demand." In such situations, various interests may motivate different types of actors to come out and frame the situation. Government leaders and their supporters appear in the media to define the situation from their perspective. Professional signifying agents such as academics voice their observations and opinions in public, but their intention may or may not be to mobilize others in protest. Still, their "diagnostic" work may contribute to an emerging collective action frame, as activists may build on such signifying work and complement it with prognostic and motivational definitions. As Gamson (1992:111) has argued, collective action frames emerge in ongoing negotiations about shared meanings. I thus will look not only at the signifying work appearing at public meetings and protest events, that is, in speeches and performances, but also at the framing work of critics and intellectuals who stepped out in the public debate to counter the government's framing of the crisis (see Appendix A for methodological description). Thus, in addition to studying public meeting speeches, I examine texts by prominent government critics and left-wing intellectuals (articles, media interviews), and by government leaders (e.g. media interviews, press conferences). In Iceland, independent actors mainly influence the public debate by writing columns[4] for national newspapers and online media websites, and by providing media interviews. I focus on such "texts" but also study meanings conveyed in protest performances.[5]

Neutralizing the crisis: the diagnostic framing of government leaders

When the financial crisis struck Iceland in early October 2008, government leaders immediately appeared in public defining it as the unfortunate consequence of global forces. The message appeared first in Prime Minister Haarde's October 6 address to the nation (see pages 1–3). A historical landmark of the collapse, the address informed the public about the dire position of Iceland's economy, a state bail-out of the Icelandic banks being impossible because their foreign liabilities were many times larger than Iceland's GDP, and therefore saving them could result in a "national bankruptcy." But, while the stated goal of the address was to inform the public of the factual situation of the crisis and of the authorities' intention to guarantee the public's savings and rescue the domestic banking system through the implementation of emergency legislation, it contained a political message: forces outside of government were to blame for the crisis. Seemingly aware of the underlying tension and potential challenge, Haarde and other government leaders immediately framed the crisis as a global problem, emphasizing that Iceland was only one of many victims of the global crisis. Again, from Haarde's address:

> The *whole world* is currently going through a *great financial crisis* and its effects can be equated with an *economic catastrophe*. Large and stable banks *on both sides of the Atlantic* have been *victims* of the crisis and *governments in many countries* are now fighting for their lives to save what can be saved at home. [...] The Icelandic banks, *like other international banks* have been affected by this *great bank crisis* and their position is now very serious [italics added by the author].[6]

In this vein, in interviews and at press conferences, government leaders and their delegates defined the crisis as an "international financial storm" and "economic hurricane" – their message was that a global storm had struck Iceland, but its impact had been much more severe in Iceland than in other countries. The reason was Iceland's small size, not its government. International regulations had enabled the banks to increase their foreign debt regardless of the size of their home countries. According to Haarde, there had been "limits to how much a government can dictate to private firms regarding their internal affairs and organization."

> We thought we had the best laws in that area, founded on the EEA (European Economic Area) Agreement. The most [*unfortunate loophole in those regulations…*] is that banks were able to promise state guarantees […] for [*the Icesave*] savings accounts created in other countries [*namely, in the United Kingdom and the Netherlands*]. This is an enormous problem that has arisen, but the Icelandic government did not create it, even though we have to deal with the problem now.[7]

Government leaders thus identified the causes of the crisis as lying outside of the sphere of government. The global banking system, not the Icelandic government, had failed. It had been difficult to restrain the growth of the private banks, and in fact it was only after the unexpected crisis occurred that it became unwise to have allowed the banks so much freedom. However unfortunate the financial crisis was for Iceland, the authorities had handled state affairs prior to the crisis in a legitimate and normal manner; they had followed the principles of the free-market economy, and doing so could be defined as wrong or unwise only after the fact.[8] After all, Iceland had been a part of international economic agreements. Blame should be assigned to global forces, and to "reckless" bankers and the financial moguls who had owned and abused the banks. As Davíð Oddsson, the Chairman of the Board of Governors of the Central Bank, stated in a televised interview at the height of the bank crash on October 7, "we will not pay the foreign debt created by reckless individuals."[9]

In short, government leaders attempted to neutralize the crisis in public opinion by defining it as a global problem and blaming it on global forces, flaws in international regulations, and the recklessness of the business Vikings. They thus argued that it was unwise to step down in the middle of a "rescue mission."

Emergence of a challenging diagnosis

But, as we have seen in Chapter 2, in the midst of the crisis government leaders, and especially the leaders of the Independence Party and their delegates, faced a severe credibility crisis. This leadership had led the liberation of capital and the privatization of the banks; it had endorsed the financial expansion and dismissed the warnings, and Iceland was the only country suffering a systemic breakdown due to the global crisis. Thus, activists and critics immediately begin to challenge the authorities' "global problem" framing of the crisis. Such signifying agents soon found a platform for their message at the public meetings (see Chapter 3). These actors downplayed the role of global forces and instead "diagnosed" the crisis as manifesting underlying problems in Icelandic democracy and government, and they criticized the authorities' handling of the crisis, especially the way it was caving in to demands from abroad.

This section discusses the major themes comprising this discourse. Four themes attribute blame to the authorities, defining them as illegitimate, identifying the government as the primary target of the protest: *political corruption*, *unfettered neo-liberalism*, *silencing*, and *a victimized public*. Two additional themes underscored the illegitimacy of the authorities and identified their ongoing rule as a major problem: *lost credibility*, and *a threat to sovereignty*.

Political corruption

As was discussed in Chapter 2, a discourse had emerged prior to the crisis about the failure of Iceland's political leadership to break away from nepotism, cronyism, and political meddling (Kristjánsson 2012). In the pre-crisis political context, this discourse entailed opposition against the long-standing rule of the Independence Party and the Progressive Party (these two parties formed successive coalition governments from the early 1990s until 2007). So when the crisis struck, critics of Iceland's government amplified this discourse, arguing that corruption and political favoritism, coupled with illegitimate consolidation of political power, had favored "the rich" and people with "party connections," creating incompetence both in government and in the business sphere. Government decisions had thus gone against the public's interest. At a public meeting broadcast on national television on November 24, 2008, a well-known academic and critic of the government, Þorvaldur Gylfason, identified political meddling and incompetence as a major cause of the bank crisis:

> Politics and business constitute an unhealthy mixture. Iceland's business life was for a long time infiltrated by politics. The privatization of banks [...] was meant to change that structure and clarify the difference between politics and business. [...] The government failed in this task. It gave the state banks to men with party connections but no experience of running banks. In their hands, the banks grew immensely and secretly imposed a heavy liability on the nation. The Central Bank, the government and the Financial Supervisory Authority did nothing, until the dam burst.[10]

But most signifying agents did not make such explicit causal links between political corruption and the crisis. More typically, they tapped into popular notions of political corruption by highlighting corruption cases associated with the current authorities in the past years, and relied on the widespread confusion, anxiety, and anger to amplify the seriousness of these practices. The message was that the crisis had occurred after the long-standing rule of this corrupt leadership. From speeches at the Saturday meetings:

> A thoroughly corrupt power-group of capitalists and party leaders controls this country. Ministers and interest-groups make the law. [...] Friends, sons and relatives are hired in important positions, and politicians speak to the public as if to a demanding kid when the acts of evil are criticized.[11]

> We have learned our lesson [...] about the consequences of corruption, greed, and blindness. [...] The largest political party believes that the state cannot be trusted to run a business. It is in the incredible position that by running state companies badly, by practicing party-based hiring and other forms of corruption, it is confirming its own ideology and strengthening its self-image. The same ministers and officials who failed in their supervisory roles now have almost total authority in Iceland, and there has been no calling to account.[12]

Many protest performances carried a similar message, as in fact did the majority of all protest signs. The slogans "CORRUPT AUTHORITIES!" and "INCOMPETENT GOVERNMENT!" appeared on protest signs and were chanted by protesters.

Signifying agents often focused on the Chairman of the governors' board of the Central Bank, Davíð Oddsson, as a personification of corruption and lack of professionalism in politics and government. Former leader of the Independence Party, Oddsson had been Prime Minister from 1991 to 2004, and then, after briefly serving as Minister of Foreign Affairs, had been appointed as the Chairman of the Board of the Central Bank in 2005. Although a standard (but debated) practice in Iceland until that point in time, the appointment was now seen to exemplify the flawed democracy in Iceland. Actors thus implied that the resulting lack of professionalism explained the inability of the Central Bank to prevent the crisis in the years leading up to it. The aforementioned speaker, Gylfason:

> In a mature democratic state it could not happen that the Chairman of the largest political party could appoint himself as the Chairman of the governors' board of the Central Bank without objections from other political parties or the media.[13]

Signifying agents also emphasized a related, pre-existing theme in Iceland's political discourse, namely, the consolidation of power in parties and party leaders at the expense of parliamentary power. Amplifying this pre-existing discourse, many actors argued that party leaders and political strongmen had been overly powerful in politics and government, and this lack of checks and balances had led to mistakes, political favoritism, and corruption. A part of the problem, many argued, was that Iceland had no tradition of politicians resigning from their posts as an admission of responsibility when things go wrong. Thus, "one of the big reasons for the collapse," a well-known novelist wrote in a newspaper column on January 15, 2009, "is that democracy has broken down, the system doesn't work [...] Therein lies the problem. We are ruled by parties, not democracy."[14] The problem was thus defined as an established pattern of flawed governance, a problem that, in the light of the crisis, called for democratic reform.

Unfettered neo-liberalism

As is discussed in Chapter 3, prior to the bank crisis, "new-left" discontent with the neo-liberal reforms of the 1990s and early 2000s, and "global justice" activism, did not resonate much with the Icelandic public. The majority supported the ruling authorities in the voting booths, and the Left-Green Party was portrayed as being "against everything." But after the bank collapse, critics perceived an opportunity to challenge the authorities, now in the new context of economic disaster. As the first quotation at the opening of this chapter illustrates, a prominent theme in the emerging discourse was that the neo-liberal reforms had created the conditions for the crisis. The quotation defines the crisis as the result of a "global financial system" that "politicians," inspired by the neo-liberalist ideology, "[... allowed to take control of] Iceland's economy." The crisis was not a "natural catastrophe" but manifested the key flaw of the neo-liberal project, namely, the reduced ability of the state to look out for the common good.

In this vein, signifying agents argued that due to their one-dimensional faith in the invisible hand of the free market, the authorities, led by the Independence Party, had reduced state restraints, allowing "the rich" to profit by victimizing the public. The authorities had privatized the banks and enabled capital to flow freely across national borders, but they had done so without putting sufficient resources into regulating and controlling the expanding financial operations. Such arguments echoed in the writings and speeches of many well-known academics, intellectuals, and protest activists:

> They talked about the state with contempt [...] had the Financial Supervisory Authority performed its duties they would have called it abnormal state interference.[15]

> Neoliberalism is based on a simple law: privatize the profit, nationalize the losses [...] when the rich fare badly, the casino capitalists, the masses take the fall.[16]

> [*In the privatization process...*] a few chosen individuals were invited to get the goods of the society, based on the firm belief that unrestrained greed would somehow benefit society as a whole. The golden boys earned

> the annual pay of a worker in two or three days [...] People asked: how is this possible? And the answer was a) none of your business, and b) it is the market. And now the bill has been sent to the same public who posed the question.[17]

Thus, the belief in free-market mechanisms had led the Icelandic authorities to de-emphasize control of the financial sphere, enabling investors and banks to profit by creating enormous risk and liabilities for the state and the public. The implementation of neo-liberalist reforms had resulted in an unjust winner-take-all-society that had created a financial elite, which was now exposed as lavish, incompetent, and extremely wealthy, but at the expense of the public. The Icesave affair was frequently cited to demonstrate this point. Again (see Chapter 2), Landsbankinn had been able to collect deposits directly in the United Kingdom and the Netherlands, and after the collapse it seemed that the Icelandic state would have to pay back the enormous sum collected (exceeding the country's annual GDP).

Often, though, signifying agents did not make claims about a direct causal link between the neo-liberal reforms and the crisis, but rather simply emphasized what they saw as the flaws of the neo-liberalist project, relying on the context of the crisis to make people realize the seriousness of these flaws. In particular, a classic theme of amoral materialism appeared; critics argued that the authorities had led Iceland into a culture of greed. "We were told that greed was good," a well-known novelist and activist argued, "but now we know from bitter experience that greed is a force of destruction."[18] In this vein, the culture of greed had led to overconsumption in Iceland, and it had pushed aside social goals and promoted a utilitarian attitude toward the law (leading to immoral behavior in the financial sector). The "virus of liberalism," a known intellectual wrote in a national newspaper in early January 2009, infects "the social body and paralyzes its immune system. It has [...] poisoned sports and cultural life."[19] "A new class emerged in Iceland," another well-known novelist wrote shortly after the bank crash, "which made middle-class people look like losers and low-class people like beggars."[20] Social goals had become inferior to business goals in the years leading to the crisis:

> In Iceland, dental care was taken out of the schools and the dental health of children deteriorated [...] Greed did not even leave children's teeth alone. Still the liberalists should have looked at long-term interests; prospective buyers need good teeth. It also just happens that neo-liberalism is largely nonsense.[21]

Silencing

Silencing is another theme in the evolving discourse, emphasizing how the established illegitimate practices of the ruling authorities had contributed to the crisis. According to many signifying agents, they had done so in part by silencing critics and warnings. Such actors pointed out that the authorities had "arrogantly" dismissed all the warnings about the unsustainability of the banks and the financial expansion. They also claimed that this practice had reflected an underlying problem in the Icelandic government, namely, that academics and scientists generally were afraid to criticize the authorities and their politics. If they did so, they could expect inconvenience, even job loss. According to this view, the years leading up to the crisis had been characterized by the suppression of criticism, made possible by the uncritical approach of the Icelandic media.[22] In the words of one critic, "people had to hide their opinions; the time of neo-liberalism was also a time of [...] silencing."[23] From a public meeting speech:

> Journalists know this, scientists know it, and economists know it. [... *For example, environmental*] scientists could not speak as free men [...] fearing subtle punishment [...] Politicians [...] kept some at bay, kept others out of projects and highly qualified people did not advance in their jobs. Who distorted democracy to serve their own ideology or interests and so caused international humiliation of the nation and bankruptcy?[24]

A victimized public

Many signifying agents averted blame from ordinary people, defining the public as an innocent victim of the financial elite and of the failures of the authorities. A two-fold message emerged. First, while many Icelanders had participated in the financial boom by engaging in overconsumption and extensive borrowing for bigger homes, new cars, and so on, they could not be blamed for the aggregate economic development, since the authorities, the banks, and the media had indicated that the economy could afford it. Hence, ordinary people had done what was expected of them. As one speaker put it:

> Don't listen to voices that say: "The whole nation is responsible. The whole nation lived beyond its means." It is not true! Some never felt the good times. Others maybe participated [...] because they trusted the words of the men in power, who said everything was all right.[25]

Second, signifying agents argued that the banks' accumulation of debt should not be blamed on the public, because it had not been made aware of the underlying problems. It was thus defined as extremely unfair that the public was being held accountable for this debt. In the words of a writer: "Never have so few plunged so many into so much debt."[26] Another critic noted that "I am not going to declare my innocence, but I'd never heard of the Icesave accounts until suddenly I was hit by terrorist legislation."[27] According to such messages, the public had not steered the course of events, and so it was unfair to hold it accountable for the enormous debt that had been created.

Lost credibility

All these themes assigned blame for the crisis to the authorities; others described the intention of the government to stay in power as a threat to the public interest and as a violation of democratic principles. The Haarde government was identified as the primary target of the protests. First of all, the major themes discussed above – political corruption and the neo-liberal reforms – were cited as reasons for not trusting the current leaders to defend the public interest in the crisis, and to press for them to step down. They had "arrogantly" dismissed the warnings (many used the phrase "sleeping on the job") and they had allowed the financial elite to create enormous risk for Iceland, due to their corruption, incompetence, and blind commitment to free-market ideology. Many claimed that the government would continue this course in the crisis, allowing the rich to protect their interests at the expense of the public. From newspaper columns written by a well-known intellectual in the wake of the bank crash:

> Who can we trust? The Prime Minister who for many months assured us that everything was fine and nothing needed to be done – and that the króna would soon become stronger? [...] Can we trust a central bank where both the Chairman of the board of directors and the main director are former politicians who have no knowledge or qualifications in economics?[28]
>
> Just the fact how [... *the government leaders*] went with the financial moguls [*to Europe in 2006*] as representatives of a corrupt banking system and tried to defend it instead of doing something about it makes them completely incompetent in leading us out of the situation that they have gotten us into.[29]

Thus, many claimed, the only way that the authorities could regain credibility, both within Iceland and abroad, was by stepping down:

> Iceland has no credibility, because it is still ruled by the same people, believe it or not, that giggled into their champagne glasses while leading us over the cliff. We cannot accept the burdens that these people have laid on us unless they step down.[30]
>
> The reason why Icelanders are not being helped [*by other countries*] is simply that the government no longer has any credibility.[31]

Threat to sovereignty

The important theme of a threat to the nation's sovereignty also emerged in the discourse. Signifying agents emphasized that the authorities were reacting to foreign pressure and liability claims in illegitimate ways; they were giving away democratic control of public affairs, and they were not serving the interests of the Icelandic public but rather those of wealthy international capitalists. Thus, by signing an agreement with the IMF and accepting the Icesave debt (see Chapter 2) the Haarde government was caving in to foreign pressure and foreign interests, at the expense of the interests of the Icelandic public. Many protest signs displayed this message in various ways (for example: "IceSlave").

> [*Government leaders*] told us, blue-eyed, that they had to accept this gigantic loan, which will burden coming generations, because the European Union told them to do so. Moreover, they said that they would not take the matter to court because the European Union did not allow it! [... *Instead, Prime Minister Haarde*] should have said: '*We* will not be oppressed.' [...] BUT, there is a good chance that they will let them oppress *you*, the Icelandic people. By so doing they violated our human rights [...] we have the right to go to impartial courts. This right has been taken away from us.[32]

The crisis had created conditions for a "fire sale" whereby Icelandic resources and property could now be sold cheap to foreign capitalists:

> Let's not forget for one minute that the International Monetary Fund aims first and foremost to ensure the most powerful member nations have cheap access to the resources of countries in financial trouble. Iceland is no exception, as our resources are good.[33]

Critics also emphasized that the agreement with the IMF had taken democratic control out of the loop; the public would have no control of events through democratic representation.

> By asking the International Monetary Fund for help we have in reality sold control and supervision of state financial affairs out of the country.[34]
>
> The International Monetary Fund probably [*will take the...*] best bits out of the welfare system, privatizing power resources and the health system and thus fully realizing the objectives of neo-liberalism.[35]

Action framing

Framing theory argues that a diagnostic frame like the one described above, that is, a frame identifying a public problem and blaming it on the illegitimate practices of the authorities, needs to emerge and become widely adopted, for a significant proportion of a population to engage in anti-government protests. But merely identifying a problem is not enough for mass protests to break out. The co-emergence of action-oriented "prognostic" and "motivational" definitions is also needed. As explained above, prognostic definitions specify what type of action is needed to remedy the identified problem and motivational definitions provide individuals with compelling reasons to participate in protests or other forms of collective action.

Such action framing became prominent in the framing work of many signifying agents, especially as the protests progressed. Appealing to ideals of democracy and civic duty, and emphasizing the seriousness of flaws in the democratic process and the threat to national sovereignty, protest organizers and meeting speakers often tried to appeal to the emotions and inspire individuals to participate in the protests. They also began to call for higher-profile protests to create anticipation and to put more pressure on the government to resign. The dynamics of the public meetings encouraged signifying agents to amplify emotions by making radical claims. Stefanía delivered an emotional speech at a large public meeting, threatening that protesters would "carry out" the political leadership unless they resigned. She recalled:

> There were, I think, 10,000 people or more and there was live television. When I saw all those old faces and serious faces [...] I became very angry, I never get angry you see, but I recall that I got extremely angry when I saw all those people and realized how incredibly serious this was. You know, all these people had been betrayed and we had to do something. So as a result the speech was more emotional and more direct, I was so angry all of a sudden, and therefore it got through better. There were so many who came to me afterwards and were just, greatly affected.[36]

In late November, prognostic and motivational framing was becoming more radical, especially as it became clearer that government leaders had no intention of stepping down.

Prognostic framing: the formulation of shared (minimum) demands

As noted in the earlier chapters, actors used the public meetings from the beginning to establish a consensus about the specific demands of the protest. As the following quotation from protest leader Torfason underscores, actors strategically formulated the demands by talking to many people, to maximize the potential of the demands in mobilizing the general public:

> I was constantly talking to people, asking people what they wanted [...] 18 hours a day [...] my phones did not stop ringing ... [*I asked people*:] "Wait; you are angry, what do you want to do about it?" [...] there were all kinds of squirts, but [everyone] wanted the government out. [...] I listened and I summarized [...] that is how I came up with these demands. I laid out these demands at each and every meeting and asked the people: "IS THIS WHAT YOU WANT?" And everyone shouted "YES!"[37]

Importantly, this strategic consensus framing made it clear early on in the protest what protesters wanted. Specifically, three demands were stated at the conclusion of each Saturday meeting. Protesters demanded: 1) the resignation of the government and a new parliamentary election; 2) the resignation of the Chairman of the governors' board of the Central Bank and former Prime Minister and leader of the Independence Party, Davíð Oddsson; and 3) the resignation of the director of the Financial Supervisory Authority.

The demand for the resignation of the coalition government of the Independence Party and the Social Democratic Party became the key stated aim of the protest campaign. As the weeks went by signifying agents emphasized that the protests needed to continue and would escalate until the demands were met. Protest was defined as necessary to force government leaders to resign and to have a new election. For instance, echoing this discourse, a well-known novelist and intellectual wrote in a national newspaper on November 20, 2008:

> A government that cannot fire those who need to be fired will itself be fired […] If not next Saturday, then the following Saturday […] A promise of a new election soon is the only promise that the nation can accept from this government.[38]

Two days later, at a large Saturday meeting, a more threatening message emerged:

> If you hinder us from expressing ourselves in the voting booths, we will vote in a different way, with protests […] and carry you out of the state buildings that you are hiding in.[39]

The demand for government resignation and a new parliamentary election had a strong mobilizing potential in Iceland. Not only did it resonate with ideals of democratic procedure and justice, but it unified different "new-left" groups, such as feminists, environmentalists, and anarchists, in protest. As discussed in Chapter 2, despite their differences, such groups were already aligned against the ruling authorities, especially the Independence Party and its neo-liberalist agenda (again, the Left-Green Party represented this opposition in the parliament) prior to the crisis. The demand for government resignation thus served as a "master frame" (Gerhards and Rucht 1992). Not only did it chime with mainstream ideals of democracy but it appealed to the existing opposition of new-left groups to the authorities. Indeed, underscoring the role of the demands stated in the protests, mass mobilization lasted only as long as the government remained in power. As soon as it resigned on January 26, the protests ceased to attract large numbers to Austurvöllur square (see Chapter 3).

But if the stated demands resonated with the general public and new-left activists, they fell short of the radical goals that appeared in the protest discourse about reforming the political system, about grassroots and direct democracy, about "revolution," and about creating a "new republic" in Iceland. From a speech at a public meeting held a few days after the government resigned:

> The demands that we had put forward – about elections and resignations – were not radical demands. They were minimum demands. By getting them through, a new mass movement was showing its claws, practicing for the real battle. Because the minimum demands were a compromise, short-term action to clear the battlefield for struggle about the fundamental aspects in our social structure.[40]

Such collective struggle for fundamental changes never occurred, although earnest attempts would be made in the subsequent years (Árnason 2015). The broad consensus attained by emphasizing "minimum" demands determined an end-point to the public's participation in protest, in the sense that once this stated goal was achieved, the public lost interest in protesting. Small groups of activists continued to protest, but protest events no longer attracted public participation and thus faded out within a few weeks (see Chapter 3).

Motivational framing

As the protests progressed in the fall of 2008, signifying agents amplified moral emotions of injustice to encourage individuals to protest. They emphasized the seriousness of the violations of democratic ideals, claiming that the authorities had aided the rich in victimizing the innocent public. For example, stories were told of how the banks, with the help of the government, had told people to invest their savings in dubious funds, and to borrow extensively prior to the crisis. Now these people were in trouble. Moreover, as is typical of social movement actors (see Benford 1993), the signifying agents tried to motivate individuals to participate in the protests by defining participation as a moral duty. A well-known novelist wrote in a national newspaper on January 15, 2009, a few days before the explosive pots and pans protest broke out:

> Everyone must take a stand. Every person must decide what kind of society she wants to live in, and create for her offspring. If she wants a society of corruption, inequality, and domination by parties and ministers, then she will not participate in anything. She will not go to Austurvöllur, will never go to a citizens' meeting: she will support the status quo by staying home. […] But those who want change must show it in action […] it is our civic duty to rise up. And it can be done in various ways. Write in the papers. Attend citizens' meetings and the protest meetings at Austurvöllur. Throw eggs. Each person chooses her own way. But she has to choose. She has to do something.[41]

According to such messages, choosing not to participate in the protest meant taking a stand against change and reform.

In line with Benford's (1993) work on activists' "vocabularies of motives," actors not only defined the protest as a moral necessity and civic duty, but tried to motivate others to participate by emphasizing the urgency of the situation and the efficacy of the protests. Bringing down the government was an urgent matter because its ongoing rule not only posed a threat to Iceland's democracy and national sovereignty, but also because the government would not protect the vulnerable public from capitalist exploitation in the crisis. While the capitalists were getting away with their immoral behavior, in particular by having their enormous debt written off by the banks, ordinary people were about to lose their savings and homes and be stuck with all of their debt. In the words of one speaker:

> In this situation [...] there are great possibilities, but also serious threats. Was the year 2008 a good year or bad – for the Icelandic people or the rich capitalists? Let's see to it that [... *it*] turns out to be a good year for the nation, but not the year that the power elite managed to establish its dream system where only moneyism rules. It is within our power, our fate is in our own hands![42]

Furthermore, the signifying agents emphasized the timeliness of the protests (and thus their efficacy) by arguing that due to the system failure a new society could now be rebuilt on the basis of democratic principles (as opposed to corruption and neo-liberalism). Speakers emphasized that it was the right time for taking action: "The system has failed," one speaker argued, "and thus now we can change it." Again, as discussed in Chapter 3, some actors were instrumental in producing anticipation of huge protests, for example, by claiming in media interviews that the protests were "just beginning," that they were about to "start for real," and that protesters had so far "just been practicing" for what was coming.

Furthermore, some of the efforts to motivate others in protest appealed to feelings of social solidarity and even nationalist emotions ("we Icelanders"). In the words of one speaker:

> Dear protesters, are you with me to get this government of destruction from power? If so, you have the assignment to find three to four friends who agree with you and bring them with you next Saturday at three o'clock. We are gathering our forces. 20,000 angry Icelanders is a number that they cannot ignore [...] Solidarity is a force that nothing can resist.[43]

Finally, signifying agents tried to destigmatize protest participation, countering the way in which the government defined protesters as "a mob." Thus, speeches and published articles often emphasized that protesters were not a mob but individuals performing important civic duties. (As we will see in the following chapter, some individuals had to overcome their fear of such labels to be able to participate in the protests.)

Framing through performance

Framing is not just what is spoken or written, but also entails dramaturgy and performance. It is well known that strategic uses of dramaturgy and performance convey and connect meanings and emotions in powerful ways (McAdam 1996). As Johnston (2009:9) argues, there is often a strong "performance-oriented emphasis" in how mobilization actors "craft public messages to attract public attention, influence public opinion, and draw members to a movement." We have already seen in Chapter 3 how social activists began to use the public meetings to stage contentious performances, inspiring them to stage performances outside of the meetings as well. Not surprisingly, the messages given in these performances echoed the framing work described above, emphasizing political corruption and the other themes.

Such performances played a crucial role in associating diagnostic and action framing. Contentious performances provided models of contention, raised shared emotions among those present (encouraging them to engage in protest action), and created anticipation that future protests could become a threat to public order. For example (see Chapter 3), at one large Saturday meeting, a young activist used a ladder to climb on top of the parliament building and raise the flag of a food chain store ("Bónus"), which was associated with a major shareholder in one of the defunct banks. By performing acts of contention and creating shared emotions among those present, he put across a clear message: the rich controlled the state. This event led to an intense situation and physical conflict between police and protesters when the latter tried to prevent the police from arresting the young activist. In addition to creating shared emotions at the protest site, and sometimes unrest, many of these acts received substantial media coverage and thus created anticipation of threat to public order at future public meetings and protest events.

Conclusion

This chapter has studied how various signifying agents, that is, protest organizers and activists, as well as public intellectuals and social critics, countered the neutralizing framing of government leaders by defining the financial crisis not as a mere consequence of the global bank crisis (as the authorities would have it), but as a crisis of democracy. These actors thus defined the crisis as a manifestation of underlying political and moral problems, and called for protest to push for democratic reform. According to this discourse, the authorities' corrupt practices and one-dimensional commitment to neo-liberalist reform made Iceland so extremely vulnerable to the global crisis. After privatizing the banks by means of political meddling, the authorities had silenced warnings about the unsustainability of the subsequent financial expansion and national accumulation of risk, allowing the rich to victimize the innocent public. Moreover, the discourse identified the intention of the authorities to lead the country through the crisis as an urgent threat. Not only because the authorities had lost all credibility, but because they were caving in to foreign capitalist pressure, disregarding the interests of the Icelandic people, and compromising the nation's sovereignty.

The convergence of the political context and the factual reality of the Icelandic crisis made the critical framing of it resonate with a substantial proportion of the public. (As we will see in the following chapter, the great majority of the Icelandic public ended up blaming the Haarde government for the crisis.) The unfolding crisis created a shared need among the public to define the situation, while at the same time it undermined the credibility of the authorities. The situation created an opening for critics to counter the authorities' global problem framing of the crisis. We saw in Chapter 3 how actors instigating the protest perceived this as a mobilization opportunity. As Oberschall (1996:94) has argued, the "loss of legitimacy puts a regime at a disadvantage in the contest for framing issues in a crisis." The factual reality of the Icelandic crisis made it fairly easy for critics to blame the authorities for it. After all, they had privatized the banks and liberated capital, they had ignored the warnings and claimed that everything was just fine, and they had failed to prevent a serious currency crisis from developing. And, of course, there was the Icesave "blunder." Moreover, Iceland was the worst-hit casualty of the global crisis at this point in time, making it difficult to blame it on global forces. Thus, blaming the authorities for the crisis rang true after the bank crash.

The Icelandic case illustrates how collective action framing relies on strategic uses of available culture (Johnston 2009; Swidler 1986, 2003). The crisis undermined the credibility and legitimacy of the authorities, so critics were able to frame it in a way that amplified pre-existing discontent and criticism of the authorities. Prior to the crisis, in a period of rising prosperity and economic boom, there had been claims about political corruption and strongman politics, but these had not received much attention (the majority kept supporting the ruling political forces in the voting booths). But after the collapse the familiar claims about democratic failures seemed more credible and more serious. Building on the available discourse about political corruption and naïve neo-liberalism made the protest discourse "culturally believable" (Benford and Snow 2000:620). Moreover, building on left-wing sentiments, the protest discourse strongly appealed to individuals with left-wing political attitudes (I demonstrate this point with survey data in Chapter 5). Finally, the theme of political corruption and failed democracy had seemingly not affected the everyday life of Icelanders prior to the crisis, but now it was used to explain widespread personal loss and anxiety. The issues now mattered in terms of everyday life.

Despite the fact that the financial crisis was a complex phenomenon, to the point of being incomprehensible to many economists and financial analysts at the time, framing it was in demand and became a political issue from the moment it struck Iceland. The conflict over the framing of the crisis followed political and ideological alliances and interests. We have seen that efforts to define and explain the financial crisis in the public debate were not "balanced" attempts to analyze the complex reality of the crisis. The actors who tried to frame the crisis, both the authorities and their critics, appealed to available beliefs and sentiments, strategically and selectively, usually in ways reflecting their political and ideological commitments and alignments. The authorities tried to neutralize the situation by blaming global forces for the crisis, while the critics blamed the authorities for it, challenging their legitimacy. This struggle over the framing of the crisis thus amplified pre-existing ideological and political conflict in Iceland, particularly that between right-wing and left-wing politics and ideologies. The substantive oppositional themes were familiar, but the crisis temporarily changed their respective leverage on public opinion.

We have seen how protest organizers strategically formulated "minimum demands" at the public meetings to establish a broad consensus about the goals of the protest. The demands, especially that for government resignation, resonated with the public's sense of democratic procedure as well as uniting different activist and new-left groups, such as feminists and environmentalists, who were already opposed to the authorities, and especially to the Independence Party, prior to the crisis. As Gerhards and Rucht (1992) have shown, by tackling the foundational attitudes of different oppositional groups, well-crafted "master frames" can mobilize a large number of individuals, and may thus be the key to mounting large-scale protests in democratic societies. Underscoring the pivotal role of the demand for government resignation in mobilizing the public in protest, the momentum of mass mobilization passed as soon as the government had been brought down. But, having no lasting organizational base, the protests continued to attract the public only as long as their manifested goals resonated with public opinion. Thus, the broad consensus attained by emphasizing "minimum" demands determined the end of the public's participation in protest.

Notes

1 Viðar Þorsteinsson, speech at Austurvöllur, November 8, 2008.
2 Andri Snær Magnason, speech at Austurvöllur, November 15, 2008.
3 Halldóra Ísleifsdóttir, speech at Austurvöllur January 3, 2009.
4 In Iceland such columns are called *aðsendar greinar* ("articles sent in"). Icelandic newspapers have a tradition of enabling almost anyone who can deliver a coherent text to access the public debate through such articles.
5 "Texts" in this sense are the linguistic products of agents engaged in framing, such as speeches, articles, and media interviews (Johnston 2009).

6 Haarde, Geir H. "Prime Minister's Address Due to Special Circumstances in the Financial Market." Special broadcast on Iceland's State Radio and Television. Reykjavík, October 6, 2008.
7 Interview with Geir H. Haarde (article). *Morgunblaðið*, October 12, 2008.
8 Interview with Geir H. Haarde (article). *Morgunblaðið*, October 12, 2008.
9 Interview with Davíð Oddsson on National Radio and Television, October 7, 2008.
10 Þorvaldur Gylfason, speech at a public meeting in Háskólabíó, November 24, 2008.
11 Viðar Þorsteinsson, speech at a Saturday meeting at Austurvöllur, November 15, 2008.
12 Andri Snær Magnason, speech at Austurvöllur, November 15, 2008.
13 Þorvaldur Gylfason, speech at a public meeting in Háskólabíó, November 24, 2008.
14 Jón Kalman Stefánsson. (2009, January). "Nýtt Ísland, nýtt lýðveldi" (A new Iceland, a new republic) (article). *Fréttablaðið*. Available online at www.visir.is/nytt-island-nytt-lydveldi/article/2009645207582
15 Andri Snær Magnason, speech at Austurvöllur, November 15, 2008.
16 Björn Þorsteinsson, speech at Austurvöllur, December 27, 2008.
17 Pétur Gunnarsson. (2008, October). "Það sem nú tekur við" (What now takes over) (article). *mbl.is*. Available online at www.mbl.is/greinasafn/grein/1249182/
18 Andri Snær Magnason, speech at Austurvöllur, November 15, 2008.
19 Njörður Njarðvík. "Frjálshyggjuveiran" (The virus of liberalism) (article). *Fréttablaðið*, January 7, 2009.
20 Einar Már Guðmundsson. "Herhvöt úr norðri" (Call to arms from the north) (article). *Morgunblaðið*, October 16, 2008.
21 "Ótti og eymd frjálshyggjunnar" (Fear and misery of liberalism) (article). (2008, November), *mbl.is*. Available online at www.mbl.is/greinasafn/grein/1253973/
22 Many journalists and editors openly engaged in self-criticism regarding their uncritical role in celebrating the financial expansion in the years leading to the crisis.
23 Einar Már Guðmundsson. "Kryddlegin Baugshjörtu" (Marinated hearts of Baugur) (article). *Morgunblaðið*, January 18, 2009.
24 Andri Snær Magnason, speech at Austurvöllur, November 15, 2008.
25 Illugi Jökulsson, speech at Austurvöllur, November 29, 2008.
26 Pétur Gunnarsson. "Mál málanna" (The main issue) (article). *Morgunblaðið*, January 9. 2009.
27 Einar Már Guðmundsson. "Kryddlegin Baugshjörtu" (Marinated hearts of Baugur) (article). *Morgunblaðið*, January 18, 2009.
28 Njörður Njarðvík. "Hverjum getum við treyst?" (Who can we trust?) (article). *Fréttablaðið*, October 26, 2008.
29 Einar Már Guðmundsson. "Þess vegna mótmælum vér öll" (That is why we all protest) (article). *Morgunblaðið*, November 14, 2008.
30 Halldóra Ísleifsdóttir, speech at Austurvöllur, January 3, 2009.
31 Viðar Þorsteinsson, speech at Austurvöllur, November 8, 2008.
32 Katrín Oddsdóttir, speech at Austurvöllur, November 22, 2008.
33 Katrín Oddsdóttir, speech at Austurvöllur, November 22, 2008.
34 Arnar Jónsson. "Endurreisn" (Resurrection) (article). *Morgunblaðið*, October 29, 2008.
35 Einar Már Guðmundsson. "Herhvöt úr norðri" (Call to arms from the north) (article). *Morgunblaðið*, October 16, 2008.
36 Interview #26.
37 Interview #24, with Hörður Torfason.
38 Hallgrímur Helgason. "Ábyrgð Samfylkingunnar" (The responsibility of the Social Democratic Coalition) (article). *Fréttablaðið*, November 20, 2008.

39 Katrín Oddsdóttir, speech at Austurvöllur, November 22, 2008.
40 Viðar Þorsteinsson, speech at a Saturday meeting at Austurvöllur, January 31, 2009.
41 Jón Kalman Stefánsson. "Nýtt Ísland, nýtt lýðveldi" (A new Iceland, a new republic) (article). *Fréttablaðið*, January 15, 2009. Available online at www.visir.is/nytt-island;-nytt-lydveldi/article/2009645207582
42 Björn Þorsteinsson, speech at Austurvöllur, December 27, 2008.
43 Lárus Birgisson, speech at Austurvöllur, January 10, 2009.

5 Individual mobilization

> [*I was protesting*] this disgusting injustice. [...] This government failed in a big way and didn't intend to do anything about it.[1]
>
> I had always been against this right-wing government and so when they flopped I was ready to take action.[2]
>
> At my school there were many who were really into activism [...] and there was also the social factor, you know, like going to a concert or a movie.[3]
>
> Those moments were so effective, when thousands stood there on Austurvöllur, it was like a spiritual experience [...] as if we were all just one and the same mind.[4]

These excerpts provide glimpses from interviews with individuals talking about their participation in the Icelandic financial crisis protests. They illustrate not only the political incentives that commonly appeared in the interviews, but also bear witness to the social and emotional aspects of protesting. Protesting is political, but for many it is also fun, exciting, and unique. As social movement research indicates, individuals may participate in protests for different reasons, even if the reasons overlap. Individuals often protest on the basis of their political mindsets (Biggs 2006; Opp and Gern, 1993), but they are also embedded in different social contexts – shaped by their social ties and networks, and demographic, social, and economic positions – that expose them differently to various types of social and emotional incentives and disincentives. Thus, having activist or political friends may entail incentives to participate in protest (McCarthy and Paulsen 1993), whereas being a parent or having a respectable job may entail protest disincentives (costs) that thus reduce one's "availability" for protest (Schussman and Soule 2005). The social dynamics emerging at a protest site can create powerful emotional incentives to protest (Jasper 1998; Juris 2008). Finally, personal deprivation or loss may create frustration, motivating individuals to participate in protest (Davies 1962; Gurr 1970).

The previous chapters have discussed how the crisis inspired individuals to create a platform for protest, igniting a dynamic process of protest action, waxing and waning participation, and framing, ultimately resulting in threatening mass protests. While the high level of public participation and support was thus a key to the "success" of the protests, we have yet to study the frames, experiences, and characteristics of the protest participants.[5] This chapter focuses on this topic by using semi-structured interviews with a group of protesters and participation surveys of samples representative of the general population.[6] This multi-method approach allows me to address protest incentives both qualitatively and quantitatively. By exploring personal accounts I will study the frames and experiences of protesters. Employing survey data allows me to verify, at least in part, whether these frames and experiences predict individuals' protest behavior among the general public.

Political, social, and economic incentives (and disincentives)

As I have discussed in previous chapters, the financial crisis changed the political context in Iceland, inspiring activists and critics to plan protests and frame the crisis as a democratic crisis rooted in the authorities' corruption, incompetence, and naïve ideology. In such a context, political attitudes, beliefs, and alliances – political incentives – should play pivotal roles in the protest behavior of individuals. If, as political opportunity theory emphasizes (Tarrow 2011: 157–182), a change in the political or social context often provides an opportunity for challengers to mobilize others in protest in support of the challengers' ideologies and interests, such protest should appeal most strongly to individuals whose political attitudes are congruent with the given ideologies and interests. As Swidler (1986, 2006) argues, ideology influences individual behavior in particular in "unsettled times"; when individuals need to choose a side in a conflict they tend to do so based on their pre-existing ideologies, beliefs and allegiances. Moreover, if collective action frames play an important role in translating opportunity into mass protest (Benford and Snow 2000), "frame alignment" should play a key role in individual protest behavior (Snow et al. 1986). Individuals participate in collective action when their frames are in alignment with the frames that movement agents create and project (Snow et al. 1986). This, of course, is why, as we have seen (in Chapter 4), such agents try to appeal to existing cultural discourses to achieve widespread frame alignment, or resonance.

By implication, if, as I have argued, the crisis changed the political context in Iceland, inspiring left-wing critics and new-left activists to challenge the country's right-wing political leadership by framing the crisis as a manifestation of unfettered neo-liberalism, incompetence, and corruption, then frame congruence with this critical discourse should play an important role in driving individual protest behavior.

Indirect effects of frames through social and situational-emotional incentives

Cultural frames influence behavior not only through internalization and commitment, but do so more broadly by providing a meaning context for social interaction and individual interpretation of the situation (Johnston 2009). As Swidler (1986, 2006) argues, culture also influences behavior from the "outside," that is, shared meanings, beliefs, and values influence the behavior of individuals even if they are not committed to them. Moreover, as sociologists often emphasize, culture always entails moral directives, codes, or situational expectations that limit what individuals think they can say and do, regardless of what they believe or what they "really" want to do (Anderson 1999; Bernburg and Thorlindsson 2005).

In this vein, when a collective action frame spreads in a given social network, social incentives to participate in protest emerge. In particular, frames influence protest behavior of individuals through their social ties. Behavioral research has generally emphasized the pivotal effects of social ties on human behavior (Akers 1985), and this applies to protest behavior also. Interpersonal ties to individuals committed to a specific action frame entail exposure to definitions that promote collective action, as well as role models, opportunities, situational motivations (e.g. not to be left alone when friends go protesting), and even sanctions (e.g. moral evaluation, contempt) that motivate participation (McAdam and Paulsen 1993; Opp and Gern 1993). Individuals committed to an action frame may often bring friends, siblings, and so on, to protests, appealing to moral duty or simply asking them to accompany them (some protesters may therefore be only vaguely familiar with the substantive issues at stake). By the same token, not having the "right" social ties may lead commitment to a given action frame to "fail" to result in protest participation. When individuals committed to an action frame do not know like-minded others or are unable to mobilize their friends, they may not want to go and protest alone (McAdam and Paulsen, 1993).

Furthermore, the social dynamics emerging at a protest may produce emotions and perceptions that reinforce protest behavior and attract even more individuals. A protest that involves a mass of people and is ongoing for a time may become a social attraction; individuals go to the protest site to meet friends and acquaintances in a novel, exciting situation. Also, as scholars (Jasper 1998; Juris 2008) have emphasized, the social dynamics emerging at a protest can create powerful emotional incentives to protest. Individuals may be attracted to a dynamic social site where they experience rare emotions stemming from affective solidarity emerging in shared activities (singing and dancing) and shared moral indignation. And there is the thrill of pushing boundaries and participating in unique events. Moreover, as we have already seen while studying the perceptions of important protest actors in Chapter 3, a growing protest may create widespread perceptions of protest efficacy, attracting even more individuals. In contrast, since protesting often involves crossing the boundaries of legality, individuals may experience internal barriers to participation as they struggle with their social identity as law-abiding citizens.

Economic loss, social comparisons, and relative deprivation

Relative deprivation theory argues that the shattered expectations and blocked goals that many individuals experience in a time of crisis may create feelings of unjust deprivation, motivating them to participate in rebellious action (Davies 1962; Gurr 1970). This notion is based on the idea that objective deprivation creates a perception of disadvantage if individuals perceive their situations negatively relative to reference points that have salience for them (Runciman 1966; see Bernburg et al. 2009; Smith et al. 2012). Using this approach to explain participation in protest, scholars have argued that expectations and goals may be salient reference points for individuals when sudden change makes them unattainable, creating widespread relative deprivation (Davies 1962; Gurr 1970). Davies (1962) has argued that many revolts have occurred at such historical moments, that is, when a long period of growing prosperity and rising expectations suddenly ends in a reversal such as an economic crisis. In Chapter 2 I discussed how the Icelandic crisis ended a long period of rising economic prosperity, creating widespread perception and anticipation of economic loss.[7]

While social movement scholars have criticized relative deprivation theory for ignoring the social-political context (see Chapter 2), the process of relative deprivation may motivate individual protest behavior in a crisis, especially if people believe that the crisis is caused by illegitimate practices. As Lind and Tyler (1988) have argued, people tend to evaluate their perceived deprivation as unjust if they attribute it to illegitimate procedures, as opposed to, say, natural disasters. The message that corruption caused the crisis may have made Icelanders prone to experience personal economic loss as unjust (Ragnarsdóttir et al. 2013), motivating them to participate in the protest.

While some work has studied the effect of worsening economic conditions on protest participation (McVeigh and Smith 1999), research has rarely studied the effect of economic loss on protest behavior in a sudden crisis. Exceptions include a recent survey study on participation in the large-scale anti-austerity protests in Greece in 2010 (Rudig and Karyotis 2013a, 2013b). This study found rather modest support for relative deprivation effects; individuals experiencing a worsening economic situation were more likely to support the protests, but they were not significantly more likely to participate in them.

However, as theorists have long argued (Runciman 1966), social comparison is pivotal in shaping how individuals evaluate their situation. The social comparisons that arise in a shared crisis may moderate the effects of economic loss on protest behavior. In a recent paper on individual distress in the Icelandic crisis, my colleagues and I (Ragnarsdóttir et al. 2013) argue that crises may evoke social comparisons that buffer the tendency for economic loss to create perceptions of injustice. The reason is that in a shared crisis, individuals evaluate the fairness of personal loss in reference to the perceived loss of others. In support of this notion, our survey work found that individuals experiencing a reduction in their standard of living in the crisis felt more anger and frustration, but only if they believed that the crisis had harmed them more than "most others." We also found that the great majority of individuals, however, felt that they had not been harmed more than others, and thus "the widespread perception that one's loss during the crisis is no worse than the loss of others appears to buffer the overall effect of perceived economic loss on some forms of distress in the Icelandic crisis" (p. 17).

Thus, social comparison moderates the tendency for economic loss to produce relative deprivation. In a shared crisis such as the Icelandic crisis, perceived economic loss may motivate only those who believe that the crisis is harming them more than others to protest.

Biographical availability

Scholars studying protest participation have pointed out that demographic, economic, and social characteristics of individuals may influence their protest behavior, depending on the broader social context. McAdam (1986:70) uses the concept of "biographical availability" to discuss these characteristics; they shape the person's availability for protest. Thus, some characteristics, such as being a parent, employed, or older, entail responsibilities that may make it more difficult or costly for individuals to protest (Petrie 2004; Schussman and Soule 2005). Moreover, having a high stake in conformity, for example, a well-paying job, may in some contexts entail an increased perceived cost of protesting (one might lose the job if arrested). The Icelandic protests provide an interesting setting to test the role of biographical availability, especially given the widespread public participation. As the activists quoted in Chapter 3 believed, individuals attending public meetings and protest events were not merely the "usual suspects," but a cross-section of Icelandic society. It is therefore interesting to see how social and economic location influenced protest behavior in the Icelandic crisis protests.

Political incentives and protest behavior in the Icelandic setting

Most of my interviewees, both those who defined themselves as activists and those who played more passive roles in the protest, expressed at least partial alignment with the diagnostic framing of the crisis discussed in Chapter 4. Thus, although many expressed the substantive themes vaguely, most said they had protested not against the bankers or business leaders, or the global capitalist system, but against the failures on the part of the Icelandic authorities; their violations of democratic principles, flawed neo-liberal reforms, and refusal to accept responsibility for the crisis. Many had defined their protest participation as a moral duty. Furthermore, interviewees defining themselves as leftists and activists, discontent with the long-standing reign of right-wing and neo-liberal politics in Iceland, perceived the crisis and the protests as an opportunity to challenge the authorities. My survey work verifies the role of these political incentives in the public's protest behavior, showing that leftist attitudes and allegiances, beliefs in the reality of political corruption and failed democracy, and blaming the authorities for the crisis were all strongly related both to protest participation and protest support among the general public.

Exposure, illegitimacy, and (lack of) accountability

Several interviewees used the word "exposure" (in Icelandic: *afhjúpun*) to describe how they perceived the financial crisis as having revealed previously hidden, "rotten" elements in Icelandic society, especially in politics. To them, the crisis revealed that Iceland was not the "good society" that it had always seemed; instead, its politics were corrupt and its politicians were untrustworthy, especially the country's political leaders. The crisis had exposed the "true nature" of politics and power: the leading politicians had acted not in the best interests of the public, but in the best interests of the rich and the powerful. "It felt to me," said 50-year-old salesman Jón, "that the government and the parties had been exposed for what they truly were."[8] Such comments were common but rarely elaborated. Likewise, in the words of 29-year-old college student Hanna:

> [*It was*] a collapse of ideas that we [*Icelanders*] had about ourselves [..., namely] that we were somehow better than others. It came to light that we were like all the other countries in the world. [*We were discovering that*] in Iceland there was corruption and there was power play.[9]

Whether or not the interviewees described the crisis as exposure, most of them explained their protest behavior by stating that illegitimate practices of the authorities had caused the crisis, although they seldom explained this causal link. Some interviewees said they had protested against government corruption, demanding political reform. To them, political corruption had caused the crisis. "I was protesting the corruption in the Icelandic government," said 51-year-old real-estate agent Gunnhildur, "which caused a total system collapse."[10] In this vein, 60-year-old working-class male Víkingur said:

> It was endless corruption to give certain men state property [*referring to the sale of the banks in the early 2000s*] and let them do what they wanted [... *for example,*] helping themselves to tens of millions in monthly wages. Like the election funds of politicians, if I give you 20 million I expect something back, that's just how it works.[11]

Many interviewees expressed the view that the authorities had failed, and/or were still failing, to defend the public's interests. Due to corruption, incompetence, or naïve neo-liberalism, or all of these, the political leaders had failed to restrain the financial sector, allowing the rich to victimize the public. And they were apparently continuing on this course. Middle-aged truck driver Daði said: "I protested because this government failed to protect us; they were elected to do so but they didn't."[12] Forty-year-old female artist Erna said:

> We were just robbed, you see [...] and [the politicians] just stood and helped them rob us, and they placed no limits on them [...] like you put a baby in a candy shop and it just eats and eats and knows no limits.[13]

A few interviewees specifically argued that the authorities' neo-liberal agenda had led them to ignore the risks, not controlling the financial sphere. In the words of Gunnhildur:

> The authorities just brought all normal defenses, almost paralyzed the Financial Supervisory Authority and never listened to any warnings [...] even when foreign experts said something [*one of the ministers*] said that they needed re-education.[14]

The perception that the country's political leaders were not being held accountable for their failures was a prominent theme in the interviews. Many interviewees said that they had protested because the political leaders would otherwise not accept any responsibility for the crisis. "They acted as if the responsibility was not theirs," 29-year-old writer Sigurður said, "and this I thought was just complete nonsense."[15] To him and several other interviewees, the denial of responsibility violated democratic principles and further illustrated the illegitimacy of the authorities. Again, young female protester Hanna noted:

> It is so much injustice to have represented some [*neo-liberal*] ideals, and when the ideals do not work just keep on in government and refuse to admit it.[16]

The interviews illustrate how the reactions of the authorities to the evolving protest bolstered their legitimacy problems. A few interviewees described how they perceived the reactions of government leaders to the public meetings and other protest events as proof of "arrogance" and "lack of understanding of the public's discontent." The interviewees brought up several incidents that to them demonstrated how government leaders dismissed them as "kids," or "radicals," or as "a mob," thus denying that the protesters represented the opinions of the majority of the Icelandic nation. Several interviewees brought up the same incident in illustration of this point. As has been described in Chapter 3, at a large citizens' meeting which was broadcast live on national television on November 24, 2008, Minister for Foreign Affairs

Ingibjörg Sólrún Gísladóttir stated that the meeting participants "may not necessarily represent the opinions of the entire nation" (Sveinsson 2013:89). Her words became rephrased and were used by signifying agents to demonstrate the arrogant stance of the authorities and their lack of understanding of the widespread public discontent. The incident is mentioned by several interviewees:

> [*I recall*] when Ingibjörg Sólrún [*the Minister for Foreign Affairs…*] said to the thousands of individuals attending the meeting: "You are not the Icelandic people" […] it was a horrible tactic on her part.[17]

The interviews illustrate how the demands stated in the protests, especially the demand for the resignation of the government, provided consensus among various groups of protesters. As I have discussed in Chapter 4, this demand united players, signifying agents, and activists, and it also united ordinary protesters. Most of my interviewees mentioned how they had felt that the government needed to step down and that an election was needed to "clean out the bad elements" and "get rid of those who slept on the job." As one interviewee put it: "[*the aim to*] get rid of this government may have been the only thing that tied us together, very loosely, but it was enough to form this unity."[18]

Related to this is how a few interviewees talked about experiencing an urge to take part in sending a message to the authorities, letting them know that they, the citizens of Iceland, were "standing up"; that they were unwilling to simply accept their violations and failures. "A big part of [the protests] was letting them know that we cared," 22-year-old music teacher Saga said, "letting them know that we knew we had been had, and that people had to accept responsibility for their actions."[19] "I acted crazy outside of the parliament building," says marketer Jón, "because I wanted the parliament members to know that I was angry."[20]

But, while the qualitative work illustrates how individuals saw themselves protesting against political corruption, incompetence, and failures on the part of the authorities, to verify the effects of these beliefs on protest behavior, we need to compare the beliefs of protesters and non-protesters. I do so in Tables 5.1–5.2, using two separate surveys of samples that were representative of the adult population of the Reykjavík area.[21] (Note: Each table reports results from two separate regression models, which statistically estimate simultaneous effects, and control for social and economic characteristics. The first model examines the effects of political attitudes, beliefs, and alignments on the probability of participating in the protests. The second model tests the effects of these measures on the probability of supporting the protests. The numbers in the tables are predicted probabilities that have been calculated to illustrate the estimated statistical effects of the characteristics on protest behavior.)

The regression statistics in Table 5.1 show that both corruption beliefs and dissatisfaction with Icelandic democracy significantly predict protest

Table 5.1 The effects of political views on the probability of participating in and supporting the pots and pans protests, January 2009

	Probability of protest participation	*Probability of protest support*
Believes that political connections are important to "get ahead in Iceland"		
Yes	0.35	(≈ 0.56)
No	0.18	(≈ 0.56)
Trust in Icelandic politicians		
Low	(≈ 0.26)	0.64
High	(≈ 0.26)	0.47
Leftist identity		
Yes	0.38	0.67
No	0.20	0.51
Party identity		
Left-Green Movement (new-left)	0.39	0.82
Social Democratic Coalition (left-center)	0.26	0.58
Progressive party (center)	0.31	0.47
Independence party (center-right)	0.08	0.34
Other party	0.44	0.56
Undecided	0.36	0.60

Data: Reykjavík Area Social Survey

Note: Table 5.1 reports predicted probabilities from logistic regression of protesting at least once (Appendix C, Table C6, Model 1) and being in favor of the protest actions (Appendix C, Table C6, Model 2). The probabilities are estimated by setting other independent variables at their grand means. Differences in predicted probabilities are statistically significant. Insignificant differences are denoted by reporting the base probabilities of protest participation (0.26) and of protest support (0.56).

Table 5.2 The effects of political views on the probability of participating in and supporting the financial crisis protests

	Probability of protest participation	*Probability of protest support*
Satisfaction with democracy in Iceland		
Not satisfied at all	0.35	(≈ 0.56)
Very satisfied	0.14	(≈ 0.56)
Perception of political corruption		
It hardly takes place at all	0.13	0.54
It is very widespread	0.32	0.78

Data: Icelandic National Voting Study (Reykjavík area sample)

Note: Table 5.2 reports predicted probabilities from logistic regression of protesting at least once (Appendix C, Table C7) and being in favor of the protest actions (Appendix C, Table C8). The probabilities are estimated by setting other independent variables at their grand means. Differences in predicted probabilities are statistically significant. Insignificant differences are denoted by reporting the base probabilities of protest participation (0.26) and of protest support (0.56).

behavior. The results indicate that individuals who believe that political connections are important for success attainment are about twice as likely to participate in protest as those who believe that such connections are unimportant (the probability of participation is .35 for those who think that connections are important, but .18 for others). Likewise, the results in Table 5.2 indicate that those who believe that corruption takes place in Icelandic politics are more than twice as likely to participate in protests as those who do not share this belief (the probability of participation is .32 for those who believe that there is corruption, but .13 otherwise). Table 5.2 also shows that individuals who are dissatisfied with Icelandic democracy are more than twice as likely to protest as those who are satisfied with it.

The findings in the second column in the tables show some effects of these beliefs on protest support among the Icelandic public as well. Thus, low trust in Icelandic politicians significantly predicts higher probability of protest support, as does the belief that there is considerable political corruption in Iceland.

Blame

A major theme emerging in the discourse analysis in Chapter 4 was the notion that the Icelandic authorities were responsible for the crisis. Indeed, the survey findings in Table 5.3 demonstrate that this core message of the diagnostic framing work of critics and mobilization players resonated well with the Icelandic public. The findings indicate that a great majority ended up blaming the Haarde government and the state supervisory institutions for the financial crisis.

Still, the data contain a good deal of variation among individuals regarding the strength of these beliefs, which allows us to study the effects of such beliefs on protest behavior. The regression findings in Table 5.4 show that those who believed that the authorities were highly responsible for the crisis

Table 5.3 Who is responsible for the financial collapse?

	Not responsible (%)	*Somewhat responsible (%)*	*Very responsible (%)*
Geir Haarde's coalition government	6	24	70
The Central Bank	4.5	18.5	77
The Financial Supervisory Authority	2.5	14.5	83
The commercial banks	2.5	7	90.5

Data: Icelandic National Voting Study, national sample (sample size = 1,230).

Note: Respondents originally indicated their position on a scale ranging from 0 (labeled "no responsibility") to 10 (labeled "a great deal of responsibility"). Table 5.3 collapses scores ranging 0 to 4 (not responsible), 5 to 7 (somewhat responsible), and 8 to 10 (highly responsible).

Table 5.4 The effects of political views on the probability of participating in and supporting the financial crisis protests

	Probability of protest participation	*Probability of protest support*
Perceived responsibility for the crisis: the authorities		
The authorities are not responsible	0.07	0.35
The authorities are very much responsible	0.41	0.84
Perceived responsibility for the crisis: the banks		
The banks are not responsible	(≈ 0.26)	(≈ 0.56)
The banks are very much responsible	(≈ 0.26)	(≈ 0.56)

Data: Icelandic National Voting Study (Reykjavík area sample)

Note: Table 5.4 reports predicted probabilities from logistic regression of protesting at least once (Appendix C, Table C7) and being in favor of the protest actions (Appendix C, Table C8). The probabilities are estimated by setting other independent variables at their grand means. Differences in predicted probabilities are statistically significant. Insignificant differences are denoted by reporting the base probabilities of protest participation (0.26) and of protest support (0.56).

were about five times more likely to protest than those who believed that they were not responsible. They were also much more likely to support the protests. Furthermore, these findings corroborate a major finding from the interview work, namely, that protesters were challenging Icelandic politics and government, and not bankers or business people. Blaming the crisis on the banks, a widespread view indeed in Iceland, was not significantly related to protest behavior.

Political views and perception of opportunity

The interviews illustrate how individuals, whose frames were already strongly aligned against the authorities prior to the crisis, especially the long-standing reign of the Independence Party and neo-liberal politics, embraced the arising protest discourse. But they also reveal how such individuals defined the crisis and the subsequent wave of public meetings and protests as an *opportunity* for challenge. Thus, interviewees who expressed commitment to left-wing or new-left politics, including environmentalism, feminism, and global justice, perceived the evolving situation as an opportunity to have their voice heard and challenge the authorities. They had been discontent with the neo-liberal reforms of the past decades:

> I am a leftist and just hate the Independence Party, and I am not going to hide it. And the Progressive Party is no better.[22]
>
> I was discontented with what had been going on, not just the financial business, but how much had been privatized, institutions and banks and Iceland Telecom [...] I was angry about the policy of building huge power plants [...] I wanted this government out.[23]

Like the players and critics instigating the protests (see Chapter 3), individuals with such political views perceived the unfolding situation as a political opportunity. To them, the crisis had tilted the social and political context in their favor by revealing the authorities as incompetent and corrupt, and exposing their neo-liberal policies as flawed. In their minds, the crisis validated what they had said (or thought) all along. Few had been ready to listen to them, until now. Leftists and activists who had been discontent with the authorities during the illusionary economic boom thus now felt that they could say "I told you so."

> I have always been on the left politically, so I was very skeptical about the *expansion* [...] I had been reading about what the Independence Party was doing to the country [...] and *then all this happened and then it was like an "I-told-you-so moment" for me and others who had been on the left wing* [italics added by the author].[24]

But the political attitudes of protesters were not confined to discontent with the current coalition government, although, again, the various groups strongly agreed on that point. The public meetings and other protest events provided an opportunity for various activist groups to stage protest and challenge the establishment. Twenty-six-year-old college student Eydís said:

> It doesn't take much to get me to protest against the Independence Party [... But the protests were] also a forum for different issues of contention [...] some brought flags "Iceland out of NATO" and there was "Iceland-Palestine" [...] it wasn't just one issue and that also made the protests so much fun.[25]

We have already seen in an earlier chapter (Chapter 3) how the initiatives of the various activist groups shaped the dynamics evolving at the protest site.

Again I can use survey data to verify whether political attitudes and alignments influenced protest participation and support among the Icelandic public. The survey statistics in Table 5.1 confirm that leftist political attitudes and party allegiance significantly predicted both protest participation and support. The findings indicate that framing the crisis as a manifestation of the failures of right-wing politics appealed to leftists, and the effects are substantial. Holding all background controls constant at their mean levels, left-wing attitudes almost double the probability of participating in the protests (the probability is 0.38 for leftists but 0.20 for non-leftists), and substantially increase the probability of supporting the protests (the probability is 0.67 for leftists but 0.51 for non-leftists). Furthermore, party allegiance predicts protest behavior in the manner expected (again, net of all background variables and left-wing ideology). As expected, supporters of the Independence Party have the lowest probability of protesting (0.09), while supporters of the new-left party (the Left-Green Movement) have the highest probability (0.39). Likewise, the probability of supporting the protest is lowest among the supporters of the Independence Party (0.34) but highest among the supporters of the new-left party (0.82).

Motivational definitions

Defining protest participation as *a duty* was a major motivational definition expressed by my interviewees. I have no survey data to verify the general effect of this definition on protest behavior, but many of my interviewees mentioned that they had seen it as their duty to go to the public meetings and the protests. They felt compelled to play their role as citizens in a democracy by protesting against the authorities' violations of democratic principles and the refusal of the political leaders to be held accountable for their illegitimate practices and utter failures. For example, 50-year-old marketer Jón recalled:

> My strongest experience was the feeling that it was my civic duty to have my voice heard and to express my discontent [...] often during this long period I felt it was my duty to go, I felt that it was lousy just to stay home and watch it on TV. Because I felt that it was a movement [...] maybe I felt a little bit like a soldier in a movement."[26]

Likewise, 40-year-old artist Erna said:

> I just felt moral pressure. You know, like you say, my grandparents are not coming because they live out in the countryside, so I thought if I go to the protest I am going for ten other people. I was there representing more people than just myself, although I never had anything in writing![27]

Social ties and protest incentives

While I have no survey data linking social ties with protest behavior, the interviewees' accounts revealed a few themes illustrating the potential importance of social ties in creating protest incentives for individuals. First, the interviews revealed how interpersonal ties with individuals who were committed to protest action explicitly or implicitly entailed incentives to protest. Second, they illustrated how the growing crowd of protesters at times became an exciting social attraction. Finally, interviewees talked about how their networks of strong and weak social ties formed important communication networks via social media.

Interpersonal "encouragement"

Although the interviewees rarely admitted to putting direct pressure on their friends or other acquaintances to go and protest, their accounts bear witness to interpersonal influence on protest behavior, so illustrating how subtle and unconscious such effects can be. Though they denied having put direct pressure on anyone, some interviewees talked about trying to "encourage" others to participate in the protests, but leaving it up to them to do this on their own terms. "I didn't try to force my opinions upon others," 19-year-old activist Guðmann recalled, "but of course you talked to your friends and tried to encourage them, and talked with them about what was going on here."[28] Such interpersonal "encouragement" was not confined to friendship ties, but also occurred in workplaces. The following two quotations are from professionals working in the public sector:

> At work we discussed the societal situation all the time, during lunch and coffee breaks [...] it wasn't in an organized fashion, you see; maybe I would say something like "Why don't you just go there and speak your mind by showing up?"[29]

> It always started around three or four and then you went down there and I even got enormous support from my work [...] I worked at a public institution at the time [...] and we were encouraged to go down there.[30]

Although the interviewees rarely acknowledged having experienced or having been affected by social pressure, some accounts indicate the subtle, unconscious influences at work. Although some interviewees usually went by themselves to protest, most went with someone they knew. Many mentioned going to protests with friends, spouses, co-workers or parents. "You know, if I went, someone came with me," 22-year-old female music teacher Saga recalled, "and if I wasn't going to go, someone would drag me along, so there was always a group dynamic."[31] Revealing her need for interpersonal ties at the protest site, Saga continued: "I wouldn't have protested all by myself, you always need your safety net, you know." In some cases, potential disapproval from significant others created an incentive to protest. Twenty-four-year-old female sports coach Kristín said:

> I don't remember asking anyone to go with me, except maybe I asked my siblings if they wanted to join me when I was on my way out to the protests. But maybe I was unconsciously creating pressure through Facebook messages. [...] Maybe there was pressure. *I think that my dad would not have been pleased if I hadn't gone to the [pots and pans] protest, since we had talked so much in the fall.* But I wasn't thinking about it; if there was pressure I wasn't paying attention to it [italics added by the author].[32]

Of course social ties can have the opposite effects when one's significant others are strongly opposed to a protest. The interviews rarely revealed cases of such disincentives (perhaps because I did not have any personal accounts from individuals who did not participate in the protests), but there were a few remarks indicative of such effects. For example, 19-year-old

Guðmann described how his grandfather became "furious" when discovering that he was participating in the protests. "Suddenly he had a picture of Davíð Oddsson on the wall, and told me to get the hell out of his house and not come again."[33]

Social networks, communication networks, and social media

Social ties and social networks were, of course, crucial for communication. The interviews illustrate how information on planned protest events spread through networks of strong and weak social ties. Information on planned protest events flowed through interpersonal ties by word of mouth and also through calling campaigns ("we asked everyone to call ten friends") and mass e-mailing. Many planned events were even announced in the news media. Furthermore, the interviews revealed the pivotal role of social media (e.g. Facebook) in spreading information on upcoming events. Social media networks, which span large networks of strong and weak social ties, made it possible for small groups to plan protest events at short notice and quickly spread the word.[34] Many interviewees mentioned social media in this way. As 20-year-old activist Ágúst said:

> The best way to get people to an organized protest is clearly on Facebook, because people check Facebook many times a day."[35]

The protest site as a social attraction

As the quotations at the beginning of this chapter illustrate, the accounts by the protesters described how the protest site became a social attraction, especially perhaps for younger individuals. As more and more public meetings and protests took place, these sites became places to meet friends and acquaintances in a novel situation. Going to the meetings and the protests to meet people became an exciting social activity. As many interviewees mention, the protests became "fun." A female in her twenties said:

> I usually went by myself, because you knew that your friends would be there and not just some protest friends but, you know, you met your school-mates, and everyone was curious, many college students [...] and I always met incredibly many people that I hadn't seen for many years. And that was so much fun. This social aspect was very much a part of the whole thing.[36]

Perceptions and emotions emerging at the protest site

The semi-structured interviews illustrate how the dynamics that, at times, emerged at the protest ground, especially at the growing public meetings in November 2008 and during the January 2009 pots and pans protest, produced not only growing expectations and perceived efficacy among protesters, but also joyful emotional experiences of "magical moments." These perceptions and experiences may have been a big part of the attraction of the protests. Still, many interviewees experienced negative emotions when witnessing disruptive or unlawful actions that, to their minds, spoiled the protests, and some individuals struggled with self-awareness as they crossed the boundaries to become protesters. I have no survey data to verify the general effects of these experiences on protest behavior, but the accounts given in the interviews are strongly indicative in this respect.

Expectations and perceived efficacy

I have already discussed (in Chapter 3) how growing participation in public meetings in late October and November 2008 raised expectations and increased the protest efficacy perceived by activists. Ordinary protesters similarly experienced heightened expectations due to growing protest participation. Many interviewees emphasized how their expectations had grown when they saw that "all sorts of people" were participating in meetings and protests. "It wasn't just some activists demanding something," 29-year-old Hanna recalled, "but old women and old men, people on the margins of society as well as professors and truck-drivers, and there were well-known faces in the crowd."[37] As the number of participants grew, both at the public meetings and at the January pots and pans protests, protesters experienced a thrilling sense of the power they seemed to have. "When there are so many people, we had such a momentum," 38-year-old town mayor Kristinn remarked, "then I was certain that [protesting] would have an effect."[38] Some interviewees talked about having been certain that the authorities could not ignore such large-scale, ongoing protests. As the January protests came closer, some individuals were expecting a huge protest with unforeseeable consequences:

> It was foreseeable that there would be many people there, and that is always a motivation [...] suddenly these protests started to be fun, not the usual boring protest [... *There was the social aspect, but also there were unspoken expectations; that is, it also made it exciting that we*] were wondering what would happen next.[39]

The lure of "magical moments"

When asked to talk about their most memorable experiences during the protests, many interviewees mentioned the powerful emotions that they had felt in moments of shared purpose and action at the protest site. Using phrases such as "magical," "higher," "spiritual," or "historical," interviewees emphasized how remarkable and joyful such moments had been.[40] Thus, the interviewees described how they had felt when protesting with others, singing and chanting and finding a common rhythm while beating pots and pans. These accounts are typical of the joyful emotions that emerged at such moments:

> People had pots and pans and then suddenly we were in tune together. It wasn't organized, we somehow started chanting: "INCOMPE-TENT GOVERN-MENT." And there was this strong rhythm. It felt so unique.[41]
>
> I felt this great force of unity that was binding us together. It was very beautiful.[42]
>
> All the little moments are so memorable [...] once a bonfire was lit in front of the Central Bank and we sat close together around it. It was so much fun.[43]

Such experiences became a part of the attraction of the protest site. "I called a few of my friends to tell them about this great experience," an interviewee recalled, "I said to them: " 'You don't want to miss out on this experience, no matter what your political convictions are.' "[44] Several interviewees thought the protests had been a "historical moment" that they wanted to be a part of. In Hanna's words: "I went down there because I was certain that this was a historical event."[45] Seeing the pots and pans protests as a historical moment was a common theme in the interviews. Kári recalled:

> When you are living your life you rarely feel that you are experiencing something historical. But at this point in time I thought that I was witnessing something that would be in books about the history of humanity.[46]

Consistent with the work of Leeuwen et al. (2014), the soft approach of the police at the protest site (discussed in Chapter 3) made the protest site more "harmonious" in the eyes of many protesters. It also reduced the perceived cost of protesting. Although some of my interviewees, particularly those who played active roles in the protests, talked about how the police had, in their view, reacted harshly and aggressively in various situations, most of them recognized that the police had actually taken a very soft approach. Many protesters felt that both the police and the protesters were "in the same boat," being forced to cooperate in a difficult situation and in fact sympathizing with each other's predicaments. In the words of middle-aged protester Jón:

> I have a very powerful image where this young girl or woman is talking to a police officer and she is very emotional, really crazy, and the officer has put up his helmet and he is explaining to her: 'Look I also have trouble, my wife has lost her job, but I just have to do my job here; I understand how you feel.' She had just spat on him and now they were bonding. This is how I experienced the cooperation between the protesters and the police. To me, this was the spirit of the protest.[47]

Disagreement and protest spoilers

But, as could be expected given the spontaneous nature of the protests, not all protesters agreed on method. The survey work presented in Chapter 3 shows that although a large majority of the public supported the pots and pans protests, many felt that the actions at these protests "went too far." The interviews illustrate experiences underlying this finding. Again, social activists kept busy during the protests, performing acts such as burning benches and lighting bonfires, and some wore masks to conceal their identities. According to police officers, a few individuals took shelter in the crowd to perform outright acts of aggression and even hooliganism by throwing not only eggs and paint at the police, but also stones and human feces.[48] Many interviewees who had been passive protesters and also more prominent activists felt some of these acts were bad and had spoiled the protests. Some felt that social activists were using the occasion to "put on their own show," and worried that their actions had given the authorities reason to label the protesters as "a mob." These individuals were concerned when the media focused on such actions and interviewed the individuals involved. The following account is typical of this prominent theme in the interviews.

> I thought that the acts of activists were good, for the most part, but it bothered me that there were some stupid people trying to fire up the protest [...] which meant [...] that people could call us a mob, but we were just ordinary people protesting.[49]

Self-image

The interviews did not focus much on self-image and social identity, but they still revealed a few insights into these issues. Some interviewees talked about struggling with engaging in unlawful behavior while maintaining their image of self as law-abiding citizens. A few interviewees recalled the struggle to "step outside of their comfort zone" by engaging in unlawful behavior. "I was fully aware that it was a tremendous barrier to overcome," Jón recalled, "I am a respectable citizen who abides by the law, but there I actually was, standing on Austurvöllur and acting like a lunatic." On entering the protest site, some individuals thought about the potential consequences for their social status. Obviously such concerns had not stopped my interviewees from protesting but they probably deterred many other individuals who wanted to protest from actually going to the protests. This position is illustrated by Kristín, a 24-year-old female who stopped playing an active frontline role in the protests after she became concerned about her social status:

> I'm a football coach and train young girls [...] I don't think I should be telling them what to think or deciding for them what is wrong and right. So I was a bit aware of myself [...] there was this one clip from the

> protest shown on television where I was in a frontline struggle. I don't think that it was easy to recognize me, but after this I kept to the back a little bit.[50]

Absolute and relative economic loss

While my interviewees rarely talked about personal economic loss as a reason for why they protested, a few talked about experiencing substantial, unexpected, and painful, economic losses. Of course, the effects of strain stemming from economic loss on protest behavior may be unconscious to some extent. While many interviewees mentioned experiences that were common among Icelanders in the crisis – their mortgages had shot up while the value of their houses had dropped and their standard of living had worsened – a few had been harmed more drastically, losing all or most of their savings in the bank crash. The following account is a typical version of such experiences, which often surfaced in the Icelandic media during the crisis. College student Eydís said:

> The bank crash was a tremendous shock for me, indirectly, because my husband had invested all of his insurance money – he had been in an accident – in bonds [...] So there were millions in his account but then the next day there was just zero. It was horrible and, you know, played a part in my protest behavior.[51]

As I have argued above, the effects of economic loss on protest behavior may be particularly pronounced among individuals such as Eydís, who believe that the crisis is harming them more than others. My survey data include two separate measurements of perceived economic loss, enabling me to test this hypothesis.[52] The first is of the respondents' perceived reduction in their standard of living since the crisis started (see Appendix B, Table B2). A substantial majority (63 percent) of the survey sample experienced some reduction in their standard of living. The second measurement is of the social comparison dimension. It asks respondents whether the crisis has harmed their financial situation more than it harmed the situation of most others. Only a minority (18 percent) of the sample believed that the crisis had harmed them more than others (again, see Table B2).

Figures 5.1–5.2 show the effects of these factors on protest behavior. Specifically, they show the probability of protest participation and protest support, respectively, by level of perceived economic loss (holding the social, economic, and demographic characteristics constant at their mean levels). The findings support the argument that social comparison moderates the effect of economic loss on protest behavior. In the language of statistics, the results reveal a significant interaction effect; the effect of perceived economic loss on protest behavior is contingent on the level of perceived economic loss relative to (see Appendix C, Table C3).[53]

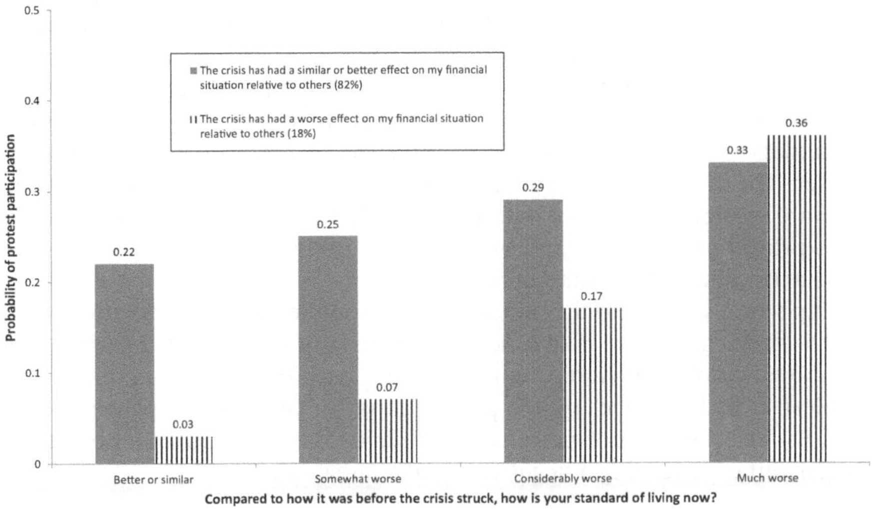

Figure 5.1 The effect of perceived reduction in standard of living on the probability of protest participation, by level of perceived financial loss relative to others (Note: the probabilities are based on Model 1, Appendix C, Table C4)

Source: Reykjavík Area Social Survey (Appendix B)

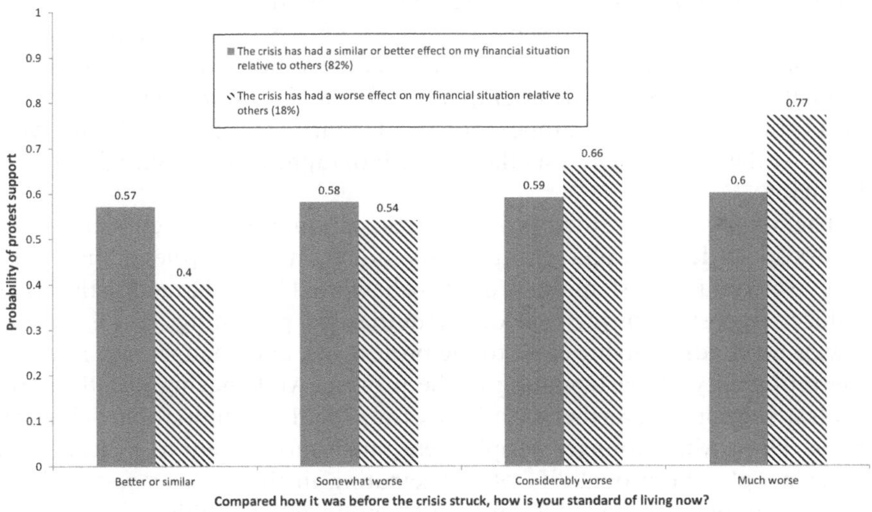

Figure 5.2 The effect of perceived reduction in standard of living on the probability of protest support, by level of perceived financial loss relative to others (Note: the probabilities are based on Model 2, Appendix C, Table C5)

Source: Reykjavík Area Social Survey (Appendix B)

Figure 5.1 shows that there is a substantial association between perceived economic loss and the probability of protest participation, *but only among individuals who thought that the crisis had harmed their financial situation more than that of others*. Among the majority of the sample, that is, among those who believed that the crisis had not harmed their financial situation more than that of others, economic loss has no effect on protest participation whatsoever. The findings in Figure 5.2 regarding protest support are substantively similar. In short, the survey data indicates that perceived economic loss predicts protest participation and support *only* if individuals think that the crisis has harmed them more than others.

Importantly, again, only 18 percent of respondents thought that the crisis had harmed them more than others, while the majority did not. Therefore, the overall effect of perceived economic loss on both outcomes is actually quite modest: it had no effect on the protest behavior of about 82 percent of the sample. Yet, the effect of perceived economic loss is substantial among those 18 percent experiencing a negative social comparison.

Social and economic characteristics of protesters (and supporters)

As I have discussed both in Chapter 3 and the current chapter, a prominent theme in the interviews was the perception that the high number of individuals coming to meetings and protests were not the usual protest "suspects" but represented a cross-section of society. (Again, this perception seemingly bolstered expectations and sense of protest efficacy among the protesters.) The survey analysis in Table 5.5 addresses the validity of this perception, estimating the effects of demographic, social, and economic characteristics on participation in and support for the January 2009 pots and pans protests. At the same time it tests the role of biographical availability in protest behavior.

The findings show that protest participation was in fact widespread across socio-demographic groups, while highlighting the role of biographical availability in shaping protest behavior. Thus, characteristics that reduce the cost of, or increase opportunities for, protesting, that is, having few or no children, living close to the protest site, and younger age, increase the probability of participating in the protests while having no effects on protest support. Nevertheless, all the groups had substantial participation rates. Thus, while younger people were much more likely to protest than older people, the probability of participating in the protests was as high as 0.26 among 40-year-olds and 0.18 among 60-year-olds, when all the other characteristics are set at their mean levels. Individuals who had children in their homes were less likely to protest, but their participation was still substantial. Finally, living close to the protest site (the midtown area) increased the probability of participating substantially. The probability of

Table 5.5 Biographical availability predictors of participation in, and support for, the January 2009 pots and pans protests

	Probability of protest participation	*Probability of supporting protest actions*
Gender		
Male	(≈ 0.26)	(≈ 0.56)
Female	(≈ 0.26)	(≈ 0.56)
Residential location		
Reykjavík Center	0.43	(≈ 0.56)
Reykjavík West (within 3–5km radius)	0.26	(≈ 0.56)
Reykjavík East (outside 5km radius)	0.22	(≈ 0.56)
Neighboring town of Reykjavík	0.18	(≈ 0.56)
Employment		
Employed	0.29	(≈ 0.56)
Not employed	0.17	(≈ 0.56)
Age		
20	0.36	0.67
40	0.26	0.60
60	0.18	0.52
80	0.12	0.45
Children in household		
0	0.28	(≈ 0.56)
1	0.22	(≈ 0.56)
2	0.17	(≈ 0.56)
3	0.13	(≈ 0.56)
Educational attainment		
Less than secondary	0.16	0.49
Secondary	0.25	0.59
College	0.27	0.63
Household income (ranked 1–17)		
Low (income rank = 5)	(≈ 0.26)	0.65
Average (income rank = 10)	(≈ 0.26)	0.57
High (income rank = 15)	(≈ 0.26)	0.51

Data: Reykjavík Area Social Survey

Note: Table 5.5 reports probability of protesting at least once and of being in favor of the protest actions. The probabilities are estimated from the regression models in Table C1, by setting other independent variables at their grand means. Differences in predicted probabilities are statistically significant. Insignificant differences are denoted by reporting the base probabilities of protest participation (0.26) and of protest support (0.56).

participating was over 0.40 among those living within a short walking distance of Austurvöllur, but decreased with greater distance from the protest site. If perceived cost impacted protest behavior, residential proximity did so in particular. Indeed, several of my interviewees lived downtown at the time of the protest.[54] They all mentioned this factor; it had been easy for them to protest. Young female Ingibjörg recalled:

> I lived with mom and dad downtown and could always hear when the speaker-system was turned on at Austurvöllur, and then I rushed out to walk the dog.[55]

Furthermore the association of education and employment with protest participation illustrates the "mainstream profile" of protesters. Prior research has indicated that protest participants tend to be more highly educated than non-participants, presumably because education increases interest in, and knowledge of, politics (Norris et al. 2005; McVeigh and Smith 1999; Shussman and Soule 2005). Likewise, the current findings show that education is significantly associated with protest participation. The probability of protesting was 0.16 for those with less than secondary education, but 0.25 and 0.27 for those with secondary or college education, respectively. Moreover, individuals who were employed were significantly more likely to protest than other groups; this is consistent with some prior research (McAdam 1986; Rudig and Karyotis 2013b). Thus, holding other characteristics at their average levels, the estimated probability of protest participation is about 0.29 for employed individuals but 0.17 for others.

Household income was not significantly related to protest participation; participation appeared not to be motivated by social class position. Still, lower income individuals were significantly more likely than high income earners to support the protests, but this effect disappears when political attitudes are controlled for (see Appendix C, Table C6). Thus, low income seemingly influences protest support through its effects on political attitudes.

Conclusion

If the broader social context contextualizes the processes underlying individual mobilization in protest (Klandermans 1993; Norris et al. 2005), the empirical work in this chapter helps to link the context of the Icelandic crisis with the protest behavior of individual citizens.[56] As I have discussed in previous chapters, the financial crisis disrupted not only shared aspects of the political and social context, spurring protest dynamics and collective action framing, but also created widespread, personal economic disruption and shattered expectations. This chapter illustrates how, in this context, several types of incentives – political, social, situational, and economic – conspired to mobilize individuals to participate in, and support, protests.

The research has demonstrated, first, the role of frame alignment in individual mobilization (Snow et al. 1986), emphasizing the pivotal role of collective action framing in protest mobilization in the Icelandic setting. Leftist activists and critics, inspired by perception of opportunity, framed the crisis as a democratic crisis rooted in the authorities' failed neo-liberal agenda, corrupt practices, and incompetence, and my interview work illustrates a strong alignment with this discourse among protest participants. Moreover, like the actors who engaged in protest planning and innovation, some protesters interpreted the situation as an opportunity to challenge the long-standing reign of right-wing politics in Iceland – experiencing the protest as an "I-told-you-so moment." Furthermore, my survey work shows not only widespread frame alignment among the public – a great majority of people in fact blamed the Haarde government for the crisis – but it verifies that individuals whose political attitudes, beliefs, and allegiances were congruent with this discourse were much more likely to participate in and support the protests.

But, as cultural theorists emphasize (Johnston 2009:22; Swidler 1986, 2006), shared frames influence behavior in diffused, non-deterministic, and situational ways; they provide a context of meanings that shape behavior even if individuals do not deeply internalize the meanings themselves. Shared frames influence behavior not only through internalization but in part through social ties and situational dynamics. The experiences of my interviewees illustrate the social and affective dimensions of protest mobilization. Thus, illustrating the role of social incentives (McAdam and Paulsen 1993), committed protesters encouraged friends and family to protest; some protested only in the company of friends, family, or co-workers; social networks became communication networks (including via social media) about upcoming events; and the protest site, at times, became an exciting location to meet with friends and acquaintances. Moreover, the dynamics of participation and innovation created anticipation as well as powerful emotions of affective solidarity (Jasper 1998; Juris 2008), reinforcing protesters and attracting even more individuals to the protest site.

The soft approach of the police, that is, tolerating even disruptive protest actions, such as burning benches and throwing paint and eggs at the parliament, made the protest site less risky and more attractive to the general public. Protesters did not fear being arrested or being subject to police brutality. Instead, the respectful attitude of the police probably shaped the mood of the protest, making it more harmonious (Leeuwen et al. 2014). Still, some individuals struggled with identity issues when they felt that other protesters went too far and when they themselves crossed the boundaries to become protesters.

Since research has rarely tested the effect of personal economic loss on protest behavior in the historical setting of a sudden crisis (but, see Rudig and Karyotis 2013a, 2013b), it is noteworthy that I find support for such an effect. But the effect is more complex and limited than theorists have posited (Davies 1962; Gurr 1970). Although my interviewees rarely mentioned economic loss as a reason for protesting, the survey work supports the conditional role of economic loss in protest behavior. Specifically, perceived economic loss predicts both protest participation and protest support, but only if individuals think that the crisis is harming them more than others. As my colleagues and I have argued (Ragnarsdóttir et al. 2013), in a shared crisis people evaluate the justice of their losses with reference to how they perceive the losses of others. But since only a minority of Icelanders (18 percent of my survey sample) thought that their economic losses were worse than those of most others, the much more common perception of losing no more than others buffers the effect of perceived economic loss on protest behavior. Still, for the minority of the population experiencing unfavorable social comparisons, economic loss ignites a strong protest incentive.

The survey work reveals the "mainstream" profile of protesters, while verifying that biographical availability influences protest behavior. The findings support the external validity of prior research (Petrie 2004; Schussman and Soule 2005) by showing that females, people with children, and older people protest less. Also, living close to the protest site (downtown Reykjavík) was associated with greater protest participation but not greater protest support, underscoring the role of "availability" in participation. Still, participation was widespread across social and economic groups. Thus, protest participation was over 20 percent among 50-year-olds, the employed protested more than the unemployed, the educated protested more than those with little formal education; and the data do not support an association between household income and protest participation.

Notes

1 Interview #18.
2 Interview #7.
3 Interview #6.
4 Interview #22.
5 Actually, this is not entirely true. In Chapter 2 I relied on the interviews with protesters to illustrate how individuals experienced a need to define the confusing crisis situation, and hence attended public meetings.
6 This chapter relies on semi-structured interviews with twenty-four individuals who participated as protesters in the pots and pans protest in midtown Reykjavík in January 2009 (see Appendix A for methodological detail). Appendix B provides methodological detail on the two social surveys.
7 In Chapter 2 I referred to this theory as an individual-level variant of breakdown theory. There I examined the shared social disruption caused by the crisis, but here I am focusing on individual-level processes.
8 Interview #2.
9 Interview #1.
10 Interview #12.
11 Interview #16.
12 Interview #13.
13 Interview #17.
14 Interview #12.
15 Interview #6.
16 Interview #1.
17 Interview #6.

18 Interview #6.
19 Interview #4.
20 Interview #2.
21 Note that the survey data were obtained months after the protests. While this practice is common in protest research it creates concerns that I address in Appendix B.
22 Interview #18.
23 Interview #3.
24 Interview #6.
25 Interview #8.
26 Interview #2.
27 Interview #17.
28 Interview #7.
29 Interview #10.
30 Interview #19.
31 Interview #4.
32 Interview #3.
33 Interview #7.
34 In fact, the police was usually able to plan its operations in advance by monitoring Facebook discussion (Interview #28).
35 Interview #9.
36 Interview #3.
37 Interview #1.
38 Interview #5.
39 Interview #6.
40 The coding of the interviews revealed three overlapping themes tackling these experiences: *higher moment*, *unified mind*, and *part of history*.
41 Interview #12.
42 Interview #4.
43 Interview #8.
44 Interview #6.
45 Interview #1.
46 Interview #10.
47 Interview #2.
48 Interview #25, with Reykjavík Police Chief Stefán Eríksson.
49 Interview #10.
50 Interview #3.
51 Interview #8.
52 See Appendix B (section: *Methodological Consideration: Time of Survey Interview*), for discussion of potential measurement error due to the timing of survey interviews. Ragnarsdóttir et al. (2013) also used these data.
53 Elsewhere (Bernburg 2015a) I have used ordered regression to test the simultaneous effects of political views and perceived economic loss on protest participation and protest support (controlling for biographical characteristics). The findings from this analysis, including the statistical interaction effects, are substantively similar to the findings reported here.
54 The midtown area is disproportionally inhabited by highly educated people, including artists (my survey data confirm this point). While my analysis controls for educational attainment, income, employment status, and other factors, it does not control for the effects that the "atmosphere" of this area may have on protest behavior. Still, the analysis in Table 5.5 shows that, even if we leave out the Reykjavík Center, participation rates decrease as people live further away from the midtown area.
55 Interview #20.

56 As I have emphasized elsewhere (Bernburg 2015a, 2015b), this work is of some value to protest research. In particular, surveys often study participation in protests without distinguishing between different types of protest and they rarely focus on specific protest events (see discussion by Norris et al. 2005). This approach prevents the research from linking contextual dynamics with the processes underlying protest behavior, and in particular it makes it difficult to study the role of specific values and beliefs in protest behavior (important exceptions include the work of Biggs 2006; Opp and Gern 1993; and Rudig and Karyotis 2013a).

6 Conclusion

This book contributes to the scholarship of protests and social movements in several ways. First of all, it broadly addresses the applicability of social movement theory. Using mixed methods to study the forces underlying the Icelandic financial crisis protests, the study cuts across the levels of sociological analysis, moving across the historical-political context of the crisis, through the interpretations and actions of mobilization actors, and to the personal frames, experiences, and characteristics of individual protest participants. The work has studied these topics by applying major social movement theories, including theories of political process/opportunity and quotidian disruption, theories of agency and framing, and individual mobilization theories. Applying the theories has helped me to interpret the data and offer a comprehensive account of how the October 2008 collapse of the Icelandic banking system resulted in a dynamic wave of protest, culminating in threatening mass protests that brought down the country's government in January 2009.

More specifically, the study addresses a classic topic that the global pattern has in recent years brought to the forefront of social movement research, namely, the triggering effects of economic crises on protests. While the effect of crisis on protest is a classic theme in social movement theory, it has not received much attention in contemporary research, that is, until the recent global protest wave of the "movements of the crisis" began to capture the attention of social movement scholars (della Porta and Mattoni 2013; Tejerina et al. 2013). The current study contributes to research on the global protest wave by studying the intermediate processes by which the financial crisis spurred protest in a particular national context. Specifically, the study has addressed three questions: 1) How was the context of the financial crisis conducive to the emergence of protest? 2) How did "agents" play a role in translating these conditions into protest mobilization? 3) What individual-level processes drove individuals' protest behavior in this time of crisis?

The Icelandic case offers not only a convenient microcosm – a particular national setting – for studying the processes by which crises evoke protest, but examining this case is significant also because Iceland "launched" the global protest wave. Being the first major victim of the global crisis, Iceland was the first country to respond to it with popular protest, starting in early October 2008. This early start means that the national conditions and processes evoked by the financial crisis in Iceland could not be influenced by the subsequent spread of protest frames and methods in the crisis protests in Europe and beyond, allowing us to isolate better the local-national processes underlying the Icelandic protests.

The context of the financial Crisis: convergence of conditions conducive to protest

Figure 6.1 summarizes the findings of this book, displaying the major processes by which the crisis led to the protests. The bank crash and the resulting fiscal and diplomatic crisis created economic loss and financial trouble for many, directly making a substantial proportion of the public receptive to protest motivation (I address this individual-level process below). Moreover, the crisis created societal conditions that inspired goal-driven actors to set the wheels of protest in motion. First of all, it disrupted the quotidian. Snow et al. (1998) have argued that accidents and disasters are conducive to collective action because they disrupt the quotidian, which refers to people's daily routines and taken-for-granted assumptions. The Icelandic crisis not only plunged many people into uncertainty about their current and future way of life, but shattered their ideas about economic prosperity and security. This situation also destroyed the credibility of major institutions and created a threat to the national identity of Icelanders. Borrowing from George Herbert Mead (via Snow et al. 1998), a "problematic present" emerged; the crisis plunged people into uncertainty about their assumptions and their future.

The quotidian disruption created a widespread need among the public to define the situation in a collective manner, while the crisis created a credibility crunch for the authorities that undermined the resonance of their "global problem" framing of the crisis. In the decade leading up to the crisis, under the same political party (the Independence Party) that headed the current government, the authorities had freed capital from state constraints and privatized the country's state banks; they had then endorsed the expansion of the banks, celebrated success myths, and dismissed all warnings. After the collapse, the authorities' outspoken faith in free-market forces appeared naïve and ill-guided. Moreover, the enormous cost of the crisis for the state made the authorities vulnerable to criticism for having allowed the rich to victimize the public. Moreover, as often happens in Third World countries (Ortiz and Béjar 2013), the authorities were forced to negotiate with foreign entities, making them vulnerable to criticism for giving up sovereignty and caving into foreign capitalist pressure. That no other country had suffered a comparable collapse of its banking system at that time made it even more difficult for the authorities to blame the crisis on global forces.

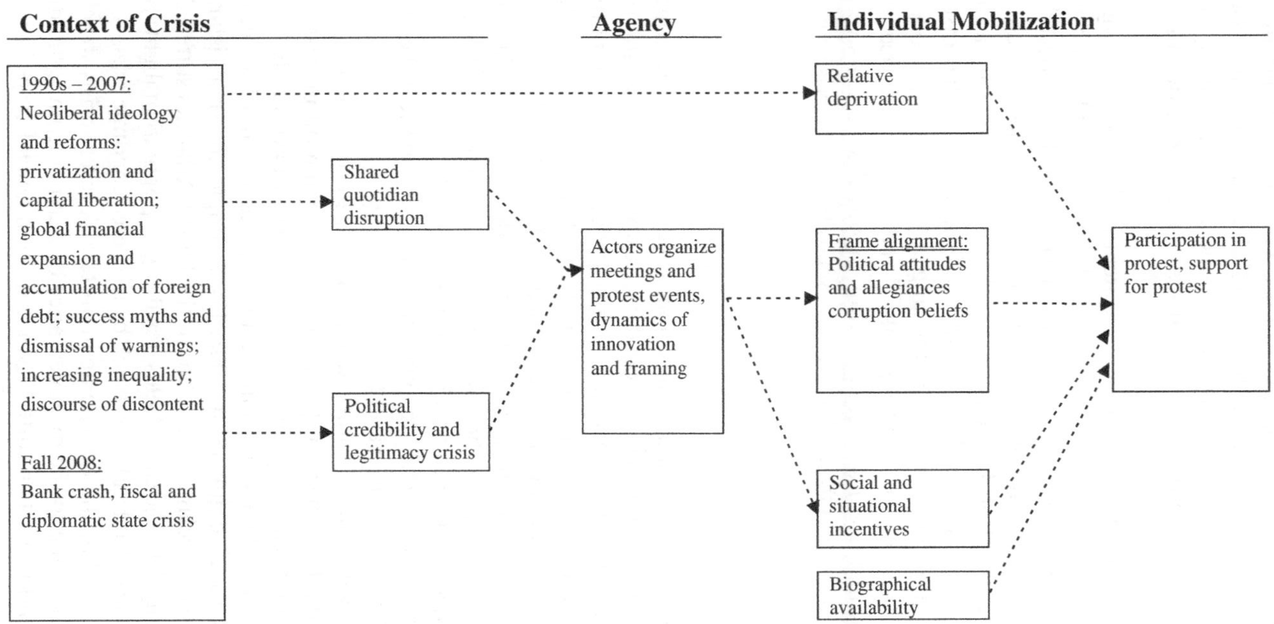

Figure 6.1 An overview: the context of the Icelandic crisis and the forces of mass protest

In short, the financial crisis made the Icelandic public receptive to protest mobilization by creating two conditions: a shared disruption of the quotidian and a credibility crunch for the authorities. The confused and anxious public was in need of a shared frame to explain what had happened. But, due to an unfolding crisis of political credibility and legitimacy, many people did not believe the global problem explanations of the authorities, making them receptive to alternative frames.

The emergence of a discourse of discontent in the years leading up to the crisis, however invisible it was during the boom years, plays an important role in the Icelandic story of historical convergence. In the decade preceding the crisis, new-left and global justice critiques of neo-liberalist reforms and political corruption had emerged in Iceland. Inspired by an emerging opportunity, activists and critics would build on these familiar discourses in the new context of the crisis that, in the language of framing theory (Benford and Snow 2000), enhanced the "credibility" and "relative salience" of the critiques. The available cultural context thus provided a "discursive opportunity" (Koopmans and Olzak 2004) for actors to frame the crisis as a crisis of democracy.

Implications

Early social movement scholarship emphasized that crises are conducive to mass protest because they create social breakdown, by producing social disintegration and widespread personal strain. In contrast, contemporary social movement research mostly ignores breakdown theories, assuming that explanations of protests and revolts need to focus on the political and cultural context. While I have emphasized the role of breakdown in the Icelandic protest, I agree that protests, even those resulting from a major social breakdown, must be situated in the historical, political and cultural context. Certainly, the political processes and shared meanings emerging in the wake of disasters and crises differ across place and time.

The reason why contemporary scholarship has not focused on economic crises is that the topic has not been salient in research on protest in affluent democratic countries. Even severe economic crises have rarely led to mass protests in affluent democracies in recent times, that is, until the global crisis began to strike such countries in 2008. For example, the small island-nation the Faroe Islands (Iceland's neighbor in the North Atlantic) suffered a major economic collapse in the early 1990s, resulting in population flight, but not in protests. Similarly, Finland was struck by a severe economic crisis in the same period, but the public did not rise up in protest. A severe crisis struck Iceland in the late 1960s, due to the disappearance of herring from Icelandic fishing grounds, but no protests resulted. Nor did the financial crisis in the United States, causing the Great Depression in the 1930s, spur protests.

In contrast, economic crises have played prominent roles in spurring protests and violent uprisings in the Third World in recent decades. Scholars studying such protests have noted that at the periphery of the global system of economic and financial dependency, economic crises often undermine the legitimacy of the ruling authorities, and thus create fertile ground for popular protest (Ortiz and Béjar 2013; Walton and Ragin 1990). One important reason has been that crises in the Third World often result in foreign-imposed economic and state restructuring (austerity) measures. As the recent wave of global crisis protests bears witness to (Kousis 2013), and the Icelandic case illustrates, something similar has been occurring in countries in the affluent world since the global crisis began to strike them in 2008.

While emphasizing the necessity of studying the historically specific, political and cultural processes underlying the financial crisis protests, I have argued that the nature of the Icelandic financial crisis, namely, the sudden reversal of growth and prosperity, provides reason and opportunity to revisit breakdown theory. My work has illustrated how in the crisis "breakdown" processes converged with economic, political, and cultural processes, creating a societal context that was conducive to protest mobilization.

If the present work establishes how the historical context shapes the effect of social breakdown on protest, it encourages the research on the movements of the crisis to focus on the role of quotidian disruption in protest mobilization. While the existing research has not paid enough attention to this issue, there is some work that supports the external validity of this approach. Borland and Sutton (2007) studied the experiences of women in the Argentinian financial crisis in the early 2000s, showing that the disruption of routine life and taken-for-granted reality that many women experienced in the crisis rendered them open to the acceptance of radical frames and identities.[1] Moreover, some work on the recent crisis protests has illustrated how people experienced the crisis as a "shock" to their shared reality. For example, Woolfson's (2010) ethnographic work on the protests in Lithuania showed how the crisis shattered widespread expectations of growing prosperity that had emerged in Lithuania in the years of growth leading up to the crisis. I suspect that the global crisis created such disruption in many places, as it did in Iceland, but research is presently lacking on this topic.

But, again, the consequences of quotidian disruption for collective action are contingent on the national-local political and cultural context in which disruption occurs. In some ways the political developments leading to the financial crisis were similar in many of the countries that were badly hit by it. In other ways, the national context differed in important ways (Pappas and O'Malley 2014). In Iceland the disruptive effects of the crisis occurred alongside a developing crisis of political credibility and legitimacy that was partially rooted in the neo-liberal reforms instituted by the authorities in the decades leading up to the crisis. This development mirrored the global development of neo-liberal reforms in the 1980s and 1990s. As in Iceland, these neo-liberal reforms included capital liberation and spurred growth, but they also entailed increased social inequality, both within and between nations, spurring a global current of left-wing and new-left discontent (including the global justice movement). As Woolfson (2010) found in his work on the protests in Lithuania in 2009, and as the Icelandic case illustrates, once the financial crisis broke the promise of growth, the underlying discontent about the social (and the environmental) consequences of the neo-liberal project was unleashed.

Importantly, however, the political crisis in Iceland was rooted not only in neo-liberal reforms, but also in a long-standing discourse in Iceland about corrupt practices and violations of democratic principles in Icelandic politics (Bergmann 2014:68; Kristinsson 2006; Kristjánsson 2012). As we have seen, the protest discourse in Iceland emphasized issues of government corruption and failed democracy. In this regard, Pappas and O'Malley's study (2014) of protest outcomes in Ireland and Greece adds a comparative dimension to my discussion. Both these countries were harmed greatly by the financial crisis, and both responded to it with severe austerity measures. Moreover, people in both these countries suffered a major setback to their standard of living. But in Greece a discourse of political corruption and government inefficiency had existed prior to the crisis; this was not the case in Ireland. Greece experienced major protests but Ireland did not. As in Iceland, the financial crisis in Greece spurred protests in part through the amplification of pre-existing discontent with the state of the nation's democracy (e.g. Kousis 2013).

Comparative work is needed to study how the national political context influenced the effect of the quotidian disruption created by the financial crisis on popular protest. The current work suggests that countries where popular discontent with national democracy was widespread prior to the crisis may have been particularly receptive to protest motivation. The lessons from the research on Third World protests (Ortiz and Béjar 2013; Walton and Ragin 1990) suggest, as does the Icelandic case, that in such contexts, negotiating with foreign entities on austerity and state debt may be particularly harmful for the legitimacy of the authorities.

Agency, opportunity, and the dynamics of protest

A major guiding assumption in the present study has been that historical contexts entailing opportunity for challenge lead to collective action only through the actions of goal-driven individuals. As social movement theorists have emphasized (McAdam et al. 1996; Tarrow 2011), social changes that offer "political" or "discursive" opportunities for challenge do not automatically trigger popular protest. Not only is "opportunity" meaningless without individuals interpreting the given situation as such, but it cannot influence real-world events unless actors are willing and able to engage in effective mobilization work. For example, individuals need to plan protests and frame the issues to motivate others to participate in them. Motivated by political and ideological goals, such actors are "agents," and their deliberate goal-driven actions constitute "human agency."

The work contributes to this general approach by illustrating how the interpretations and actions of goal-driven agents play a role in translating abrupt change into large-scale protest mobilization. The Icelandic bank crash did not automatically trigger protest. It took many weeks of ongoing public meetings and protest events and phases of waxing and waning public participation before explosive mass protest finally broke out. The context of the unfolding crisis made the public receptive to protest mobilization, but the development of protest was contingent on the initiatives of mobilization actors, timely employment of novel tactics, effective framing, and also on coincidences and chains of events.

Social movement scholars have argued that when a change in the social and political context entails an opportunity for challenge, such opportunity may often be temporary and thus the timely and novel initiatives of "early risers" may be crucial in igniting a protest dynamic (Koopmans 2004:24–26; Tarrow 2011:201). In Iceland the key instigators of protest were independent actors with no organizational or formal political ties. In the middle of the turmoil caused by the collapse of the three Icelandic banks, inspired by a perception of the problematic present and emotional need among the public to define the crisis, and by their pre-existing political goals, a handful of individuals used informal ties and social media to call on people to come to public meetings in midtown Reykjavík to define the crisis. The meetings initially attracted few people, but the actors persisted in organizing more meetings. As the crisis developed into a fiscal and diplomatic crisis, meetings began to attract a growing number of people of all social and economic backgrounds. The actions of these determined individuals thus set the wheel of collective action in motion by creating a platform for protest. Pre-existing political and social movement organizations in Iceland, including the political parties and the trade unions, played no role in planning meetings and protest events.

Theorists have emphasized that protest events may create opportunities for more protest (della Porta 2012a; Koopmans 2004). They may attract new players and participants, lead to the formation of new social ties and organizational forms, and they may facilitate the emergence of new frames. The pattern of the Icelandic protests illustrates such a process. The public meetings created a platform for a dynamic development of protest, public participation, framing, and ultimately threatening mass protest. As participation in the meetings grew during the unfolding of the crisis in October and November 2008, other activists, inspired by a growing sense of protest efficacy and solidarity, began to perform their own acts of contention at the meetings and organize their own events, creating anticipation of public disorder. During the holiday month of December 2008, a month in which all normal routine is interrupted by preparations for traditional celebrations in the Christmas and New Year period, when public participation almost vanished, this developed activism was pivotal in "keeping the protests alive" until participation increased again in January, culminating in the threatening pots and pans protests.

Agency-driven protest dynamics have their own momentum, independent of the broader conditions that make them possible (Koopmans 2004), but the specific social, cultural, and global context of the financial crisis shaped the strategic actions of individuals. First of all, as scholars commenting on the subsequent wave of global crisis protests have noticed (della Porta and Mattoni 2013:8), independent agents, including both new actors and "usual" grassroots activists, played a key role in spinning the wheel of "spontaneous" protest in Iceland. Again, neither formal organizations, such as trade unions, nor established political actors, such as the political parties, planned or brought resources or organization to the protest events. Nor did the protest campaign have a central leadership. A handful of key actors were crucial in organizing public meetings and major protest events, but no single mind or organization planned or controlled the myriad of protest actions at the meetings, and there were different groups of actors that instigated and planned protest events outside of the meetings. Sometimes the different actors cooperated, but usually they did not. Disagreement thus often emerged among and between major actors as well as average protesters about protest methods.[2]

As scholars studying protests in various national contexts in recent years have observed (Postill 2014; Tufekci and Wilson 2012), social media communication technology made it possible for independent actors and small groups to plan and effectively use informal networks to spread information about protest events, often at very short notice. But such communication technology was effective only as long as the frustration and confusion of the crisis made the public receptive to protest mobilization. As in many other countries struck by the crisis after Iceland, the absence of lasting organizational structures explains why protest mobilization did not last beyond the shared experience of the unfolding financial crisis.

Importantly, while I have focused on the "local" evolution of the Icelandic protests, the deployment of protest tactics had an important global dimension. As della Porta (2013) has argued, activists often try to translate protest methods that have been successful in one historical context into their own context. For example, Fominaya and Jiminéz (2013) have studied how activists in Spain's housing crisis movement from 2011–2013 adopted tactics from the Argentinian late 1990s "dirty war" protest. As these authors argue, cross-national diffusion of protest methods "does not only happen from one nation to the next within a single protest cycle: it can also happen across time" (p. 19).

Likewise, although Icelanders were the first to respond to the global financial crisis with popular protests, global repertoires of contention played an important role in the development of the protests. The collection of mobilization actors – both the key organizers and the groups of activists on the ground – were inspired by known protest methods. In particular, aside from the fundamental impact of the deployment of public "town meetings," the timely and strategic deployment of a South American-style *cacerolazo* (pots and pans) protest on January 20, 2009 was a turning point in the protest because it introduced a well-timed innovation into the situation, sparking threatening mass protest. If the contextual similarities of Iceland to some of the South American crises are obvious, particularly to the early 2000s Argentinian financial collapse and subsequent protests, the deployment of this protest method shows how activists' strategic choices drive the diffusion of protest between nations (della Porta 2013), not only across space (as in the transcontinental spread of the *acampada*, that is, the occupation of squares, in 2011) but also across time.

Emergence of protest discourse: framing in political, cultural – and global – context

Framing theory emphasizes that objective problems (crisis, war, inequality, etc.) can be defined in different ways, and hence mobilization agents usually try to frame problems and situations in ways that rationalize protest and motivate others to participate (Snow and Benford 1988; Benford and Snow 2000). The current study illustrates how framing work was integral to the development of protest in Iceland; deliberate, strategic production of meanings and symbols played a pivotal role in protest mobilization. The emerging protest discourse was rooted in discontent with the transformation of democracy in an age of neo-liberal globalization.

Although the global financial crisis was incomprehensible to many economists and financial analysts when it struck, it disrupted the public's taken-for-granted reality, and framing it was thus "in demand." But the framing of the crisis was a political issue from the moment that it struck Iceland; the framing work appearing in the public debate followed political and ideological allegiances and interests. Thus, anticipating criticism, government leaders hastened to neutralize the crisis by defining it as an "international storm," portraying Iceland as a victim of global forces. But government critics, social activists, and protest advocates immediately countered this view. Their broad message, appearing in the media as well as at the emerging public meetings, was that the authorities' long-standing corruption, incompetence, and naïve commitment to free-market ideology had made Iceland vulnerable to the global bank crisis. The intention of the authorities to lead Iceland through the crisis was not only a violation of democratic principles, but constituted a threat to the Icelandic public since the authorities were caving in to the demands of the rich, compromising the country's sovereignty and disenfranchizing the public.

The public meetings were crucial in facilitating the development of protest discourse. The meetings provided a platform for collective action framing; in the language of framing theory (Benford and Snow 2000), the meetings associated the emerging "diagnostic" definitions with "prognostic" and "motivational" definitions. Thus, as opponents of the government, critics, and intellectuals began to diagnose the crisis as a democratic crisis in the public debate, the public meetings associated this discourse with collective action, defining protest actions, including civil disobedience, as a way to remedy the democratic problems. Moreover, in line with Benford (1993), the framing work at the meetings conveyed "motivational" definitions, by appealing to, and amplifying ideas and emotions of, injustice, moral duty, urgency, nationalism and solidarity, and the efficacy of the protests.

A particularly effective framing action at the public meetings was the establishment of "minimum demands." By making the resignation of the government the key stated goal of the protest campaign, protest actors strategically construed a shared "master frame" (Gerhard and Rucht 1992). The demand resonated with the public's sense of democratic procedure, while uniting various new-left groups as well as moderate segments of the public aligned with the political left. All of these groups had been discontent with the authorities prior to the crisis. However, this most resonating element of the protest discourse also pre-defined the end of the protests. Having no lasting organizational base, the protests attracted the public only as long as the stated goals resonated widely with public opinion. Once these goals had been attained, mass mobilization ended, leaving radical activists protesting by themselves for a time before giving up.

To understand why the framing campaign resonated with the Icelandic public, we must situate it in the national historical-political, and ultimately also the global, context of the financial crisis. Framing theory implies that the social context constrains framing innovation; for frames to resonate with a substantial part of a population they need to ring true in the given context, and they need to appeal to shared values and beliefs and everyday experiences (Benford and Snow 2000; Snow et al. 1986). My work has shown how, as the disruption of the taken-for-granted created a widespread demand for framing (the entire nation was anxiously focusing on the crisis), the political and discursive context in Iceland entailed opportunities for framing that could resonate with many. By breaking the promise of economic prosperity, the crisis undermined the credibility of the authorities that had implemented profound neo-liberal reforms in the name of economic prosperity. The new context of the economic crisis enabled critics and activists to amplify the pre-existing discontent with the neo-liberal reforms. The familiar criticisms of the authorities' corruption, incompetence, and naïve commitment to neo-liberalism now were relevant to the everyday anxieties and frustrations of many people, greatly enhancing the mobilizing potential of these frames.

In one sense, then, the Icelandic story is a microcosm of a global story; the financial crisis unleashed popular discontent with the democratic implications of neo-liberal globalization in many places. As in Iceland, the discourses of the crisis protests in the different countries have usually emphasized the implications of the global financial crisis for the current state of national democracy and national sovereignty in an age of neo-liberal globalization (della Porta and Mattoni 2013; Kousis 2013; Roos and Oikonomakis 2013; Woolfson 2010). As scholars studying protests in Third World countries began noticing decades ago (Walton and Ragin 1990), the economic and financial interdependencies that prevail in the contemporary globalized world, which the financial crisis revealed so well, do not chime so well with the public's traditional notions of national sovereignty and democratic ideals. Thus, although Icelanders were the first to the respond to the crisis with protests, the protest discourse that emerged had a global dimension, just like the methods used by protesters.

Individual mobilization: protest incentives in times of crisis

The final major aim of this work has been to study the individual-level processes underlying protest behavior in a time of crisis. While crisis-evoked protests often involve enormous public participation, and this applies to the global wave of crisis protests in particular, research on individual mobilization in crisis protests has up to now been limited (Bernburg 2015a, 2015b). The current work contributes to this research by using mixed methods to study the frames, experiences, and characteristics of ordinary protesters.

The right-hand side of Figure 6.1 summarizes the findings pertaining to the individual-level mobilization processes. Firstly, as in many of the subsequent crisis protests (Rudig and Karyotis 2013a), protest participation in Iceland went far beyond the usual grassroots activists. My survey data show that about 25 percent of the adult population of the Reykjavík metropolitan area participated in the protests, at least in some capacity, and a majority of the nation supported the protests. Accordingly, while biographical characteristics (McAdam 1986), such as gender, age, and residential proximity influenced protest behavior, protest participation was widespread across the major social and economic groups. Underscoring the mainstream profile of protesters, protest was more prevalent among the employed and the educated, and it was unrelated to income. The widespread participation of the societal mainstream played an important role in the emerging sense of protest efficacy among activists, encouraging them to spin the wheel of protest. Moreover, the high level of participation in the explosive pots and pans protest was of course essential in creating the pressure needed to bring down the government in January 2009.

The work illustrates how, in the context of the crisis and the developing protests, several different processes conspired in motivating many individuals to participate in, and support, the ongoing protests. The data support the pivotal role of "frame alignment" (Snow et al. 1986) in individual mobilization, illustrating the effects of framing on the growth of the protests. Thus, mobilization agents framed the crisis as a democratic crisis rooted in the authorities' failed neo-liberal agenda, corrupt practices, and incompetence, and my work illustrates a strong alignment with this discourse among protesters. Moreover, it illustrates how some protesters, particularly leftists and new-left activists, defined the protest as an "I-told-you-so moment." Thus, like the actors instigating the protests, they viewed the situation as an opportunity to challenge the long-standing reign of neo-liberal politics in Iceland. My survey work verifies that attitudes, beliefs, and allegiances congruent with this discourse strongly predict both protest participation and protest support among the general public. As Swidler (1986, 2006) argues, ideology influences behavior in "unsettled" times; having to choose a side in an evolving conflict, individuals tend to rely on their existing frames, including their political ideas, beliefs, and ideologies. Thus, I have found that individuals were much more likely both to participate in and to support the protests if they had leftist political attitudes and allegiances, if they believed in the reality of political corruption and deterioration of democracy, and if they blamed the Haarde government for the crisis.

Furthermore, confirming the diffuse effects of cultural frames on social interaction and on actors' interpretations of their situations (Johnston 2009), my work reveals how the social and situational dynamics emerging at the protests created powerful incentives for individuals to protest. Illustrating social incentives entailed in social ties (McCarthy and Paulsen 1993), committed protesters encouraged friends and family to protest; some protested only in the company of friends, family, or co-workers; social networks became communication networks (including via social media) about upcoming events; and the protest site, at times, became an exciting location to meet with friends and acquaintances. And the dynamics of participation and innovation created anticipation as well as powerful emotions of affective solidarity (Jasper 1998; Juris 2008), reinforcing protesters and attracting even more individuals to the protest site.

The police adopted a "negotiation model" (della Porta and Diani 2006:198), that is, instead of trying to prevent the protest, the police tried to tolerate it and allowed protesters to engage in disruptive and illegal forms of protest while refraining from using coercive methods (Gíslason 2014). As Leeuwen et al. (2014) have suggested, the "soft" approach of the police made more room for experiences of joy and solidarity. Still, some individuals struggled with identity issues when other protesters went too far and when they themselves crossed the boundaries to become protesters.

Finally, the financial crisis created a widespread experience of economic loss that made a sizable minority of the population receptive to protest mobilization. As my survey work indicates, almost two thirds of Icelandic adults perceived some reduction in their standard of living in the crisis, and a sizable minority (a little less than one fifth) believed that the crisis was harming them more than others. In the latter group, experiencing a reduction in the standard of living had a pronounced positive effect on both protest participation and protest support. Elsewhere, my colleagues and I (Ragnarsdóttir et al. 2013) have found that individuals experiencing reduction of their standard of living in the Icelandic crisis felt more status injustice, especially if they thought that the crisis had harmed them more than others. Apparently, this type of unfavorable social comparison motivated some individuals to participate in the protests.

Research on the recent crisis protests in Europe and elsewhere has rarely tested the role of economic loss in protest behavior among the public. A rare exception is a study by Rudig and Karyotis (2013a) who surveyed public participation in the austerity protests in Greece in 2011. It found that perceived economic loss in the crisis predicted only protest support and not protest participation. But the study did not include the social comparison dimension that I have emphasized. Again, economic loss may influence protest behavior among only a part of the population, namely, among those who think that they are being harmed more than others. The current work is among the first to demonstrate, with individual-level data, that relative deprivation influences protest behavior in a time of crisis (Bernburg 2015a). I suggest that incorporating economic loss and social comparison into the research may help to explain protest participation in the global wave of crisis protests.

But the effect of the crisis on protest behavior through relative economic loss has been a small part of our story. Personal loss and relative deprivation did not directly motivate actors to plan protest events or produce a protest discourse. The major actors spinning the wheel of protest were not motivated by personal loss, but by political goals. Still, widespread individual loss probably influenced their general perception of opportunity. It was only after the shared social disruption and a change in the political context had inspired protest action and framing that individuals experiencing relative deprivation became motivated to protest. At the same time, a much larger part of the population became motivated to participate in the protests on the basis of their political attitudes, and as the protests grew in size, social and situational incentives amplified the dynamics of the protests, resulting in Iceland's first revolutionary situation.

Epilogue

In the years that have passed since the economic and political turmoil of the winter of 2008–2009, the strong shared emotions have faded into distant memory. The state is still burdened by debt from the financial crisis, but the country's economy has stabilized and currently there is growth in Iceland. These years have seen more protest activity than before, but while political protests have at times attracted a substantial number of individuals they have not spurred a dynamic process of participation and activism such as occurred after the collapse.

However, significantly, in 2009–2010 substantial grassroots activism emerged, protesting the efforts of the Icelandic authorities to settle the Icesave dispute with the United Kingdom and the Netherlands. Activists were motivated by moral reasoning rooted in the discourse emerging in the financial crisis protests; focusing on issues of natural justice and sovereignty, they viewed the Icesave dispute as a test of democracy (Hallgrímsdóttir and Brunet-Jailly 2014). The Icelandic parliament accepted a debt repayment agreement in December 2009, but in a context of growing public pressure, President Ólafur Ragnar Grímsson vetoed the parliament's decision, forcing the issue to a referendum. An overwhelming majority of Icelanders rejected the agreement in March 2010. Several years later, in 2014, the EFTA Court ruled that Iceland had neither breached the Deposit Guarantee Directive nor discriminated against depositors in a manner contrary to EEA law.[3]

Still, the long-term effects of the protests have disappointed many of those who had hoped for fundamental change and democratic reform. In the years following the protests, ambitious attempts were made to ignite institutional processes of democratic reform. The parliament set up a Special Investigation Commission (2010) to "search for the truth" about the financial crisis, and a nationally representative platform was created to re-examine the proposed changes to the country's Constitution (Árnason 2015). But these efforts have not yet led to any fundamental institutional changes in politics or government in Iceland.

While the shared emotion of indignation has waned, public trust in Icelandic politics has not been restored (Bjarnason 2014). The crisis and the protests have changed party politics in Iceland. New parties have emerged and undermined the power of the traditional parties (Proppé 2015). In the April 2009 national parliamentary election, three months after the pots and pans protests brought down Haarde's government, the Independence Party lost about one third of its traditional vote. A new party, The Citizen's Movement, was founded by individuals who had been active in the protest movement. This party received about 7 percent of the national vote. Moreover, the two left-wing parties, the Left-Green Movement and the Social Democratic Alliance, made substantial gains. Jointly these parties received more than 50 percent of the national vote. For the first time in the country's history, left-wing parties jointly received a majority of the vote and were able to form a coalition government.

However, the government's major task in the following years, that is, dealing with the aftermath of the financial crisis, both within Iceland (cutbacks in state welfare, restoring the domestic banks) and internationally (cooperation with the IMF and negotiations with the United Kingdom and the Netherlands about the Icesave debt) made it unpopular among voters. Struggling with the economic situation, additional strain on the welfare system, and diplomatic after-shocks of the crisis, the left-wing coalition government gradually lost the public's trust. In the 2013 election, inspired by the post-collapse critique of traditional politics, the political left disintegrated into several new parties, ironically leading voters to re-establish the majority rule of the two parties that had led the neo-liberal reforms of the 1990s and 2000s, that is, the Independence Party and the Progressive Party. But these parties have not restored trust in politics. To the contrary, according to polls, a new party, the *Pirate Party*, has gained ground. Rooted in the Citizen's Movement, this party emphasizes government transparency and constitutional change. What voters do in the next general election (in 2017) remains to be seen, but the Pots and Pans Revolution may still change Iceland. Up to this point, however, the political development bears witness to the momentary nature of political opportunity arising in a time of crisis and the limited ability of a small nation to change in a globalized world.

Notes

1 Gemici's (2013) study of protests that broke out in Turkey after an economic crisis hit the country in 2001 may also be interpreted as support for the quotidian disruption explanation. Gemici found that shopkeepers who experienced moral outrage because the government's reaction to the crisis posed a threat to their subsistence routines or way of life were most active in the protests.

2 Related, my survey work in Chapter 3 mirrors a conflict in public opinion between supporting protest and opposing radical action. The majority of Icelandic adults supported the financial crisis protests, but many still felt that the protest actions had gone too far.

3 Icelandic Ministry for Foreign Affairs. (2013, January). "Iceland Welcomes Acquittal in Icesave Case" (article). Available online at www.mfa.is/news-and-publications/nr/7515

Appendix A

Grounded work

Appendix A presents the grounded research used in this book. The grounded work consists of two data collection modes: 1) a discourse analysis of texts (speeches, articles, blogs) and performances, and 2) semi-structured interviews with actors and protest participants.

Discourse analysis

Textual material and a sample of performances were obtained for the discourse analysis presented in Chapter 4. This analysis focused on framing work performed by prominent signifying agents in the period from when the banks collapsed in early October 2008 until the January pots and pans protests. The major platforms for these actors included opinion articles and interviews in national newspapers and online media, and the Saturday and citizen meetings. I studied twenty public meeting speeches, fifty articles and interviews in major news media by prominent intellectuals and critics, and twenty media articles (interviews, press releases, announcements) by government leaders or their delegates in the Central Bank or the Financial Supervisory Authority. I obtained fifty samples of social media discussion among activists. Finally, a sample of protest performances was obtained via news media, YouTube, and semi-structured interviews (see below). I coded all the texts and performances for thematic content, following the method of grounded theory (Glaser and Strauss 1967).

Semi-structured interviews

Semi-structured interviews were conducted with thirty individuals. Table A1 provides an overview of the interviewees and their primary roles in the protests. The table lists the interview numbers and the pseudonyms used for reference in the main text of this work. However, due to their well-known roles in the protests, real names are used for five individuals (who all agreed to be named in this work). Hörður Torfason, the leading organizer of the Saturday meetings, was interviewed, as was Gunnar Sigurðsson, the leading organizer of the citizens' meetings. An interview was also taken with well-known

Table A1 Semi-structured interviews: interviewees' characteristics and roles in the protests (n = 30)

	Date of interview	*Real name/(Pseudonym)*	*Gender (Age)*	*Occupational status*	*Main role in the protests*
#1	23-05-12	(Hanna)	Female (29)	College student	Protester, passive participant*
#2	30-05-12	(Jón)	Male (50)	Marketer	Protester, ground-level activist**
#3	07-06-12	(Kristín)	Female (24)	Sports coach	Protester, ground-level activist**
#4	05-07-12	(Saga)	Female (22)	Music instructor	Protester, passive participant*
#5	17-07-12	(Kristinn)	Male (38)	Town mayor	Protester, passive participant*
#6	23-07-12	(Sigurður)	Male (29)	Writer	Protester, passive participant*
#7	25-07-12	(Guðmann)	Male (19)	Unemployed	Protester, ground-level activist**
#8	01-08-12	(Eydís)	Female (26)	College student	Protester, passive participant*
#9	14-08-12	(Ágúst)	Male (20)	Unemployed	Protester, ground-level activist**
#10	23-09-12	(Kári)	Male (44)	Professional	Protester, passive participant*
#11	20-11-12	(Lárus)	Male (22)	Waiter	Protester, ground-level activist**
#12	11-10-12	(Gunnhildur)	Female (51)	Real-estate agent	Protester, ground-level activist**
#13	11-10-12	(Daði)	Male (59)	Truck driver	Protester, ground-level activist**
#14	15-11-12	(Hlín)	Female (61)	Unemployed	Protester, ground-level activist**
#15	21-11-12	(Böðvar)	Male (30)	Artist	Protester, ground-level activist** / Signifying agent (via social media)
#16	27-11-12	(Víkingur)	Male (60)	Skilled worker	Protester, passive participant*
#17	29-11-12	(Erna)	Female (40)	Artist	Protester, passive participant*
#18	14-12-12	(Ingimar)	Male (29)	College student	Protester, ground-level activist**
#19	17-12-12	(Björk)	Female (30)	Lawyer	Protester, passive participant*
#20	19-12-12	(Ingibjörg)	Female (23)	College student	Protester, passive participant*
#21	12-12-12	(Baldur)	Male (30)	Journalist	Protester, ground-level activist**
#22	05-10-12	(Freyr)	Male (67)	Politician	Protester, passive participant*
#23	23-10-12	Einar Már Guðmundsson	Male	Novelist	Prominent signifying agent in the national media and at public meetings
#24	18-10-12	Hörður Torfason	Male	Artist, activist	Leading organizer of the Saturday meetings
#25	01-11-12	Stefán Eiríksson	Male	Chief of police	Chief of the Reykjavík Area Police
#26	25-09-14	(Stefanía)	Female (32)	College student	Protester, ground-level activist** / Signifying actor (spoke at a public meeting)
#27	16-11-14	(Þórður)	Male (51)	Journalist	Organizer of meetings and protest events outside of the Reykjavík area
#28	01-11-14	Hörður Jóhannesson	Male	Assistant police chief	Assistant chief of Reykjavík Area Police
#29	06-12-12	(Hávarður)	Male (40–50s)	Sergeant	Manager of police operations at the protest site
#30	11-10-14	Gunnar Sigurðsson	Male	Theatrical director	Leading organizer of the citizens' meetings

* Participated by "joining" the protest, e.g. by shouting slogans and banging pots and pans, but did not plan protest events or acts, or engage in vandalism or other illegal acts.

** Played a role in planning protest events and acts at public meetings and pots and pans protests, engaged in vandalism or other illegal acts.

Icelandic novelist Einar Már Guðmundsson, a prominent signifying agent at public meetings and in the media in this period. The interviews asked about reasons for engaging in mobilization work, and about their strategies and perceptions of the post-collapse situation. Also, real names are used for the chief of Reykjavík Area Police and the assistant to the chief of police. The third police officer interviewed, a sergeant directing police operations at the protest site, is given the pseudonym Hávarður. The police interviews were conducted to obtain descriptive material about the protests, including police estimation of the size of specific events.

Twenty-four interviewees are defined as protesters, both ground-level activists, that is, individuals who took part in planning protest actions and engaged in vandalism and other types of illegal action, and passive participants, that is, individuals who "joined in," for example, by shouting slogans, and beating on pots and pans, but took no part in planning protest acts. The method of recruitment was to find individuals who had participated in the January 2009 pots and pans protests, using a blend of snowball and purposive sampling. While over-represented by active protesters, the group of interviewees is heterogeneous in other respects. Ages range from 19 to 67 years, and employment status includes unemployed, college students, workers, and professionals. The interviews contained open-ended questions about how these individuals came to participate in the protests (for example, "Lead me through how it was that you first went to the pots and pans protests"), probing their reasons for protesting (e.g. "What were you protesting against?"). They also asked about their social interactions in relation to the protests (e.g. "Did anyone go with you to protest?"). Also, interviewees were asked to recall memorable experiences of the protest. Finally, they were asked how the crisis had influenced their own financial situation.

The majority of the interviews were conducted in the period from May through December 2012. Although more than three years had passed from the protests, the interviewees expressed little difficulty in talking about their experiences. As Opp and Gern (1993) argue, people usually recall historically unique and emotion-provoking protests, even months or years later (of course, through their own subjective lenses). All the interviews were transcribed and coded for thematic content.

Appendix B

Survey data

Chapter 3 and Chapter 5 report findings from two population-representative surveys. The Reykjavík Area Social Survey measured participation in and support for the pots and pans protests of January 2009. The Icelandic National Voting Study measured participation in and support for the post-crash protests. Appendix B explains the methodology of the surveys.

Reykjavík area social survey

A simple random sample of 968 individuals was drawn from a complete list of adults with registered residence in the Reykjavík metropolitan area (sampling frame: National Registry). Trained interviewers conducted standardized "face-to-face" interviews with 610 persons in the sample, a response rate of 63 percent. Comparison of known population characteristics and the sample characteristics confirms that the sample reflects population parameters well, although males, youths, and unemployed individuals are slightly under-represented (Ragnarsdóttir et al. 2013). The majority of the interviews (76%) were conducted in the period from October 2009 through January 2010 (9–12 months after the pots and pans protests); the remainder (24%) were conducted in February through July 2010 (13–18 months after the protests). The multivariate models employed in the current study result in additional deletion of cases due to missing values. The multivariate models include between 489 and 542 cases (80–89 percent of completed interviews).

Measurement

Table B1 lists the measures used in Chapters 3 and 5, along with descriptive results. It also shows the final coding of all measures for the regression models shown in Appendix C.

Protest Support and Protest Participation. The survey asked respondents about their participation in, and support for, the "pots and pans" protests, the ongoing demonstrations, and protests that went on for three days, from 20–22 January 2009. Specifically, respondents were asked to think back to January 2009 when the "most determined protests took place in Reykjavík Center, for

Table B1 Descriptive results: Reykjavík area social survey

	Ordinal/Nominal variables		*Interval/Ratio variables*		
	Percent	*Final coding*	*Mean*	*Standard deviation*	*Range*
Participation in the pots and pans protests					
Never	74.5	0	—	—	—
Once	9.5	1	—	—	—
Two or three times	10	1	—	—	—
Four times or more often	6	1	—	—	—
Support for the pots and pans protest actions					
Very much opposed	9.7	0	—	—	—
Rather opposed	13.6	0	—	—	—
Neither opposed or in favor	19.7	0	—	—	—
Rather in favor	34.9	1	—	—	—
Very much in favor	22.1	1	—	—	—
Survey interview later than January 2010	27	0, 1	—	—	—
Biographical availability					
Residential area	—	—	—	—	—
Reykjavík Center (reference)	8	0	—	—	—
Reykjavík West	27	0, 1	—	—	—
Reykjavík East	27	0, 1	—	—	—
Neighboring towns	38	0, 1	—	—	—
Female	52	0, 1	—	—	—
Age	—	—	45.0	16.9	18–89
Number of children	—	—	.83	1.09	0–6
Married/cohabiting	72	0, 1	—	—	—
Educational attainment	—	—	—	—	—
Less than secondary school (reference)	26	0	—	—	—

Secondary school	37	0, 1	—	—	—
College degree	37	0, 1	—	—	—
Household income	—	—	10.5	4.62	1–17
Employed	54	0, 1	—	—	—
<u>Economic strain</u>					
Difficult to make ends meet	14	0, 1	—	—	—
Difficult to pay mortgage	19	0, 1	—	—	—
<u>Relative deprivation</u>					
Perceived economic loss	—	—	.93	.85	0–3
Perceived economic loss relative to others	18	0, 1	—	—	—
<u>Political views</u>					
Political connections important to get ahead	49	0, 1	—	—	—
Low trust in Icelandic politicians	57	0, 1	—	—	—
Leftist ideology	37	0, 1	—	—	—
Party allegiance	—	—	—	—	—
Left-Green Movement (reference)	16	0	—	—	—
Social Democratic Alliance	22	0, 1	—	—	—
Progressive Party (moderates)	5	0, 1	—	—	—
Independence Party (right-wing)	24	0, 1	—	—	—
Other party	9	0, 1	—	—	—
Undecided	24	0, 1	—	—	—

example, when protesters were beating pots and pans in front of the *Alþingi* (the parliament building)." Then two questions were asked. First: "Were you in favor of or opposed to the actions of the protesters?" The ordinal scale was: "1" (very much opposed), "2" (rather opposed), "3" (neither opposed nor in favor), "4" (rather in favor), and "5" (very much in favor). Second: "Did you go and participate in the protests?" The ordinal scale was: "1" (never), "2" (once), "3" (2–3 times), and "4" (four times or more often).

Biographical availability. Respondents were asked about household income on a scale ranging from "1" (monthly income less than ISK 99,999) to "17" (ISK 1,200,000 or more). Employment is coded "1" for full- or part-time work, "0" otherwise. Educational attainment is measured with dummy variables for secondary and university education, with primary education (or less) for reference. Gender is coded "1" for women, "0" for men. Age is measured in years. The number of children in the household can range from "0" (none) to "6" (six or more). Marital status is coded "1" for individuals who are married or living with a partner, and "0" otherwise.

Last, residential location is measured using three dummy variables: Reykjavík West (lives 3–5 kilometers from the protest site), Reykjavík East (lives 5–10 kilometers from the protest site), and neighboring towns (lives 5–15 kilometers from the protest site), using Reykjavík Center for reference (lives within three kilometers from the protest site).

Economic strain. Respondents were asked two questions about economic strain. First, they were asked about the current financial situation of their household, coded "0" (the household can make ends meet), and "1" (it is difficult to make ends meet). Second, they were asked whether the household was experiencing difficulty in paying a mortgage or some other loan, coded "0" (no difficulty), and "1" (rather difficult, very difficult, not possible).

Relative deprivation. Following the previous work of Ragnarsdóttir et al. (2013) on this survey data, two measures are used for tackling relative economic deprivation due to the crisis. First, *perceived reduction in economic standard of living (perceived economic loss)* is measured with the following item: "Compared to the way your standard of living was before the crisis hit in Fall 2008, how is your standard of living today?" Shown in Table B2, initially this is a seven-point scale ranging from "1" (much better than before the crisis) through "4" (about the same as before the crisis) through "7" (much worse than before the crisis). Since the aim of the current study is to measure perceived economic loss (not gain), the scale has been recoded so that it ranges from "0" (living standard is better or the same as it was before the crisis) through "3" (living standard is much worse than before the crisis).

Second, *perceived financial loss relative to others* is measured with the following item: "Many people in Iceland have had financial problems because of the crisis. What effect do you believe the crisis has had on your financial situation compared to other Icelanders?" The survey item initially ranges from "1" (much better effect) through "5" (same effect) to "11" (much worse effect). But, to simplify the analysis, the scale has been recoded as a dichotomous

Table B2 Measures of relative deprivation; survey instrument, final coding, and distribution of answers

Perceived reduction in standard of living	*Survey scale*	*Final coding*	*Distribution of answers (%)*
Standard of living much better now than before the crisis	1	0	1.0
Standard of living considerably better now than before the crisis	2	0	2.5
Standard of living a little better now than before the crisis	3	0	3.6
Standard of living about the same as before the crisis	4	0	29.1
Standard of living a little worse now than before the crisis	5	1	41.9
Standard of living considerably worse now than before the crisis	6	2	16.4
Standard of living much worse now than before the crisis	7	3	5.6
Perceived financial loss relative to others			
Compared to most others, the crisis has had a much worse effect on my financial situation	−5	1	1.5
(no label)	−4	1	2.3
(no label)	−3	1	3.3
(no label)	−2	1	4.6
(no label)	−1	1	6.0
About the same effect as on most others	0	0	47.0
(no label)	+1	0	5.6
(no label)	+2	0	13.1
(no label)	+3	0	11.4
(no label)	+4	0	3.0
Compared to most others, the crisis has had a much better effect on my financial situation	+5	0	2.2

Data: Reykjavík Area Social Survey

variable, coded "0" for those experiencing "similar" or "better" effects and "1" for those experiencing "worse effects."

Political views. Several items are used to measure political attitudes and beliefs. To tackle *belief in reality of political corruption* respondents were asked about the importance of "having political connections" for "getting ahead in Iceland" (items from the 2009 "Inequality Module" of the International Social Survey Programme; see www.issp.org). The original scale ranged from "1" (not important at all) to "5" (necessary), but it is coded here as "1" (rather important, very important, necessary) and "0" (not very important, not important at all). Also, measure of *trust in Icelandic politicians* is coded "1" (low trust, that is, scores "1" through "5" on a 11 point scale ranging from "no trust" to "perfect trust"), and "0" (scores 6 through 11).

Leftist ideology is coded "1" for respondents who score between 1–4 on a political orientation scale ranging from "1" (far to the left) to "10" (far to the right), and "0" otherwise. Finally, dichotomous variables are used for *party allegiance*. Respondents were asked to indicate which political party they "support the most": The Social Democratic Alliance, Progressive Party (pragmatists), Independence Party (right-wing), other party, and undecided, with the Left-Green Movement (socialists, new-left) as the reference group.

Methodological consideration: time of survey interview

It is important to note that the Reykjavík Area Social Survey was conducted over a fairly long period, from October 2009 to July 2010, that is, between nine and seventeen months after the January protests. That the interviews were conducted so long after the protests creates potential problems in measuring both the dependent variables (protest participation, protest support) and the independent variables (economic strain, relative deprivation, and political views).

Asking about participation in a protest months afterwards is common practice in protest research. Opp and Gern (1993:665) have argued that individuals can recall "unique, highly consequential, unexpected, and emotion-provoking" protests, as the Icelandic protests were, months later. The fact that only one survey respondent (out of 610) had a missing value on participation supports this view. Still, all models estimated on the basis of this survey control the timing of the survey interview, coded "0" for interviews obtained earlier (9–12 months after the protests), and "1" for later interviews (13–18 months after the protests).

The focal independent variables studied in Chapter 5, that is, perceived economic loss, relative deprivation, and political views, are all subject to substantial measurement error. Thus, perceptions of economic strain and economic loss several months after the protests may have changed. However, we may assume that these items capture both experienced and also in part anticipated economic loss at the time of the protests. For example, many of those who had experienced reduction in their standard of living due to increased mortgage payments would have been able to foresee this difficulty by January

2009. Moreover, many of those who suffered substantial loss in the crisis, for example, those who lost their savings or borrowed for investing in stocks, probably had already experienced these losses by January 2009. Presumably, anticipated deprivation is as important as experienced deprivation in mobilization (Kowalewski and Porter 1992).

Still, some of those reporting economic loss at the time of interview may not have anticipated it in January 2009, thus creating measurement error. The same can be said about political views, which may have changed since the protests. To address this problem (not shown), I divided the survey data into two sub-samples: 1) early interviews (about 360 cases obtained within 12 months of the protests, and 2) late interviews (about 130 cases obtained between 13 and 17 months after the protests). I then estimated all regression models separately in each of these sub-samples. Although none the effects were significantly different between the early and late interviews (I used multiplicative terms testing whether the effects of relative deprivation and political attitudes interact with time of interview), the observed effects were larger in the early interviews. Thus, economic strain and perceived economic loss influence protest behavior significantly in the early interviews only, while the observed effects of most of the political view indicators are larger in the early interviews. Thus, measurement error due to the timing of survey interviews likely creates an underestimation of focal effects, especially of the relative deprivation indicators. The fact that the more reliable earlier data lend stronger support for the key hypotheses indicates that my data underestimate the effects of the focal predictors on protest participation and support (presumably, more reliable data might lend even stronger support for the key hypotheses than found here). It appears that surveying participation more than a year after a protest event creates a serious risk of underestimation of the predictors of protest behavior (see Bernburg 2015a).

Icelandic national voting study

The Icelandic National Voting Study was conducted in May 2009, four months after the protests (the survey data is is open access: www.fel.hi.is/2009). The survey is a national survey on voting behavior, but included questions about protest participation and protest support in the post-crash period. Only the Reykjavík area sample is used in the current work. The survey interviewed 817 adults in the Reykjavík area via telephone (57 percent of an initial random sample of adults from the National Registry). In the multivariate analysis, about 655 individuals had non-missing data (80 percent of interviews).

Measurement

Table B3 shows the coding and descriptive statistics for all the variables used in the analysis in Chapters 3 and 5. It also shows the final coding of all measures for the regression models shown in Appendix C.

Table B3 Descriptive results: Icelandic national voting study 2009 (only residents of Reykjavík metropolitan area)

	Ordinal/Nominal variables		*Interval/Ratio variables*		
	Percent	*Coding*	*Mean*	*Standard deviation*	*Range*
Protest participation					
No	75	0	—	—	—
Yes	25	1	—	—	—
Protest support (ordinal scale)					
Very much opposed	7	0	—	—	—
Rather opposed	10	0	—	—	—
Neither opposed or in favor	11	0	—	—	—
Rather in favor	35	1	—	—	—
Very much in favor	37	1	—	—	—
Biographical availability					
Residential area	—	—	—	—	—
Reykjavík City	41	0, 1	—	—	—
Reykjavík area outskirts / neighboring towns	59	0, 1	—	—	—
Female	48	0, 1	—	—	—
Age	—	—	44.0	15.3	18–80
Number of children	—	—	0.74	0.96	0–4
Educational attainment	—	—	—	—	—
Less than secondary school (reference)		0	—	—	—
Secondary school	38	0, 1	—	—	—
College degree	37	0, 1	—	—	—
Employed	77	0, 1	—	—	—
Household income	—	—	5.3	2.6	1–5

Political views					
Happy with Icelandic democracy (Likert scale)	—	—	2.8	.79	1–4
Icelandic politicians are corrupt (Likert scale)	—	—	3.1	.78	1–4
Authorities to blame for the crisis (sum index)	—	—	8.45	1.60	0–10
The banks to blame for the crisis (Likert scale)	—	—	9.2	1.5	0–10
How much do you like the…	—	—	5.3	2.6	1–5
Social Democratic Alliance	—	—	5.3	2.6	0–10
Progressive Party	—	—	3.8	2.5	0–10
Independence Party	—	—	3.8	2.9	0–10
Left-Green Movement	—	—	5.0	2.7	0–10
Liberal Party	—	—	2.3	2.2	0–10
Citizens' Movement	—	—	4.1	2.7	0–10

Protest participation and protest support. The survey asked about participation in "a protest or a demonstration after the bank crash," coded "0" (no) and "1" (yes). Also, respondents were asked a general question about protest support: "Were you in favor or opposed to the protests that occurred after the banks collapsed, coded "1" (very much in favor, rather in favor), and "0" (neutral or opposed to them).

Biographical characteristics. Residence is coded "1" (lives in the City of Reykjavík), and "0" (lives in a neighboring town of Reykjavík). Gender is coded "1" for male and "0" for female. Age is measured in years. Household income is measured in deciles, ranging from "1" (monthly income is ISK 192,000 or less) to "5" (monthly income is more than ISK 700,000). Number of children ranges from "0" (no child in household) to "3" (three children or more). Employment is coded "1" for full- or part-time work, "0" otherwise. Educational attainment is measured with dummy variables for secondary and university education, with primary education (or less) for reference.

Political views. Four measures are used in the current analysis. First, attitude toward Icelandic democracy is measured with a single item asking how satisfied respondents are with how democracy works in Iceland, ranging from "1" (not at all satisfied) to "4" (very satisfied). Second, perception of political corruption is measured with a single item asking how widespread respondents think that corruption is among Icelandic politicians, ranging from "1" (hardly takes place at all) to "4" (very widespread). Third, blaming the ruling authorities for the crisis is measured by calculating average scores on four separate 0–10 scales measuring the extent to which respondents blame specific entities for the bank crisis: 1) the Independence Party, 2) Prime Minister Geir Haarde, 3) the Central Bank, and 4) the Financial Supervisory Authority. The summary scale's internal (Chronbach's Alpha) reliability is .85, and ranges from "0" (minimum blame) to "1" (maximum blame). Finally, a separate 0–10 scale measures blame assigned to the banks, ranging from "0" (minimum blame) to "1" (maximum blame).

Appendix C

Regression tables

Table C1 Association of biographical characteristics with the odds of participating in and supporting the pots and pans protests, January 2009: binary logistic regression

	Dependent variables	
Independent variables	*Model 1* *Participation*	*Model 2* *Support*
Survey interview conducted January 2010 or later	1.21	1.44
Residential location		
Lives in Reykjavík Center	-reference-	-reference-
Lives in Reykjavík West (within 3–5km radius)	0.47*	0.97
Lives in Reykjavík East (outside 5km radius)	0.39**	1.06
Lives in a neighboringtown	0.30**	1.23
Educational attainment		
Less than secondary school	-reference-	-reference-
Secondary school	1.71	1.48
College degree	1.90*	1.78*
Female	0.67	0.78
Age	0.98**	0.99*
Married/cohabiting	1.07	1.35
Number of children in household	0.70*	1.05
Employed	1.60**	0.96
Household income (ranked 1–17)	0.95	0.94*
Nagelkerke R Square	0.16	0.06
Sample size	541	538

Data: Reykjavík Area Social Survey

Note: Table C1 reports odds ratios. Participation is coded: 1 = attended the pots and pans protest once or more; 0 = never attended. Support is coded: 1 = in favor of the protest actions; 0 = neutral or not in favor.

* $p < 0.05$; ** $p < 0.01$ (two-tailed tests)

Table C2 Association of biographical characteristics with the odds of participating in and supporting any protest in the post-collapse period: binary logistic regression

	Dependent variables	
Independent variables	*Model 1 Participation*	*Model 2 Support*
Residential area		
Reykjavík City	-reference-	-reference-
Reykjavík area outskirts / neighboring towns	0.46**	0.74
Female	0.86	0.95
Age	0.98**	1.0
Number of children	0.88	1.1
Educational attainment		
Less than secondary school	-reference-	-reference-
Secondary school	0.75	0.97
College degree	1.2	1.0
Employed	1.3	1.1
Household income	0.91	1.1
Nagelkerke R Square	0.08	0.08
Sample size	595	585

Data: Icelandic National Voting Study (Reykjavík area sample)

Note: Table C2 reports odds ratios. Participation is coded: 1 = participation in protest in the post-crash period; 0 = no protest participation. Support is coded: 1 = in favor of the protests that have broken out in the post-crash period; 0 = neutral or not in favor of the protests.

* $p < 0.05$; ** $p < 0.01$ (two-tailed tests)

Table C3 Effects of relative deprivation on the odds of participating in and supporting the pots and pans protests, January 2009: binary logistic regression

	Dependent variables	
Independent variables	*Model 1 Participation*	*Model 2 Support*
Relative deprivation		
Perceived economic loss since before the crisis	1.21	1.02
Perceived economic loss relative to others	0.19**	0.45*
Perceived economic loss since before the crisis* Perceived economic loss relative to others	1.97*	1.70*
Control variables		
Survey interview conducted January 2010 or later	1.21	1.49
Residential location		
Lives in Reykjavík Center	-reference-	-reference-
Lives in Reykjavík West (within 3–5km radius)	0.50	1.01
Lives in Reykjavík East (outside 5km radius)	0.41*	1.12
Lives in a neighboringtown	0.34**	1.33
Educational attainment		
Less than secondary school	-reference-	-reference-
Secondary school	1.70	1.62*
College degree	2.02*	2.02**
Female	0.66	0.76
Age	0.97**	0.99*

Table C3 (*cont.*)

Independent variables	*Dependent variables*	
	Model 1 *Participation*	*Model 2* *Support*
Number of children in household	0.69**	1.06
Employed	1.95**	0.96
Household income (ranked 1–17)	0.96	0.95*
Nagelkerke R Square	0.20	0.08
Sample size	542	540

Data: Reykjavík Area Social Survey

Note: Table C3 reports odds ratios. Participation is coded: 1 = attended the pots and pans protest once or more; 0 = never attended. Support is coded: 1 = in favor of the protest actions; 0 = neutral or not in favor.

* p < 0.05; ** p < 0.01 (two-tailed tests)

Table C4 Effects of perceived economic loss on the odds of protest participation in two subgroups: 1) among those who think that the crisis has not harmed them more than others; 2) among those who think that the crisis has harmed them more than others

Independent variables	*Subgroup 1* *Crisis has harmed me no more than others*	*Subgroup 2* *Crisis has harmed me more than others*
Relative deprivation		
Perceived economic loss since before the crisis	1.21	2.71**
Control variables		
Survey interview conducted January 2010 or later	1.00	4.66*
Residential location		
Lives in Reykjavík Center	-reference-	-reference-
Lives in Reykjavík West (within 3–5km radius)	0.43	0.58
Lives in Reykjavík East (outside 5km radius)	0.46	0.15
Lives in a neighboring town	0.37*	0.10
Educational attainment		
Less than secondary school	-reference-	-reference-
Secondary school	1.94*	1.24
College degree	2.12*	1.67
Female	0.70	0.37
Age	0.97**	0.96
Number of children in household	0.62**	1.52
Employed	2.12**	0.76
Household income (ranked 1–17)	0.96	0.94
Nagelkerke R Square	0.19	0.40
Sample size	445	97

Data: Reykjavík Area Social Survey

Note: Table C4 reports odds ratios from binary logistic regression. Participation is coded: 1 = attended the pots and pans protest once or more; 0 = never attended.

* p < 0.05; ** p < 0.01 (two-tailed tests)

Table C5 Effects of perceived economic loss on the odds of protest support in two subgroups: 1) among those who think that the crisis has not harmed them more than others; 2) among those who think that the crisis has harmed them more than others

	Subgroup 1	*Subgroup 2*
Independent variables	*Crisis has harmed me no more than others*	*Crisis has harmed me more than others*
Relative deprivation		
Perceived economic loss since before the crisis	1.04	1.72*
Control variables		
Survey interview conducted January 2010 or later	1.55	0.87
Residential location		
Lives in Reykjavík Center	-reference-	-reference-
Lives in Reykjavík West (within 3–5km radius)	0.85	2.83
Lives in Reykjavík East (outside 5km radius)	1.07	1.68
Lives in a neighboring town	1.15	4.89
Educational attainment		
Less than secondary school	-reference-	-reference-
Secondary school	1.59	1.83
College degree	2.15**	0.79
Female	0.30	0.44
Age	0.99*	0.99
Number of children in household	1.03	1.34
Employed	1.02	0.56
Household income (ranked 1–17)	0.97	0.86*
Nagelkerke R Square	0.07	0.27
Sample size	443	97

Data: Reykjavík Area Social Survey

Note: Table C5 reports odds ratios from binary logistic regression. Support is coded: 1 = in favor of the protest actions; 0 = neutral or not in favor.

* $p < 0.05$; ** $p < 0.01$ (two-tailed tests)

Table C6 Effects of political attitudes on the odds of participating in and supporting the pots and pans protests, January 2009: binary logistic regression

	Dependent variables	
Independent variables	*Model 1 Participation*	*Model 2 Support*
Belief in the reality of political corruption	2.50**	1.25
Distrust of politicians	1.04	1.97**
Left-wing identity	2.43**	2.01*
Party allegiance	—	—
Left-Green Movement (new-left)	-reference-	-reference-
Social Democratic Coalition (left-center)	0.56	0.30**
Progressive Party (center)	0.71	0.20**
Independence Party (center-right)	0.14**	0.12**
Other party	1.26	0.29*

Table C6 (cont.)

Independent variables	*Dependent variables* *Model 1* *Participation*	*Model 2* *Support*
Undecided	0.87	0.34*
Prior activism	2.51**	2.12**
Control variables		
Survey interview conducted January 2010 or later	1.09	1.24
Residential location		
Lives in Reykjavík Center	-reference-	-reference-
Lives in Reykjavík West (within 3–5km radius)	0.41*	1.20
Lives in Reykjavík East (outside 5km radius)	0.42*	1.30
Lives in a neighboring town	0.24**	1.38
Educational attainment		
Less than secondary school	-reference-	-reference-
Secondary school	1.46	1.67
College degree	1.33	1.96*
Female	0.59*	0.62*
Age	0.98*	0.99
Number of children in household	0.69**	1.06
Employed	2.12**	0.80
Household income (ranked 1–17)	0.98	0.96
Nagelkerke R Square	0.37	0.31
Sample size	498	496

Data: Reykjavík Area Social Survey

Note: Table C6 reports odds ratios. Participation is coded: 1 = attended the pots and pans protest once or more; 0 = never attended. Support is coded: 1 = in favor of the protest actions; 0 = neutral or not in favor.

* $p < 0.05$; ** $p < 0.01$ (two-tailed tests).

Table C7 The association of political attitudes (and control variables) with the odds of participating in the post-collapse protests: binary logistic regression

Independent variables	*Model 1*	*Model 2*
Satisfied with Icelandic democracy	1.49**	1.43**
Corruption in Icelandic politics	1.45**	1.16
Authorities to blame for the crisis	—	1.56**
Banks to blame for the crisis	—	.97
Control variables		
Residential area		
Reykjavík City	-ref-	-ref-
Reykjavík area outskirts / neighboring towns	0.44**	0.47**
Female	0.87	0.78
Age	0.99*	0.98**
Number of children	0.91	0.88

Table C7 (*cont.*)

Independent variables	*Model 1*	*Model 2*
Educational attainment		
Less than secondary school	-ref-	-ref-
Secondary school	0.93	1.00
College degree	1.47	1.45
Employed	1.13	1.11
Nagelkerke R Square	0.12	0.17
Sample size	666	666

Data: Icelandic National Voting Study (Reykjavík area sample)

Note: Table C7 reports odds ratios. Participation is coded: 1 = participation in protest in the post-crash period; 0 = no protest participation.

* $p < 0.05$; ** $p < 0.01$ (two-tailed tests)

Table C8 The association of political attitudes (and control variables) with the odds of supporting the post-collapse protests: binary logistic regression

Independent variables	*Model 1*	*Model 2*
Satisfied with Icelandic democracy	1.10	1.07
Corruption in Icelandic politics	1.45**	1.12
Authorities to blame for the crisis	—	1.58**
Banks to blame for the crisis	—	0.92
<u>Control variables</u>		
Residential area		
Reykjavík City	-ref-	-ref-
Reykjavík area outskirts / neighboring towns	0.63*	0.67
Female	0.78	0.64
Age	1.00	1.00
Number of children	1.15	1.12
Educational attainment		
Less than secondary school	-ref-	-ref-
Secondary school	0.82	0.91
College degree	1.02	0.99
Employed	1.13	1.07
Nagelkerke R Square	0.05	0.14
Sample size	655	655

Data: Icelandic National Voting Study (Reykjavík area sample)

Note: Table C8 reports odds ratios. Support is coded: 1 = in favor of the post-crash protests; 0 = neutral, opposed.

* $p < 0.05$; ** $p < 0.01$ (two-tailed tests)

References

Accornero, Guya, and Pedro Ramos Pinto. 2014. "'Mild Mannered'? Protest and Mobilization in Portugal under Austerity, 2010–2013." *West European Politics* 38(3): 491–515.

Akers, Ronald L. 1985. *Deviant Behavior: A Social Learning Approach.* Third Edition. Belmont: Wadsworth.

Almeida, Paul D. 2003. "Opportunity Organizations and Threat Induced Contention: Protest Waves in Authoritarian Settings." *American Journal of Sociology* 109(2): 345–400.

Almeida, Paul D. 2010. Globalization and Collective Action. In: Kevin T. Leicht and J. Craig Jenkins (eds.), *Handbook of Politics: State and Society in Global Perspective.* New York: Springer, pp. 305–326.

Anderson, Eliah. 1999. *Code of the Street.* New York: Norton.

Andrews, Kenneth T., and Michael Biggs. 2006. "The Dynamics of Protest Diffusion: Movement Organizations, Social Networks, and News Media in the 1960 Sit-Ins." *American Sociological Review* 71(5): 752–777.

Auvinen, Juha Y. 1996. "IMF Intervention and Political Protest in the Third World: A Convention Wisdom Refined." *Third World Quarterly* 17(3): 377–400.

Auyero, Javier. 2001. "Glocal Riots." *International Sociology* 16(1): 33–53.

Árnason, Mörður. 2014. Talk at a meeting entitled "Búsáhaldabyltingin 5 ára: áhrif og árangur" (The pots and pans revolution 5 years old: Impacts and results) held on January 29, Reykjavíkurakademían.

Árnason, Ragnar. 2008. "Iceland's ITQ System Creates New Wealth." *The Electronic Journal of Sustainable Development* 1(2): 35–41.

Árnason, Vilhjálmur. 2015. "Something Rotten in the State of Iceland: 'The Production of Truth' about Icelandic Banks." In: Paul Durrenberger and Gísli Pálsson (eds.), *Gambling Debt: Iceland's Rise and Fall in the Global Economy.* Boulder, Colorado: University of Colorado Press, pp. 47–59.

Aya, Rod. 1979. "Theories of Revolution Reconsidered." *Theory and Society* 8(1): 39–99.

Benediktsdóttir, Sigríður, Jón Daníelsson, and Gylfi Zoega. 2011 "Lessons from a Collapse of a Financial System." *Economic Policy* 26(66): 183–235.

Benford, Robert D. 1993 "'You Could Be the Hundredth Monkey': Collective Action Frames and Vocabularies of Motive within the Nuclear Disarmament Movement." *The Sociological Quarterly* 34(2): 195–216.

Benford, Robert D., and David A. Snow. 2000 "Framing Processes and Social Movements: An Overview and Assessment." *Annual Review of Sociology* 26: 611–639.

Beyeler, Michelle, and Hanspeter Kriesi. 2005. "Transnational Protest and the Public Sphere." *Mobilization* 10(1): 95–109.

Bergmann, Eiríkur. 2014. *Iceland and the International Financial Crisis: Boom, Bust, and Recovery*. New York: Palgrave Macmillan.

Bernburg, Jón Gunnar. 2015a. "Economic Crisis and Popular Protest in Iceland, January 2009: The Role of Perceived Economic Loss and Political Attitudes in Protest Participation and Support." *Mobilization* 20(2): 231–252.

Bernburg, Jón Gunnar. 2015b. "Overthrowing the Government: A Case Study in Protest." In: Paul Durrenberger and Gísli Pálsson (eds.), *Gambling Debt: Iceland's Rise and Fall in the Global Economy*. Boulder, Colorado: University of Colorado Press, pp. 63–77.

Bernburg, Jón Gunnar, and Sigrún Ólafsdóttir. 2012. Viðhorf Íslendinga til launaójafnaðar (Icelanders' attitudes to income inequality). In: Guðný Björk Eydal and Stefán Ólafsson (eds), *Þróun íslensku velferðarinnar 1992 til 2008* (The Icelandic welfare, 1992 to 2008). Reykjavík: Félagsvísindastofnun Háskóla Íslands, pp. 291–330.

Bernburg, Jón Gunnar, and Thorolfur Thorlindsson. 2005. "Violent Values, Conduct Norms, and Youth Aggression: A Multilevel Study in Iceland." *The Sociological Quarterly* 46(3): 455–476.

Bernburg, Jón Gunnar, Thorolfur Thorlindsson, and Inga Dora Sigfúsdóttir. 2009. "Relative Deprivation and Adolescent Outcomes in Iceland: A Multilevel Test." *Social Forces* 87(3): 1223–1250.

Biggs, Michael. 2006 "Who Joined the Sit-Ins and Why: Southern Black Students in the Early 1960s." *Mobilization* 11(3): 321–336.

Bjarnason, Helgi. 2008. "Munur á mótmælum og skrílslátum" (Difference between a protest and a mob) (article). (2008, November), *Mbl.is*. Available online at www.mbl.is/greinasafn/grein/1254283/

Bjarnason, Tómas. 2014. "Traust í kreppu: Traust til Alþingis, lögreglu, stjórnmálamanna og forseta Íslands í kjölfar hrunsins" (Trust during crisis: Trust toward the Parliament, politicians, and the President of Iceland in the wake of the collapse). *Íslenska þjóðfélagið* 5(2): 19–38.

Borland, Elizabeth, and Barbara Sutton. 2007. "Quotidian Disruption and Women's Activism in Times of Crisis, Argentina 2002–2003." *Gender & Society* 21(5): 700–722.

Boswell, Terry, and William J. Dixon. 1993 "Marx's Theory of Rebellion: A Cross-National Analysis of Class Exploitation, Economic Development, and Violent Revolt." *American Sociological Review* 58(5): 681–702.

Broddason, Thorbjörn. 2005. *Ritlist, prentlist, nýmiðlar* (The art of writing and printing, and the new media). Reykjavík: Háskólaútgáfan.

Broddason, Thorbjörn, and Keith Webb. 1975. "On the Myth of Social Equality in Iceland." *Acta Sociologica* 18(1): 49–61.

Buechler, Steven M. 2004. "The Strange Career of Strain and Breakdown Theories of Collective Action." In: David A. Snow, Sarah A. Soule, and Hanspeter Kriesi (eds.), *The Blackwell Companion to Social Movements*. Malden and Oxford: Blackwell, pp. 47–66.

Burean, Toma, and Gabriel Badescu. 2014. "Voices of Discontent: Student Protest Participation in Romania." *Communist and Post-Communist Studies* 47(3–4): 385–397.

Calvo, Kerman. 2013. "Fighting for a Voice: The Spanish 15-M/Indignados Movement." In: Christina Flesher Fominaya and Laurence Cox (eds.), *Understanding European Social Movements*. New York: Routledge, pp. 236–253.

Council for European Studies. 2014. "'Enough!' – Dispatches from researchers studying Europe's exploding social movements." Available online at http://councilforeuropeanstudies.org/critcom/enough-dispatches-from-researchers-studying-europes-exploding-social-movements-3/

Danske Bank. 2006. *Iceland: Geyser Crisis*. Köbenhavn: Danske Bank.

Davies, James C. 1962. "Toward a Theory of Revolution." *American Sociological Review* 27(1): 5–19.

della Porta, Donatella. 2012a. "Eventful Protest, Global Conflicts: Social Mechanisms in the Reproduction of Protest." In: Jeff Goodwin and James M. Jasper (eds.), *Contention in Context: Political Opportunities and the Emergence of Protest*. Stanford, CA: Stanford University Press, pp. 256–275.

della Porta, Donatella. 2012b. "Mobilizing Against the Crisis, Mobilizing for 'Another Democracy': Comparing Two Global Waves of Protest." *Interface: A Journal For and About Social Movements* 4(1): 274–277.

della Porta, Donatella. 2013. "Learning Democracy: Cross-Time Adaptation in Organizational Repertoires." In: Donatella della Porta and Alice Mattoni (eds.), *Spreading Protest: Social Movements in Times of Crisis*. Colchester, UK: ECPR Press, pp. 43–70.

della Porta, Donatella, and Mario Diani. 2006. *Social Movements: An Introduction*. Second Edition. Malden, MA: Blackwell Publishing.

della Porta, Donatella, and Alice Mattoni. 2013. "Patterns of Diffusion and the Transnational Dimension of Protest in the Movements of the Crisis: An Introduction." In: Donatella della Porta and Alice Mattoni (eds.), *Spreading Protest: Social Movements in Times of Crisis*. Colchester, UK: ECPR Press, pp. 1–18.

Durkheim, Émile (1951[1897]). *Suicide: A Study in Sociology*. London: Routledge.

Durkheim Émile (1984[1893]) *The Division of Labor in Society*. New York: The Free Press.

DV. 2008. "Íbúðalánasjóður gæti hrunið" (The Homeloan Fund might collapse) (article). (2008, December), *Dv.is*. Available online at www.dv.is/neytendur/2008/12/9/ibudalanasjodur-gaeti-hrunid/

Einarsdóttir, Anna S. 2008. "Hrópuðu "Davíð burt" (Shouted "Davíð out") (article). (2008, December), *Mbl.is*. Available online at www.mbl.is/greinasafn/grein/1258202/

Einarsdóttir, Lára H. 2008. "Magnaður borgarafundur" (An amazing citizen meeting) (blog post). (2008, November), *Lára Hanna*. Available online at http://blog.pressan.is/larahanna/2008/11/25/magnadur-borgarafundur/

Einarsson, Níels. 2015. "When Fishing Rights Go Up Against Human Rights." In: Paul Durrenberger and Gísli Pálsson (eds.), *Gambling Debt: Iceland's Rise and Fall in the Global Economy*. Boulder, Colorado: University of Colorado Press, pp. 151–160.

Erlendsdóttir, Björg Eva 2008. Þögn er gull en kjaftæðið króna (Silence is gold but nonsense is króna) (article). (2008, October), *Mbl.is*. Available online at www.mbl.is/greinasafn/grein/1247798/

Fominaya, Christina Flesher, and Antonio Montañés Jimenéz. 2013. "Transnational Diffusion across Time: The Adoption of the Argentinian Dirty War '*Escrache*' in the Context of Spain's Housing Crisis." In: Donatella della Porta and Alice Mattoni (eds.), *Spreading Protest: Social Movements in Times of Crisis*. Colchester, UK: ECPR Press, pp. 19–42.

Fominaya, Christina Flesher, and Laurence Cox. 2013. "Conclusion: Anti-Austerity Protests in European and Global Context – Future Agendas for Research." In: Christina Flesher Fominaya and Laurence Cox (eds), *Understanding European Social Movements*. New York: Routledge, pp. 236–253.

Foran, John. 1993. "Theory of Revolution Revisited: Toward a Fourth Generation?" *Sociological Theory* 11(1): 1–20.

Fréttablaðið. 2003. "Mótmæli erlendra gegn Kárahnjúkavirkjun" (Protest of foreigners against the Kárahnjúkar Power Plant) (article). *Fréttablaðið*, February 24, 2003.

Fréttablaðið. 2005. "Þorri landsmanna vill af Íraks-listanum" (The majority of people wants off the Iraq-list) (article). (2005, January: page 6), *Fréttablaðið*. Available online at www.visir.is/ExternalData/pdf/fbl/050106.pdf

Fréttablaðið. 2008a. "Krefjast þess að Davíð víki" (Demand Davíð's resignation) (article). (2008, October: page 2), *Fréttablaðið*. Available online at www.visir.is/ExternalData/pdf/fbl/081019.pdf

Fréttablaðið. 2008b. "Á fjórða þúsund mótmælti" (About four thousand protested) (article). (2008, November: page 4), *Fréttablaðið*. Available online at www.visir.is/externaldata/pdf/fbl/081109.pdf

Fréttablaðið. 2008c. "Boða skyndiaðgerðir" (Announce sudden actions) (article). (2008, December), *Fréttablaðið*. Available online at http://timarit.is/ view_page_init.jsp?pageId=4013366

Gamson, William A. 1992. *Talking Politics*. Cambridge, MA: Cambridge University Press.

Gamson, William A., Bruce Fireman, and Steven Rytina. 1982. *Encounters with Unjust Authority*. Homewood, IL: Dorsey Press.

Gemici, Kurtulus. 2013. "Moral Economy Redux: Social Protests in Turkey after the 2001 Economic Crisis." *Mobilization* 18(2): 143–160.

George, Alexander L., and Andrew Bennet. 2005. *Case Studies and Theory Development in the Social Sciences*. Cambridge, MA and London: MIT Press.

Gerhards, Jürgen, and Dieter Rucht. 1992. "Mesomobilization: Organizing and Framing in Two Protest Campaigns in West Germany. *American Journal of Sociology* 98(3): 555–595.

Gíslason, Ingólfur V. 2014. "Lögreglan og búsáhaldabyltingin" (The police and the pots and pans revolution). *Íslenska þjóðfélagið* 5(2): 5–18.

Glaser, Barney, and Anselm Strauss. 1967. *The Discovery of Grounded Theory*. Chicago: Aldine.

Goldstone, Jack A. 1980. "Theories of Revolution: The Third Generation." *World Politics* 32(3): 425–453.

Goldstone, Jack A., and Charles Tilly. 2001. "Threat (and Opportunity): Popular Action and State Response in the Dynamics of Contentious Action." In: Ronald R. Aminzade, Jack A. Goldstone, Doug McAdam, Elizabeth J. Perry, William H. Sewell, Jr., Sidney Tarrow and Charles Tilly, *Silence and Voice in the Study of Contentious Politics*. New York: Cambridge University Press, pp. 179–194.

Grétarsdóttir, Tinna, Ásmundur Ásmundsson, and Hannes Lárusson. 2015. "Creativity and Crisis." In: Paul Durrenberger and Gísli Pálsson (eds.), *Gambling Debt: Iceland's Rise and Fall in the Global Economy*. Boulder, Colorado: University of Colorado Press, pp. 93–105.

Grímsson, Ólafur R., and Thorbjörn Broddason. 1977. *The Icelandic Society*. Reykjavík: Faculty of Social Science at the University of Iceland, and Örn & Örlygur.

Gunnarsson, Pétur. 2008. "Það sem nú tekur við" (What now takes over) (article). (2008, October), *mbl.is*. Available online at www.mbl.is/greinasafn/grein/1249182/

Gunnarsson, Pétur. 2009. "Mál málanna" (The main issue) (article). *Morgunblaðið*, January 9, 2009.

Gunnarsson, Valur and Mark Tran. 2009. "Icelandic PM becomes World's First Leader to Step Down over Banking System Crisis" (article). (2009, January), *The Guardian*. Available online at www.theguardian.com/world/2009/jan/27/iceland-prime-minister-resignation

Gunnlaugsson, Helgi, and John F. Galliher. 1986. "Prohibition of Beer in Iceland: An International Test of Symbolic Politics." *Law & Society Review* 20(3): 335–354.

Gurr, Ted R. 1970. *Why Men Rebel*. Princeton, NJ: Princeton University Press.

Guðbjartsson, Steinþór. 2008. "Ráðamenn tali við fólk en ekki til þess" (The authorities talk with people but not about them) (article). (2008, November), *Mbl.is*. Available online at www.mbl.is/greinasafn/grein/1251814/

Guðmundsson, Einar M. 2008a. "Herhvöt úr norðri" (Call for arms from the north) (article). (2008, October), *Mbl.is*. Available online at www.mbl.is/greinasafn/grein/1250149/

Guðmundsson, Einar M. 2008b. "Þess vegna mótmælum vér öll" (That is why we all protest) (article). *Morgunblaðið*, November 14, 2008.

Guðmundsson, Einar M. 2009. "Kryddlegin Baugshjörtu" (Marinated hearts of Baugur) (article). *Morgunblaðið*, January 18, 2009.

Gylfason, Þorvaldur. 2008a. "Saklausir vegfarendur" (Innocent bystanders) (article). (2008, October), *Visir.is*. Available online at www.visir.is/saklausir-vegfarendur/article/2008350689856

Haarde, Geir H. 2008a. "Prime Minister's Address Due to Special Circumstances in the Financial Market." Special broadcast on Iceland's National Radio and Television. Reykjavík, October 6, 2008.

Haarde, Geir H. 2008b. "Prime Minister's Address at the Annual General Meeting of the Iceland Chamber of Commerce." Speech, Reykjavík, February 13, 2008. Reykjavík: Prime Minister's Office.

Hallgrímsdóttir, Helga Kristín, and Emmanuel Brunet-Jailly. 2015. "Contentious Politics, Grassroots Mobilization and the Icesave Dispute: Why Iceland Did Not 'Play Nicely'." *Acta Sociologica* 58(1): 79–93.

Hálfdanarson, Guðmundur. 2001. *Íslenska þjóðríkið: uppruni og endamörk* (The Icelandic national state: Origins and limits). Reykjavík: Hið íslenska bókmenntafélag og Reykjavíkurakademían.

Helgason, Hallgrímur. 2008. "Ábyrgð Samfylkingunnar" (The responsibility of the Social Democractic Coalition) (article). *Fréttablaðið*, November 20, 2008.

Icelandic Ministry of Foreign Affairs. 2013. "Iceland Welcomes Acquittal in Icesave Case" (article). (2013, January), *Icelandic Ministry of Foreign Affairs*. Available online at www.mfa.is/news-and-publications/nr/7515

Icelandic National Audit Office. 2003. *Einkavæðing helstu ríkisfyrirtækja árin 1998 til 2003* (Privatization of major state companies in the years 1998 to 2003). Reykjavík: Icelandic National Audit Office.

Jasper, James M. 1998. "The Emotions of Protest: Affective and Reactive Emotions In and Around Social Movements." *Sociological Forum* 13(3): 397–424.

Jasper, James M. 2012. "Introduction: From Political Opportunity Structures to Strategic Interaction." In: Jeff Goodwin and James M. Jasper (eds.), *Contention in Context: Political Opportunities and the Emergence of Protest*. Stanford, CA: Stanford University Press, pp. 1–36.

Johnsen, Gudrun. 2014. *Bringing Down the Banking System: Lessons from Iceland*. New York: Palgrave Macmillan.

Johnston, Hank. 2009. "Protest Cultures, Performance, and Ideations." In Hank Johnston (ed.), *Culture, Social Movements, and Protest*. Farnham, Surrey and Burlington, VT: Ashgate, pp 3–29.

Johnston, Hank, and Seraphim Seferiades. 2012. "The Greek December, 2008." In: Seraphim Seferiades and Hank Johnston (eds.), *Violent Protests, Contentious Politics, and the Neoliberal State*, Farnham, Surrey and Burlington, VT: Ashgate, pp. 149–156.

Jóhannesson, Guðni Th. 2006. *Óvinir ríkisins* (Enemies of the state). Reykjavík: Mál og menning.

Jóhannesson, Guðni Th. 2009. *Hrunið* (The collapse). Reykjavík: JPV.

Jóhannesson, Guðni Th. 2015. "Exploiting Icelandic History: 2000–2008." In: Paul Durrenberger and Gísli Pálsson (eds.), *Gambling Debt: Iceland's Rise and Fall in the Global Economy*. Boulder, Colorado: University of Colorado Press, pp. 15–22.

Jónsson, Arnar. 2008. "Endurreisn" (Resurrection) (article). *Morgunblaðið*, October 29, 2008.

Jónsson, Ásgeir. 2009. *Why Iceland? How One of the World's Smallest Countries Became the Meltdown's Biggest Casualty*. New York: McGraw-Hill.

Jónsson, Örn. 2015. "Free Market Ideology, Crony Capitalism, and Social Resilience." In: Paul Durrenberger and Gísli Pálsson (eds.), *Gambling Debt: Iceland's Rise and Fall in the Global Economy*. Boulder, Colorado: University of Colorado Press, pp. 23–32.

Jung, Jai Kwan. 2010. "Disentangling Protest Cycles: An Event-History Analysis of New Social Movements in Western Europe." *Mobilization* 15(1): 25–44.

Juris, Jeffrey S. 2008. "Perfoming Politics: Image, Embodiment, and Affective Solidarity during Anti-Corporate Globalization Protests." *Ethnography* 9(1): 61–97.

Klandermans, Bert. 1993. "A Theoretical Framework for Comparisons of Social Movement Participation." *Sociological Forum* 8(3): 383–402.

Koopmans, Ruud. 1993. "The Dynamics of Protest Waves: West Germany, 1965–1989. *American Sociological Review* 58: 637–658.

Koopmans, Ruud. 2004. "Protest in Time and Place. The Evolution of Waves of Contention." In: David A. Snow, Sarah A. Soule, and Hanspeter Kriesi (eds.), *The Blackwell Companion to Social Movements*. Malden and Oxford: Blackwell, pp. 19–46.

Koopmans, Ruud, and Susan Olzak. 2004. "Discursive Opportunities and the Evolution of Right-Wing Violence in Germany." *American Journal of Sociology* 110(1): 198–230.

Kousis, Maria. 2013. "The Transnational Dimension of the Greek Protest Campaign against Troika Memoranda and Austerity Policies, 2010–2012. In: Donatella della Porta and Alice Mattoni (eds.), *Spreading Protest: Social Movements in Times of Crisis*. Colchester, UK: ECPR Press, pp. 137–169.

Kowalewski, David, and Karen L. Porter. 1992. "Ecoprotest: Alienation, Deprivation, or Resources?" *Social Science Quarterly* 73: 523–534.

Kristinsson, Gunnar Helgi. 1993. "Valdakerfið fram til viðreisnar 1900–1959" (The political power structure 1900–1959). In: Guðmundur Hálfdanarson and Svanur

Kristjánsson (eds.), *Íslensk þjóðfélagsþróun 1880–1990: Ritgerðir* (The evolution of Icelandic society 1880–1900: Essays). Reykjavík: Félagsvísindastofnun og Sagnfræðistofnun Háskóla Íslands, pp. 321–354.

Kristinsson, Gunnar Helgi. 2006. "Pólitískar stöðuveitingar á Íslandi" (Political hiring in Iceland). *Stjórnmál og stjórnsýsla* 2(1): 5–30.

Kristjánsson, Svanur. 1993. "Stjórnmálaflokkar, ríkisvald og samfélag 1959–1990" (Political parties, state and society 1959–1990). In: Guðmundur Hálfdanarson and Svanur Kristjánsson (eds.), *Íslensk þjóðfélagsþróun 1880–1990: Ritgerðir* (The evolution of Icelandic society 1880–1990). Reykjavík: Félagsvísindastofnun og Sagnfræðistofnun Háskóla Íslands, pp. 355–398.

Kristjánsson, Svanur. 2012. "Brothætt lýðræði: Valdsmenn í sókn" (Fragile democracy). *Skýrnir* 186 (Fall): 303–337.

Kristjánsson, Arnaldur Sölvi, and Stefán Ólafsson. 2009. "Heimur hátekjuhópanna: Um þróun tekjuskiptingar á Íslandi 1993–2007" (The world of the high income groups: Income distribution in Iceland 1993–2007). *Stjórnmál og stjórnsýsla* 5(1): 93–212.

Leeuwen, Anouk van, Bert Klandermans, and Jacquelien van Stekelenburg. 2014. "A Study of Perceived Protest Atmosphere: How Demonstrators Evaluate Police-Demonstrator Interactions and Why." *Mobilization* 20(1): 81–100.

Lind E. Allan, and Tom R. Tyler. 1988. *The Social Psychology of Procedural Justice*. New York: Plenum Press.

Loftsdóttir, Kristín. 2012. "Colonialism at the Margins: Politics of Difference in Europe as Seen Through Two Icelandic Crises." *Identities* 19(5): 597–615.

Loftsdóttir, Kristín. 2014. "Building on Iceland's 'Good Reputation': Icesave, Crisis and Affective National Identities." *Ethnos* 1–26. doi: 10.1080/00141844.2014.931327

Loftsdóttir, Kristín. 2015. "Vikings Invade Present-Day Iceland." In Paul Durrenberger and Gísli Pálsson (eds.), *Gambling Debt: Iceland's Rise and Fall in the Global Economy*. Boulder, Colorado: University of Colorado Press, pp. 3–14.

McAdam, Doug. 1986. "Recruitment to High-Risk Activism: The Case of Freedom Summer." *American Journal of Sociology* 92: 64–90.

McAdam, Doug. 1996. "The Framing Function of Movement Tactics: Strategic Dramaturgy in the American Civil Rights Movement." In: Doug McAdam, John D. McCarthy, and Mayer N. Zald (eds.), *Comparative Perspectives on Social Movements: Political Opportunities, Mobilizing Structures, and Cultural Framings*. Cambridge, UK: Cambridge University Press, pp. 338–355.

McAdam, Doug, James D. McCarthy, and Meyer N. Zald. 1996. "Introduction: Opportunities, Mobilizing Structures, and Framing Processes – Toward a Synthetic, Comparative Perspective on Social Movements." In: Doug McAdam, John D. McCarthy, and Mayer N. Zald (eds.), *Comparative Perspectives on Social Movements: Political Opportunities, Mobilizing Structures, and Cultural Framings*. Cambridge, UK: Cambridge University Press, pp. 1–22.

McCarthy, James D., and Ronnelle Paulsen. 1993. "Specifying the Relationship between Social Ties and Activism." *American Journal of Sociology* 99: 640–667.

McVeigh, Rory, and Christian Smith. 1999. "Who Protests in America: An Analysis of Three Political Alternatives – Inaction, Institutionalized Politics, or Protest." *Sociological Forum* 14(4): 685–702.

Marx, Karl. 1967[1887]. *Capital, Volume 1*. New York: International Publishers.

Matthíasson, Thorolfur. 2008. "Spinning Out of Control: Iceland in Crisis." *Nordic Journal of Political Economy* 34(3): 1–19.

Mead, George Herbert. 1938. *The Philosophy of the Act*. Chicago: University of Chicago Press.

Mixa, Már Wolfgang. 2015. "A Day in the Life of an Icelandic Banker." In: Paul Durrenberger and Gísli Pálsson (eds.), *Gambling Debt: Iceland's Rise and Fall in the Global Economy*. Boulder, Colorado: University of Colorado Press, pp. 33–46.

Morgunblaðið. 2008a. "Ekki þörf á aðgerðapakka" (No need for an operation packet) (article). (2008, October), *Mbl.is*. Available online at www.mbl.is/frettir/innlent/2008/10/05/ekki_thorf_a_adgerdapakka/

Morgunblaðið. 2008b. "Lög um gjaldeyrismál samþykkt" (Legislation on currency issues passed) (article). (2008, November), *Mbl.is*. Available online at www.mbl.is/frettir/innlent/2008/11/28/log_um_gjaldeyrismal_samthykkt/

Morgunblaðið. 2008c. "Hryðjuverkalögum beitt gegn landsbanka" (Terrorist act enforced against Landsbankinn) (article). (2008, October), *Mbl.is*. Available online at www.mbl.is/vidskipti/frettir/2008/10/08/hrydjuverkalog_gegn_landsbanka/

Morgunblaðið. 2008d. "Mótmæli á Arnarhóli vekja athygli" (Protest at Arnarhóll receives attention) (article). (2008, October), *Mbl.is*. Available online at www.mbl.is/frettir/innlent/2008/10/10/motmaeli_a_arnarholi_vekja_athygli/

Morgunblaðið. 2008e. "Verðbólgan mælist 18,1%" (Inflation is 18.1%) (article). (2008, December), *Mbl.is*. Available online at www.mbl.is/vidskipti/frettir/2008/12/22/verdbolgan_maelist_18_1_prosent/

Morgunblaðið. 2008f. "Ládeyða á Austurvelli" (Little action at Austurvöllur) (article). (2008, October), *Mbl.is*. Available online at www.mbl.is/greinasafn/grein/1248750/

Morgunblaðið. 2008g. "Kröfðust afsagnar bankastjórnar Seðlabanka" (Demanded the resignation of the Central Bank's governor board) (article). (2008, October), *Mbl.is*. Available online at www.mbl.is/greinasafn/grein/1249373/

Morgunblaðið. 2008h. "Ástandi efnahagsmála mótmælt" (The economic situation protested) (article). (2008, October), *Mbl.is*. Available online at www.mbl.is/greinasafn/ grein/1249585/

Morgunblaðið. 2008i. "Fanganum sleppt" (The prisoner released) (article). (2008, November), *Mbl.*is. Available online at www.mbl.is/frettir/innlent/ 2008/11/22/fanganum_sleppt/

Morgunblaðið. 2008j. "Kryddsíld lokið vegna skemmdarverka" (Kryddsíld over due to vandalism) (article). (2008, December), *Mbl.is*. Available online at www.mbl.is/frettir/innlent/2008/12/31/kryddsild_lokid_vegna_skemmdarverka/

Morgunblaðið. 2008k. Interview with Geir H. Haarde (article). *Morgunblaðið*, October 12, 2008.

Morgunblaðið. 2008l. "Ótti og eymd frjálshyggjunnar" (Fear and misery of liberalism) (article). (2008, November), *mbl.is*. Available online at www.mbl.is/greinasafn/grein/1253973/

Morgunblaðið. 2009a. "Táragasi beitt á Austurvelli" (Teargas used at Austurvöllur) (article). (2009, January), *Mbl.is*. Available online at www.mbl.is/frettir/innlent/2009/01/22/taragasi_beitt_a_austurvelli/

Morgunblaðið. 2009b. "Jóhanna þakkaði traustið" (Jóhanna said thanks for the trust) (article). (2009, February), *Mbl.is*. Available online at www.mbl.is/frettir/innlent/2009/02/01/skjaldborg_slegid_um_heimilin/

Morgunblaðið. 2009c. "Mótmælin rétt að byrja" (The protests are just beginning) (article). *Morgunblaðið*, January 11, 2009.

Morgunblaðið. 2009d. "Fjölmenni á Austurvelli" (Many people at Austurvöllur) (article). (2009, January), *Mbl.is*. Available online at www.mbl.is/frettir/ innlent/2009/01/20/fjolmenni_a_austurvelli/

Morgunblaðið. 2009e. "Allt á suðupunkti við Alþingi" (Things at a boiling point by the Parliament) (article). (2009, January), *Mbl.is*. Available online at www.mbl.is/frettir/innlent/2009/01/20/allt_a_sudupunkti_vid_althingi/

Morgunblaðið. 2009f. "Mótmæli á Ráðhústorgi" (Protest at a town-hall square) (article). (2009, January), *Mbl.is*. Available online at www.mbl.is/frettir/ innlent/2009/01/21/motmaeli_a_radhustorgi/

Morgunblaðið. 2009g. "Mótmæli við fundarstað" (Protest by a meeting place) (article). (2009, January), *Mbl.is*. Available online at www.mbl.is/frettir/innlent/2009/ 01/21/motmaeli_vid_fundarstad/

Morgunblaðið. 2009h. "Samþykktu ályktun um stjórnarslit" (Resolution about a government breakup) (article). (2009, January), *Mbl.is*. Available online at www.mbl.is/frettir/ innlent/2009/01/21/samthykktu_alyktun_um_stjornarslit/

Morgunblaðið. 2009i. "Appelsínugul mótmæli" (An orange protest) (article). (2009, January), *Mbl.is*. Available online at www.mbl.is/frettir/innlent/2009/01/22/appelsinugul_motmaeli/

Myers, Daniel J. 2010. "Violent Protest and Heterogeneous Diffusion Processes: The Spread of U.S. Racial Rioting from 1964–1971." *Mobilization* 15(3): 289–321.

National Radio and Television. 2008. Interview with Davíð Oddsson, October 7, 2008.

Navrátil, Jiři, and Ondřej Císař. 2013. "Towards a 'Non-Global Justice Movement'? Two Paths to Re-Scaling the Left Contention in the Czech Rebublic." In: Donatella della Porta and Alice Mattoni (eds.), *Spreading Protest: Social Movements in Times of Crisis*. Colchester, UK: ECPR Press, pp. 227–252.

Njarðvík, Njörður. 2008. "Hverjum getum við treyst?" (Who can we trust?) (article). *Fréttablaðið*, October 26, 2008.

Njarðvík, Njörður. 2009."Frjálshyggjuveiran" (The virus of liberalism) (article). *Fréttablaðið*, January 7, 2009.

Norris, Pippa, Stefaan Walgrave, and Peter Van Aelst. 2005. "Who Demonstrates? Antistate Rebels, Conventional Participants, or Everyone?" *Comparative Politics* 37(2): 189–205.

Oberschall, Anthony. 1996. "Opportunities and Framing in the Eastern European Revolts of 1989." In: Doug McAdam, John D. McCarthy, and Mayer N. Zald (eds), *Comparative Perspectives on Social Movements: Political Opportunities, Mobilizing Structures, and Cultural Framings*. Cambridge, UK: Cambridge University Press, pp. 93–121.

Opp, Karl-Dieter, and Christiane Gern. 1993. "Dissident Groups, Personal Networks, and Spontaneous Cooperation: The East German Revolution of 1989." *American Sociological Review* 58(5): 659–680.

Ortiz, David G., and Sergio Béjar. 2013. "Participation in IMF-Sponsored Economic Programs and Contentious Collective Action in Latin America, 1980–2007. *Conflict Management and Peace Science* 30(5): 492–515.

Ólafsson, Stefán. 1982. Modernization and Social Stratification in Iceland. Unpublished Ph.D. thesis, University of Oxford.

Ólafsson, Stefán. 1993. "Þróun velferðarríksins" (Evolution of the welfare state). In: Guðmundur Hálfdánarson and Svanur Kristjánsson (eds.), *Íslensk þjóðfélagsþróun 1880–1990: Ritgerðir* (The evolution of Icelandic society 1880–1990: Essays). Reykjavík: Félagsvísindastofnun og Sagnfræðistofnun Háskóla Íslands, pp. 399–430.

Ólafsson, Stefán. 1996. *Hugarfar og hagvöxtur: Menning, þjóðfélag og framfarir á Vesturlöndum* (Mentality and growth: Culture, society, and progress in Western countries). Reykjavík: Félagsvísindastofnu Háskóla Íslands.

Ólafsson, Stefán. 2008. "Íslenska efnahagsundrið: Frá hagsæld til frjálshyggju og efnahagshruns" (The Icelandic economic wonder: From prosperity to liberalism and economic collapse). *Stjórnmál og stjórnsýsla* 4(2): 231–256.

Ólafsson, Stefán. 2011. "Icelandic Capitalism – From Statism to Neoliberalism and Financial Collapse. *The Nordic Varieties of Capitalism* 28: 1–51.

Önundarson, Ragnar. 2005. "Fyrst draumur svo martröð" (First a dream, then a nightmare). *Morgunblaðið*, 16 January.

Pappas, Takis S., and Eoin O'Malley. 2014. "Civil Compliance and 'Political Luddism': Explaining Variance in Social Unrest during Crisis in Ireland and Greece." *American Behavioral Scientist* 58(12): 1592–1613.

Petrie, Michelle. 2004. "A Research Note on the Determinants of Protest Participation: Examining Socialization and Biographical Availability." *Sociological Spectrum* 24(5): 553–574.

Polanyi, Karl. 1957. *The Great Transformation: The Political and Economic Origins of Our Time*. Boston, MA: Beacon.

Postill, John. 2014. "Freedom Technologists and the New Protest Movements: A Theory of Protest Formulas." *Convergence* 20(4): 402–418.

Prime Minister's Office. 2006. *Alþjóðleg fjármálastarfsemi á Íslandi* (International financial operations in Iceland). Reykjavík: The Prime Minister's Committee about International Financial Operations.

Proppé, Hulda. 2015. "'Welcome to the Revolution!' Voting in the Anarcho-Surrealists." In: Paul Durrenberger and Gísli Pálsson (eds.), *Gambling Debt: Iceland's Rise and Fall in the Global Economy*. Boulder, Colorado: University of Colorado Press, pp. 79–91.

Raddir Fólksins. 2009. "Mótmælastaða við Alþingishúsið þriðjudaginn 20. Janúar" (A protest stand by the Parliament on Tuesday January 20) (article). (2009, January), *Raddir Fólksins*. Available online at http://raddirfolksins.info/?p=370

Ragnarsdóttir, Berglind Hólm, Jón Gunnar Bernburg, and Sigrún Ólafsdóttir. 2013. "The Global Financial Crisis and Individual Distress: The Role of Subjective Comparisons after the Collapse of the Icelandic Economy." *Sociology* 47(4): 755–775.

Razsa, Maple, and Anrej Kurnik. 2012. "The Occupy Movement in Žižek's Hometown." *American Ethnologist* 39(2): 238–258.

Reynisson, Jón Trausti. 2008. "Við brugðumst ykkur" (We failed you) (article). (2008, October), *DV.is*. Available online at www.dv.is/leidari/2008/10/10/vid-brugdumst-ykkur/

Roos, Jerome E., and Leonidas Oikonomakis. 2013. "They Don't Represent Us! The Global Resonance of the Real Democracy Movement From the Indignados to Occupy." In: Donatella della Porta and Alice Mattoni (eds.), *Spreading Protest: Social Movements in Times of Crisis*. Colchester, UK: ECPR Press, pp. 117–136.

Rudig, Wolfgang, and Georgios Karyotis. 2013a. "Beyond the Usual Suspects? New Participants in Anti-Austerity Protests in Greece." *Mobilization* 18(3): 313–330.

Rudig, Wolfgang, and Georgios Karyotis. 2013b. "Who Protests in Greece? Mass Opposition to Austerity." *British Journal of Political Science* 44(3): 487–513.

Runciman, Walter G. 1966. *Relative Deprivation and Social Justice*. London: Routledge and Kegan Paul.

Sakellaropoulos, Spyros. 2012. "On the Causes and Significance of the December 2008 Social Explosion in Greece." *Science & Society* 76(3): 340–364.

Schussman, Alan, and Sarah A. Soule. 2005. "Process and Protest: Accounting for Individual Protest Participation." *Social Forces* 84(2): 1083–1108.

Sigurgeirsdóttir, Rakel. 2008. "Við sem mótmælum okkur miðar áfram" (We who protest are making progress) (blog post). (2008, December), *Rakel Sigurgeirsdóttir*. Available online at http://raksig.blog.is/blog/raksig/entry/743711/

Sigurjónsson, Throstur Olaf. 2010. "Privatization and Deregulation: A Chronology of Events." In: Robert Z. Aliber and Gylfi Zoega (eds.), *Preludes to the Icelandic Financial Crisis*. London: Palgrave Macmillan, pp. 26–50.

Sigurjónsson, Throstur, and Mar Wolfgang Mixa. 2011. "Learning From the "Worst Behaved": Iceland's Financial Crisis and the Nordic Comparison." *Thunderbird International Business Review* 53(2): 209–224.

Sigurjónsson, Throstur Olaf, David Schwartzkopf, and Auður Arna Arnardóttir. 2011. "Viðbrögð tengslanets við gagnrýni á fjármálastöðugleika Íslands" (Network reactions to criticism of financial stability in Iceland). *Stjórnmál & stjórnsýsla* 7(1): 161–184.

Skocpol, Theda. 1979. *States and Social Revolutions: A Comparative Analysis of France, Russia and China*. Cambridge, UK: Cambridge University Press.

Smith, Heather J., Thomas F. Pettigrew, Gina M. Pippin, and Silvana Bialosiewicz. 2012. "Relative Deprivation: A Theoretical and Meta-Analytic Review." *Personality and Social Psychology Review* 16(3): 203–232.

Snow, David A. and Robert D. Benford. 1988. "Ideology, Frame Resonance, and Participant Mobilization." *International Social Movement Research* 1: 197–217.

Snow, David A., E. Burke Rochford, Jr., Steven K. Worden, and Robert D. Benford. 1986. "Frame Alignment Processes: Micromobilization, and Movement participation." *American Sociological Review* 51: 464–481.

Snow, David A., Daniel M. Cress, Liam Downey, and Andrew W. Jones. 1998. "Disrupting the "Quotidian": Reconceptualizing the Relationship between Breakdown and the Emergence of Collective Action." *Mobilization* 3(1): 1–22.

Snow, David A. and Byrd, Scott C. 2007. "Ideology, Framing Processes, and Islamic Terrorist Movements." *Mobilization* 12(1): 119–136.

Special Investigation Commission. 2010. *Report of the Special Investigation Commission*. Reykjavík: Alþingi.

Stefánsson, Jón K. 2009. "Nýtt Ísland, nýtt lýðveldi" (A new Iceland, a new republic) (article). (2009, January), *Fréttablaðið*. Available online at www.visir.is/nytt-island-nytt-lydveldi/article/2009645207582

Sveinsson, Stefan Gunnar. 2013. *Búsáhaldabyltingin* (The pots and pans revolution). Reykjavík: Almenna bókafélagið.

Swidler, Ann. 1986. "Culture in Action: Symbols and Strategies." *American Sociological Review* 51(2): 273–286.

Swidler, Ann. 2003. "Cultural Power and Social Movements." In Hank Johnston and Bert Klandermans (eds.), *Social Movements and Culture*. London: Routledge, pp. 25–40.

Tarrow, Sidney G. 2011. *Power in Movement: Social Movements and Contentious Politics*. New York: Cambridge University Press.

Tejerina, Benjamín, Ignacia Perrugorría, Tova Benski, and Lauren Langman. 2013. "From Indignation to Occupation: A New Wave of Global Mobilization." *Current Sociology* 61(4): 377–392.

Thorlindsson, Thorolfur. 1988. "Equality and Educational Opportunity in Iceland." *Scandinavian Journal of Educational Research* 32(1): 9–22.

Tomason, Richard F. 1980. *Iceland: The First New Society*. Reykjavík: Iceland Review.

Tufekci, Zeynep, and Christopher Wilson. 2012. "Social Media and the Decision to Participate in Political Protest: Observations from Tahrir Square." *Journal of Communication* 62(2): 363–379.

Useem, Bert. 1998. "Breakdown Theories of Collective Action." *Annual Review of Sociology* 24: 215–238.

Visir. 2005. "Efasemdir um Kárahnjúkavirkjun" (Reservations about the Kárahnjúkar Power Plant) (article). (2005, April), *Visir.is*. Available online at www.visir.is/efasemdir-um-karahnjukavirkjun/article/2005504070413

Visir. 2008a. "Mótmæla Davíð Oddsssyni" (Protest against Davíð Oddsson) (article). (2008, October), *Visir.is*. Available online at www.visir.is/ motmaela-david-oddsssyni/article/2008944858393

Visir. 2008b. "Hundrað manna hópuppsagnir um mánaðamótin" (Hundreds laid off by the end of the month) (article). (2008, October), *Visir.is*. Available online at www.visir.is/hundrad-manna-hopuppsagnir-um-manadamotin/article/2008873968238

Visir. 2008c. "Áhlaup á Seðlabankann – varnaúða hótað" (Attack on the Central Bank – defense-spray threatened) (article). (2008, December), *Visir.is*. Available online at www.visir.is/ahlaup-a-sedlabankann–varnaruda-hotad/article/2008104292779

Visir. 2008d. "Sjö handteknir – átökum lokið" (Seven arrested – fight over) (article). (2008, December), *Visir.is*. Available online at www.visir.is/sjo-handteknir–atokum-lokid/article/2008171271402

Visir. 2009a. "Kröftug mótmæli við Alþingishúsið" (A strong protest by the Parliament building) (article). (2009, January), *Visir.is*. Available online at www.visir.is/kroftug-motmaeli-vid-althingishusid/article/2009271666814

Visir. 2009b. "Piparúða beitt á mótmælendur – tíu í handjárnum" (Pepper spray used on protesters – ten in handcuffs) (article). (2009, January), *Visir.is*. Available online at www.visir.is/piparuda-beitt-a-motmaelendur–tiu-i-handjarnum/article/200952240833

Visir. 2009c. "Óviðunandi ógn við ráðherra" (Unacceptable threat to minister) (article). (2009, January), *Visir.is*. Available online at www.visir.is/ ovidunandi-ogn-vid-radherra/article/2009138876888

Viðskiptablaðið. 2008a. "Hætta á að landið verði olíulaust" (A risk that the country may become without oil) (article). (2008, October), *Viðskiptablaðið*. Available online at www.vb.is/frettir/12986/?q=and

Viðskiptablaðið. 2008b. "Bankar undir álagi" (Banks under pressure) (article). (2008, August 15), *Viðskiptablaðið*. Available online at www.vb.is/skodun/bankar-undir-alagi/14699/

Walton, John, and Charles Ragin. 1990. "Global and National Sources of Political Protest: Third World Responses to the Debt Crisis." *American Sociological Review* 55(6): 876–890.

Woolfson, Charles. 2010 "'Hard times' in Lithuania: Crisis and 'Discourses of Discontent' in Post-Communist Society." *Ethnography* 11(4): 487–514.

Zagorin, Perez. 1973. "Theories of Revolution in Contemporary Historiography." *Political Science Quarterly* 88(1): 23–52.

Þórisson, Geir Jón. 2014. *Samantekt á skipulagi lögreglu við mótmælin 2008–2011* (Summary of police reactions to the protests in 2008–2011). Reykjavík: Lögreglustjórinn á Höfuðborgarsvæðinu.

Index

For Product Safety Concerns and Information please contact our EU representative GPSR@taylorandfrancis.com Taylor & Francis Verlag GmbH, Kaufingerstraße 24, 80331 München, Germany